Randi Mil

FUN PLACES
to Go with
Children in

New York

CHRONICLE BOOKS

SAN FRANCISCO

Printed in the United States of America.

Library of Congress Cataloging-in-Publication Data:
Millman-Brown, Randi.
    Fun places to go with children in New York / by Randi Millman-Brown.
    p.   cm.
    Includes index.
    ISBN 0-8118-1567-6 (pbk.)
    1. New York (N.Y.)—Guidebooks. 2. Children—Travel—New
York (State)—New York—Guidebooks. 3. Family recreation—New York
(State)—New York—Guidebooks. I. Title.
F128.18.M55 1998
917.47'10443'083—dc21   97-35964
                                                              CIP

Cover design: Martine Trélaün
Book design and illustration: Karen Smidth
Composition: Words & Deeds
Maps: Ellen McElhinny
Cover photograph: Bill Losh/FPG International

Distributed in Canada by Raincoast Books,
8680 Cambie Street, Vancouver, B.C. V6P 6M9

10 9 8 7 6 5 4 3 2 1

Chronicle Books
85 Second Street
San Francisco, CA 94105

Web Site: www.chronbooks.com

Contents

*This book is dedicated to my family and friends,
especially my husband Keith, who supported me throughout the
writing of the book, and my daughter Mathea and son
Gabriel, who were (and still are) the best travel critics I know.
And a very special thank you to my parents, who instilled in
me a love for travel and a thirst for knowledge.*

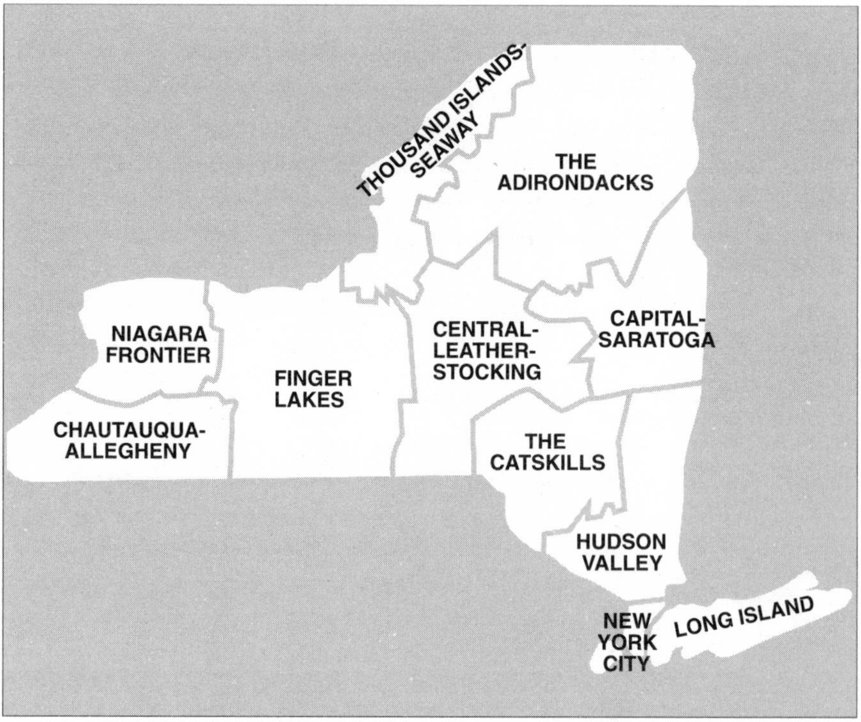

THOUSAND ISLANDS-SEAWAY

THE ADIRONDACKS

NIAGARA FRONTIER

CENTRAL-LEATHER-STOCKING

CAPITAL-SARATOGA

FINGER LAKES

CHAUTAUQUA-ALLEGHENY

THE CATSKILLS

HUDSON VALLEY

NEW YORK CITY

LONG ISLAND

Introduction

OKAY, HERE'S AN EASY QUESTION—where can you see the following sites: the Statue of Liberty, Niagara Falls, the Baseball Hall of Fame, and the Finger Lakes? Of course, New York State. But where can you also find these unusual attractions: museums consisting of only bottles or Jell-O memorabilia, a museum where the admission fee is a piece of trash, and a historical site where you can harvest ice? Yes, it's all right here in New York and the surrounding regions of northern New Jersey and western Connecticut.

New York is one of the most popular vacation destinations in the world, with over 50 million visitors per year (30 million to New York City alone). However, many potential visitors get the wrong impression of the state and come away thinking that it mainly consists of cities, concrete, and highways. But the Adirondack Park contains over 6 million acres of forest and land; there are 11 Finger Lakes in central New York; and in northern New York there is a real fairy tale castle you can visit. Within these pages, you will read about lots of places, such as these fun spots that are off the beaten track. By including the areas of northern New Jersey and western Connecticut (and a portion of southeastern Ontario), I hope that I will have encouraged you to get off the main highway every once in a while, take a few side roads, and discover some of the sights in the region that makes up the heart of the Northeast.

The state of New York holds so many attractions—museums, parks, historical sites, zoos, hiking trails, wineries, restaurants, wonderful bookstores—that if I tried to write a book that included each and every place to visit, it would be thousands of pages long. And besides, your kids wouldn't want to go to all those places anyway. The attractions listed in this book are included because they are historical, educational, fun, exciting, recreational, or just plain unusual. Two years ago I went to a bookstore with a large travel section and tried to buy a book like this one.

When I realized there wasn't such a guide available, I took it upon myself to write one, so that visitors to New York, the bordering states of New Jersey and Connecticut, and Canada would have a comprehensive guide in one source book.

A couple of pieces of travel advice, particularly when visiting New York City, although it applies generally as well. Try to visit only two major attractions per day. Any more than that, and the kids will tire out quickly. For example, visit the Statue of Liberty and Ellis Island, and then take the kids out for ice cream. Or show them the wonders of Niagara Falls, the Niagara Aquarium, and then go to a kids-friendly restaurant for dinner. The last thing you need are cranky, whiny kids screaming "I wanna go."

Before you visit a region, pick out several main attractions or sites you intend to visit, and make sure to leave room for a few last-minute changes. If you are traveling by car, consider giving each of your kids their own travel case that they can fill with small note pads, washable markers, stickers, and other little stuff to keep them occupied. My kids each have one. I also make sure they pick at least five books each that they can read in the car. And I have recently discovered that many four-year-olds love portable cassette players with headphones. On a recent trip, I gave each of our children their own players, and this kept them entertained for the entire ride home (my husband and I were actually able to have a conversation for more than half a minute). We also discovered wonderful car travel activity pads that have illustrations of 10 items each that kids check off whenever they see one of the objects (this keeps them looking out the window). One pad has city scenes, another country scenes (cow, silo, barn, and so on), another has different types of vehicles. And, of course, don't forget the standard license plate game. Remember to bring a first aid kit and wet wipes to keep in the car; the kids will inevitably get messy or dirty or spill juice all over themselves. Bring extra clothing and have it accessible (don't pack it in the bottom of the trunk of your car). If you and your family are prepared, the trip will go more smoothly.

Please note that prices change frequently. A few places we visited just last summer have increased their rates by as much as 25 percent. Also, hours and schedules change, sometimes each season, and occasionally places go out of business, so call ahead to play it safe. If a place has hours that change each season, I've tried to indicate accordingly; if I haven't specified seasonal hours, you can assume the site is open year-round. Be careful around holidays, though: many attractions are closed on holidays. Definitely call ahead if you're considering a holiday visit. Having said all that, enjoy yourselves. Your kids will have the time of their lives, and will have memories of New York and the surrounding areas that will stay with them for a lifetime. Sharing adventures with your family is an opportunity to combine learning and fun. Don't forget the camera and film, and have a wonderful visit!

An important note for members of science and technology museums:

Your local museum probably has reciprocal agreements with the museums in New York state. Check with your museum for the list of participating museums (over 190 museums throughout the country are included) or visit the Association of Science and Technology Centers Web site at www.fi.edu/astc/. In New York your membership provides free or reduced admission at the following 16 museums with your membership card:

- Brooklyn Children's Museum, Brooklyn
- Buffalo Museum of Science, Buffalo, Niagara Falls Region
- Discovery Center (at Ross Park), Binghamton, Central Leatherstocking Region
- DNA Learning Center, Cold Spring Harbor, Long Island
- The Junior Museum, Troy, Capital-Saratoga Region
- New York Hall of Science, Corona Park, Queens
- New York Transit Museum, Brooklyn
- Roberson Museum and Science Center, Binghamton, Central Leatherstocking Region
- Rochester Museum and Science Center, Rochester, Finger Lakes Region
- Rubenstein Museum of Science and Technology, Syracuse, Finger Lakes Region
- Schenectady Museum and Planetarium, Schenectady, Capital-Saratoga Region
- Science and Discovery Center, Horseheads, Finger Lakes Region
- Science Discovery Center, Oneonto, Central Leatherstocking Region
- Sciencenter, Ithaca, Finger Lakes Region
- Sci-Tech Center of Northern New York, Watertown, Thousand Islands–Seaway Region
- Utica Children's Museum, Utica, Central Leatherstocking Region

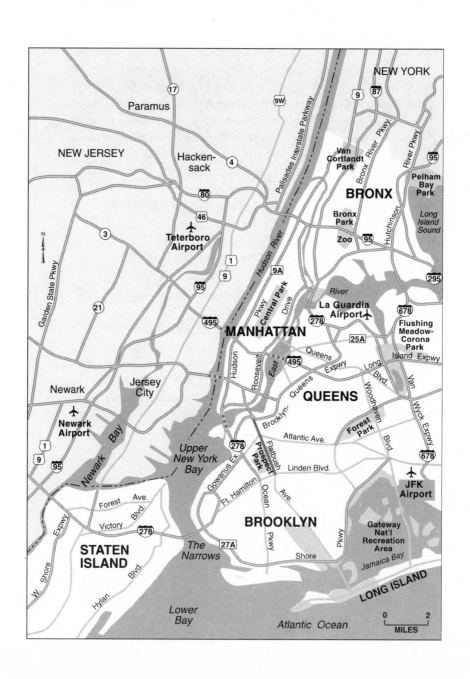

New York City

GEOGRAPHICALLY, NEW YORK CITY consists only of Manhattan, that
thin stretch of land just east of New Jersey that's encircled by rivers—
however, "the city" is politically defined by five boroughs: Manhattan,
Brooklyn, Queens, Bronx, and Staten Island. There is so much to do with
kids here, I've had to pick and choose among the many attractions in
creating this chapter. Suffice it to say that each of the listings is a starting
point for discovery. If you find an interesting museum, historical site, play
place, park, or other attraction that might be a good addition, please send
the suggestion to me. My kids and I can always use more places to visit!
My most important piece of advice? Relax. Have a great time, look,
photograph, wonder, and enjoy. There's no place like New York City. For
more information please contact the New York Convention and Visitors
Bureau at 1-800-NYC-VISIT (1-800-692-8474) or 212-397-8222 from
outside the U.S., or visit them on the Internet at *www.nycvisit.com.*

Manhattan

Manhattan is only 2½ miles wide and 10 miles long, but over 7 million people live here (that's more than 20,000 people in every square mile). To give you a sense of the scale of Manhattan, in order to eat at every restaurant here, you would have to eat out every night for 47 years.

Manhattan is made up of 13 distinct regions: Lower Manhattan, Chinatown, Little Italy, Lower East Side, Tribeca, Soho, Greenwich Village, Chelsea, Midtown Manhattan, Central Park, Upper East Side, Upper West Side, and Harlem. Each of these neighborhoods offers a wide variety of attractions and culture. I suggest purchasing a detailed New York City street map that highlights each of these areas. For convenience, I have listed each attraction in Manhattan alphabetically, rather than by neighborhood.

The area code for Manhattan is 212 unless otherwise noted.

● Abigail Adams Smith Museum
421 E. 61st Street, 838-6878. Hours: Tues.–Sun. 11–4 (Tues. until 8 in June and July, closed Aug.). Admission: Adults $3, children under 12 free. **Ages 4–14.**

This federal-style museum was built in 1799 and was converted to a country hotel during the period from 1826 to 1832. Nine period rooms with antiques and decorative arts are now open to the public and re-create the estate during the time it was a hotel. Permanent exhibits feature 19th-century New York City history. The museum holds special events and project workshops for children, such as making herbal wreaths and Mother's Day sachets.

● American Craft Museum
40 W. 53rd Street, 956-3535. Hours: Tues.–Sun. 10–6 (Thurs. until 8). Admission: Adults $5, children under 12 free (Thurs. 6–8 is pay as you wish). **Ages 3 and up.**

The exhibits of contemporary American crafts here are often more interesting to kids than the pieces in a traditional art museum. The craft museum usually has interesting sculptures and wall hangings that are very kid-appealing, since they're made from the same crafts materials and found objects that kids use at school. Call for information regarding special programs for children. Classes in the past have included hat and doll making, fish printing, tin pressing, and Japanese crafts, among many others.

● American Museum of Natural History and Hayden Planetarium

Central Park West at 79th Street, 769-5100. Hours: Mon.–Thurs. and Sun. 10–5:45, Fri. and Sat. 10–8:45. Admission: Adults $8, children 12 and under $4.50. www.amnh.org/. **Ages 3 and up.**

With over 40 exhibition halls featuring the history of people and cultures, gemstones, dinosaurs, African and Asian mammals, and more, you will want to spend quite a bit of time here. When we visited, I thought my kids were ready to leave after about three hours, but they said, "Mom, we can't leave yet, we haven't even been to the third floor!" And they were right. It took about another hour before we were ready to go (and they wanted to come back again later). If you visit, get to the museum early and rush up to the dinosaur exhibits because it gets crowded fast. The dinosaur exhibits were renovated between 1994 and 1996 and are extremely well done, interesting, and therefore time-consuming to go through. The kids loved all of them especially the two robotic dinosaur heads that show the prehistoric animals' different methods of chewing. Another area we all enjoyed was the Hall of Minerals and Gems. Located in a darkened room, the exhibits are dazzling, and you have the feeling you should be quiet and just look. This is one of those classic museums that you will return to time and time again. Across the street, at the corner of 81st and Central Park West, is a very nice playground for the kids to play in afterwards.

Note: The Planetarium will reopen in the year 2000 in a new state-of-the-art facility. It will be called the Center for Earth and Space, and will include the Hall of the Planet Earth and the Hall of the Universe.

● Cathedral of St. John the Divine

1047 Amsterdam Avenue at 112th Street, 316-7540. Hours: daily 7–5, tours are led Tues.–Sat. at 11 and Sun. after 1. Tours are $3 per person. www.stjohndivine.org/cathedral/. **Ages 5 and up.**

If you are in the neighborhood, I would highly recommend a visit to this modern Gothic cathedral in the heart of New York City. Located on 13 acres on the Upper West Side, St. John the Divine is the largest cathedral in the world. The interior is over 600 feet long and 146 feet wide (by contrast, Notre Dame in Paris is only 430 feet long). The cathedral was begun in 1892 and is still not complete. Because construction is ongoing, visitors have the opportunity to see some of the work in progress, such as the unfinished carved columns, which are very interesting. Another fascinating feature of the development of the cathedral is the

Stoneworks program. Master English stonemasons teach local residents their trade, continually passing their skills on. Officials estimate it will take approximately another 40 to 50 years to complete the cathedral. Every Saturday the stonemasons hold a medieval arts workshop that is open to adults and children. For $5 per person, you can try your hand at chiseling a block of limestone or sculpting a gargoyle. Children (and adults) are quite impressed with the cathedral's interior, and most people walk in and say "Wow."

● Central Park Zoo

5th Avenue at 64th Street (behind the Arsenal), 794-0284 or 861-6030. Hours: Apr.–Oct. weekdays 10–5, weekends 10:30–5:30; Nov.–Mar. daily 10–4. Admission: Adults $2.50, children 3–12 $.50, children under 3 free. www.wcs.org/. **All ages.**

What a wonderful treat in the middle of Manhattan. Watch polar bears swimming underwater as you look through a glass wall. Enjoy the feeding of the seals in the central square. The Central Park Zoo is a nice, small zoo and a perfect place to take smaller children. The zoo underwent an extensive renovation from 1984 to 1988.

● Central Park

Visitor's Center at the Dairy, 794-6564. www.CentralPark.org/~park. **All ages.**

Central Park is an enormous urban park (843 acres to be exact), and there are many recreational activities to enjoy here. There is a carousel, the Belvedere Castle (which in 1996 opened the Henry Luce Nature Observatory, a nature education center), the Chess and Checkers House (with 24 outdoor tables; the playing pieces are available at the Dairy), the Loeb Boathouse, and many playgrounds. You can rollerblade, ice skate, take a jog, play golf, or just sit back and enjoy the views from the horse-drawn carriages. Stop in at the Central Park Visitor's Center at the Dairy for more information, and be sure to ask for a free copy of the Central Park calendar which lists current special events and activities in the area.

● Children's Museum of the Arts

72 Spring Street, 941-9198. Hours: Tues.–Fri. 12–6, weekends 11–5. Admission: Adults and children $4 weekdays, $5 weekends, 18 months old and younger free. **Ages 2–8.**

The CMA is a great place for children to learn about and experience the arts without the crowds of an art museum. There is a creative play area in a two-story playhouse, an artist's studio, the Monet ball pond, and the

Wonder Theater, where kids can create their own theater sets. The museum also offers weekend workshops (like T-shirt painting) and other special programs.

● Children's Museum of Manhattan

212 W. 83rd Street, between Amsterdam and Broadway, 721-1234 (info. line) 721-1223 (offices). Hours: Wed.–Sun. 10–5. Admission: Adults and children $5, children under 1 free. www.cmom.org. **Ages 1–9.**

Children love to visit museums where they can touch things and play with them and that is precisely what they are encouraged to do here: touch, climb, listen, draw. With over 25,000 square feet of space, there are plenty of places to explore. They can work in the Media Center and produce their own TV shows, or climb the Urban Tree House, or try on costumes. A special Dr. Seuss exhibition will be on display until February 1999. There are no eating facilities within the museum but there are family restaurants and cafes nearby. Strollers are not allowed inside.

● Circle Line Cruise

W. 42nd Street and 12th Avenue, Pier 8, 563-3200. Hours: 3-hour cruise, weekdays, 10, 11, 12, 1:30, 2:30, and 4 departures, weekends departures each hour 10–5; 2-hour cruise, daily 9:30, 12:30 and 3 departures. Admission: 3-hour cruise, adults $20, children 12 and under $10; 2-hour cruise, adults $17, children 12 and under $8.50. **Ages 3 and up.**

Take the famous Circle Line boat tour around Manhattan Island, and see the city skyline. The three-hour cruise is too long for young children, but the new 2-hour cruises might be manageable.

● The Cloisters

Fort Tryon Park, 923-3700. Hours: Mar.–Oct. Tues.–Sun. 9:30–5:15; Nov.–Feb. Tues.–Sun 9:30–4:45. Admission: Suggested donation $8, children under 12 free. **Ages 5 and up.**

This branch of the Metropolitan Museum of Art features medieval art in a monastery-style building. The Cloisters were built with bits and pieces of many European chapels and courtyards, taken apart and rebuilt here at Fort Tryon Park. Touring *all* the rooms was a bit much for my kids, but they really enjoyed the enclosed gardens where over 250 herbs and plants that were used during the medieval period are grown. The famous Unicorn Tapestries are on display here, as is the world's earliest known set of playing cards (dating to around 1470), which are interesting because they are larger, more colorful, and only remotely resemble contemporary card sets.

● Ellis Island Immigration Museum

Museum: 363-3200 or 363-7620. Ellis Island/Statue of Liberty ferry: leaves from Battery Park, (212) 269-5755, or Liberty State Park in Jersey City, New Jersey, (201) 435-9499. Hours: Museum, daily 9:30–6:30. Ferry, daily boats leave every 30 minutes, 9:30–3:30. Admission: Museum, free; Ferry, adults $7, children ages 3–17 $3, children under 3 free. Please note that the ferry does not accept credit cards. (Note: your ferry ticket includes a stop at the Statue of Liberty.) www.ellisisland.org/ellis.html or www.i-channel.com/ellis. **Ages 5 and up.**

Tour this historic museum on the site that was the main entry point into the U.S. from 1892 until 1954. Over 12 million immigrants came through here. Ellis Island was in ruins until renovation began in 1983. The renovation, which was completed in 1990, took seven years to complete at a cost of over $150 million. The museum has more than 30 galleries filled with photos, maps, artifacts, and music installations—all of which tell the story of immigration in this county. Kids love to explore the *Family Album Kodak Exhibit* looking at all the different immigrant families, as well as the interactive learning center which was designed for children. This museum is recommended for children ages 5 and up, since some understanding of U.S. history is helpful in order to appreciate the significance of the island.

● El Museo del Barrio

1230 5th Avenue at 104th Street, 831-7272. Hours: Wed.–Sun. 11–5. Admission: Adults $4 (suggested donation), children under 12 free. **Ages 3 and up.**

This museum is the only one in the U.S. that focuses on the art and culture of Puerto Rico and Latin America. El Museo del Barrio (the Museum of the Neighborhood) features a collection of over 8,000 objects, including many paintings and photographs. If you are interested in learning about Puerto Rican and Latin American cultures, stop in for a look at this museum. Call for information regarding special programs for children. In May the museum has a Family Day, a day of art-making and family fun.

● Empire State Building

34th Street and 5th Avenue, 736-3100. Hours: daily 9:30–midnight (special hours on Dec. 25 and Jan. 1). Admission: Adults $4.50, children 6–12 $2.25, children 5 and under free. **Ages 4 and up.**

Come visit our nation's most famous modern building. When it was built in 1931, it was the tallest building in the world. Get an incredible 360-degree view (on a clear day you can see for 50 miles) from the

102nd floor outdoor observatory at 1,250 feet, or try the 86th floor indoor observatory at 1,050 feet. The fast elevators here travel at a speed of about 1,200 feet per minute. Runners who compete in the annual Empire State Run-Up climb (that is, *run*) all 1,860 steps in about 11 minutes (I'll take the elevator, thanks). A visibility notice is usually posted at ground level to help you decide if it's worth it to go to the top or not. There is also an attraction here called the New York Skyride. It is a big-screen thrill ride that you have to wear seat-belts for, because your seats actually move. There is an extra fee and I do not recommend it for small children.

● FAO Schwartz

767 5th Avenue at 58th Street, 644-9400. Hours: Mon.–Sat. 10–7, Sun. noon–6 (Thurs. until 8). **All ages.**

It's hard to resist taking your kids to the world's largest and most prestigious toy store. There is much to see, and your kids, in addition to being overwhelmed, will most definitely beg you to buy them something. (Pick a price limit and stick to it.) They've got gigantic stuffed animals and more gadgets and whatnots than you can imagine. Not only that, but the staff let kids play with any toy in the entire store! Toy demonstrations, special concerts, and celebrity appearances take place regularly.

● Forbes Magazine Galleries

62 5th Avenue at 12th Street, 206-5548. Hours: Tues., Wed., Fri., Sat. 10–4. (Note: hours are subject to change without notice, please call ahead.) Admission: free. **Ages 3 and up.**

The late Malcom Forbes (of magazine fame) was not one to throw away childhood items or interesting objects. In these few galleries you can enjoy his collection of over 10,000 toy soldiers, boats, and ships, all displayed in interesting tableaux. In addition to these is the collection of presidential memorabilia, which includes items such as Abraham Lincoln's stovepipe hat and eyeglasses, and a handwritten copy of the Gettysburg Address. To top it all off is the wonderful special collection of Faberge eggs which is sure to delight children and adults alike.

● Guggenheim Museum

1071 5th Avenue at 89th Street, 423-3500. Hours: Sun.–Wed. 10–6, Fri. and Sat. 10–8. Admission: Adults $8, children under 12 free (pay as you wish Fri. 6–8). www.guggenheim.org/. **All ages.**

Kids love this architectural masterpiece designed by Frank Lloyd Wright and built in 1959. With its circular gallery, the museum's dynamic space keeps kids interested in the modern and contemporary art exhibits. The new annex, built in 1992 by Gwathmey Siegel Architects, has increased the exhibition space, and there is a museum cafe if you need to sit and rest. Pick up a copy of the Guggenheim's family activity guide for interesting ideas to help you explore the museum. A wide variety of public programs including jazz concerts, lectures, and other special events are also offered.

● Intrepid Sea-Air-Space Museum

12th and W. 46th Street, Pier 86, 245-0072. Hours: Oct–April Wed.–Sun. 10–5; May–September daily 10–5. Admission: Adults $10, children 12–17 $7.50, children 6–11 $5, first child under 6 free, each additional child $1. www.intrepid-museum.com. **Ages 3 and up.**

Plan to spend several hours viewing this 900-foot-long World War 2 aircraft carrier, which has been converted into a museum of history and technology. Kids can sit in a fighter plane cockpit, or go up on the bridge where sailors will give detailed explanations of all the buttons and dials. You can even go below deck and walk through the rooms, where it's easy to see how hard it must have been to spend days and months aboard ship. There are displays of 50 aircraft, rockets, and space vehicles. Every year during the last week of May, the museum participates in Fleet Week, a week-long celebration of the armed forces, with special events each day. Call for specific details on this annual event. Kids are genuinely fascinated by this museum and it's easy to understand why. Note however, that there really is more to see here than you can do in one visit. (The Circle Line Cruise leaves from the pier next door, see listing above.)

● Jewish Museum

1109 5th Avenue, 423-3200. Hours: Sun., Mon., Wed., Thurs. 11–5:45, Tues. 11–8 (Tues. 5–8 free) (closed legal and Jewish holidays). Admission: Adults $7, students $5, children under 12 free. www.jewishmuseum.org. **Ages 3 and up.**

Jewish history, culture, and art are housed in this 1908 French Gothic chateau built for Felix Warburg, a financier and leader in the Jewish community at the beginning of this century. The collection has objects dating back 4,000 years, including ceremonial and archaeological objects, paintings, photographs, and more. Changing exhibitions explore Jewish life throughout the world.

● KidMazeum—Kids Village and Interactive Discovery Museum

80 East End Avenue at 83rd Street, 327-4800. Hours: weekdays 10–7, weekends 10–6. Admission: Adults free, children $8. **Ages 1–10.**

With 10,000 square feet of play space, kids can pack in a lot of activities here. In the museum, they can shop in a real kids' supermarket (they love this), stage their own performances in the theater, or play in the Lego Room, the Computer Lab, or the Music Center. In the recreation area, they can crawl and jump in the ball pit, try the maze, or, for the best part, jump and jump and JUMP in the indoor Airbounce Room. Kids will have more fun here than you can imagine (you'd better bring a book to read). You can even schedule birthday parties here. Check it out.

● Lower East Side Tenement Museum

90 Orchard Street, 431-0233. Hours: Tues.–Fri. 12–5, weekends 11–5. Admission: Gallery, free; Tenement Tours, Adults $8, children 6–18 $6; Neighborhood Walks, Adults $8, children 6–18 $6; Tour and walk combination tickets, Adults $12, children 6–18 $10. Tenement tours leave weekdays at 1, 2, and 3, weekends every 45 minutes. The Neighborhood Walk, weekends only, 1:30 and 2:30. www.wnet.org/tenement. **Ages 5 and up.**

The LESTM was the first living history museum in the U.S. and is designated a National Historic Site. Its focus is on preserving the history of this country's immigrants, many of whom settled in the Lower East Side of Manhattan. A tenement was a five- or six-story building usually built on a 25-foot lot. Each building had four apartments per floor, and each apartment had two bedrooms. As many as 14 people lived in an apartment at a time. It is very interesting to see the restored apartments, and the one apartment that was left as it was found, complete with peeling wallpaper. Call for guided tour hours because they are subject to change.

● Metropolitan Museum of Art

82nd Street and 5th Avenue, 879-5500. Hours: Tues.–Thurs. and Sun. 9:30–5:15, Fri. and Sat. 9:30–8:45. Admission: Adults $8 (suggested donation), children under 12 free. www.metmuseum.org. **All ages.**

As one of the most famous museums in the world, the Met lives up to its reputation of being the place where you can see everything. If you take kids here, try to be selective, or they'll pass out from exhaustion (and so will you) before you get a chance to see every Monet, van Gogh, Rubens, and every Egyptian artifact. One of the greatest ways I've learned to help kids enjoy art museums, is to plan a museum treasure hunt for them; the Met publishes several small booklets that lay out specific art hunts for the kids to try. The booklet we used was called *Egyptian Life: A Gallery Guide for Families*. It included not only a list of objects to find, but a bibliography, hieroglyphics, Egyptian recipes, pictures for coloring, word finds, and other activities. My son also enjoyed the medieval armor room, with its model of knights on horseback in full body armor (and horse armor). My daughter spent her time trying to find a painting of a woman in a blue ball gown (she found it, Ingres's portrait of Princesse de Broglie). Call ahead for children's programming information; the museum offers quite a number of classes and special events for kids.

● Museum of Modern Art (MOMA)

11 W. 53rd Street, 708-9480. Hours: Sat.–Tues. 10:30–6, Thurs. and Fri. noon–8:30 (closed Wed.). Admission: Adults $8.50, children under 16 free (pay as you wish Fri. 4:30–8:30). www.moma.org. **All ages.**

MOMA is a great place to take children. Founded in 1929 and at its present location since 1939, the museum has over 100,000 objects, ranging from painting and sculpture to silverware and chairs. The modern sculpture pieces usually attract children like magnets. The education department has terrific family programs geared towards children ages 4 to 10; these include gallery talks, Tours for Tots, family films, and art workshops. If you are worried whether or not your children will appreciate modern art (they will), the museum sells an interesting children's book that explains several works of art in its permanent collection. There is a museum café, and on a nice day you can try to get a table in the garden. In July and August there are free musical concerts in the sculpture garden. The museum has recently begun a massive renovation and expansion project that is expected to last almost 10 years.

● Museum of the City of New York

5th Avenue and 103rd Street, 534-1672. Hours: Wed.–Sat. 10–5, Sun. 1–5. Admission (suggested donation): Adults $5, children $4, family rate $10. www.mcny.org/. **Ages 4 and up.**

Learn about the development of New York City from the time of the Dutch settlements through modern times. Exhibits include objects such as furniture, silver, paintings, toys, costumes, and more. Children interested in dolls and dollhouses will love the extensive collection on display here. Past special exhibitions have included photographs and memorabilia relating to the history of the Empire State Building, and the history of New York City in photographs.

● Museum of Television and Radio

25 W. 52nd Street, 621-6600. Hours: Tues.–Sun. 12–6, Thurs. 12–8. Admission: Adults $6, children under 13 $3. www.mtr.org. **Ages 5 and up.**

Here you can watch TV classics at one of 96 viewing consoles (each one accommodates two people at a time); pick from the museum's extensive selection of videos and watch an old show or two from your childhood. Kids are always amazed that anyone would sit and watch, on purpose, something in black and white. The Children's Program screenings are normally on the weekends at 12:30 P.M. The Annual Children's Television Festival takes place here from October through March, when some of the world's best children's television programming is shown. The MTR has a sister museum in Beverly Hills, California.

● **National Academy Museum and School of Fine Arts**
1083 5th Avenue at 89th Street, 369-4880. Hours: Wed., Thurs., Sat., Sun. noon–5, Fri. noon–8. Admission: Adults $5, children under 16 free. www.si.edu.organiza/museums/design/. **Ages 5 and up.**

Take a trip down memory lane by visiting this 19th century Beaux Arts mansion, one of the few 5th Avenue mansions open to the public today. The former home of philanthropist Archer M. Huntington and his wife, sculptor Anne Hyatt, features exhibits of American painting, sculpture, drawing, and architecture. In the fall and spring, the education department hosts Family Fun Days which take place once a month on a Saturday. Children and their parents can come to the museum, get a tour, and then have fun with a creative project. The cost usually runs to approximately $5 per person.

● **National Museum of the American Indian**
George Gustav Haye Center, 1 Bowling Green, in the Alexander Hamilton U.S. Custom House, 668-6624. Hours: year-round daily 10–5 (closed Christmas day). Admission: free. www.si.edu/nmai. **Ages 4 and up.**

With over 1 million artifacts in its collection, this museum provides visitors with an interesting overview of Native American culture and history. Seventy percent of the collection is from the U.S. and Canada; the other 30 percent is from Central and South America. You can see all kinds of objects, such as textiles, painted hides, carvings, and jewelry. While many of the items on display are historical, the museum exhibits works of contemporary Indian art as well, and occasionally hosts Native American dancers and artists to perform or give presentations for visitors. It is a branch of the Smithsonian Institution in Washington, D.C.

● **New York City Fire Museum**
278 Spring Street, 691-1303. Hours: June–Aug. Tues.–Sun. 10–4. Admission (suggested donation): Adults $4, children under 12 $1. www.haven.ios.com/~donfdny/museum.html. **Ages 4–10.**

For those of you with children who are into fire trucks, firefighters and the like, this museum features one of the most comprehensive collections of fire-related artifacts in the country. Located in a renovated firehouse that dates back to 1904, the kids will enjoy the horse-drawn fire vehicles, the ladder truck from 1882, the wonderful 1901 La France horse-drawn steam pumper, and plenty of toys and models. The museum will even host your child's birthday party if he or she is between the ages of four and eight.

● PlaySpace

1504 3rd Avenue at 85th Street, 717-5200, second location at 2473 Broadway at 92nd Street, 769-2300. Hours: daily 9–6. Admission: Adults free, first child $9, additional children $6.50 each. **Ages 1–8.**

Unlike the well-known Discovery Zone, these play centers are geared towards younger children. At PlaySpace there is a dress-up area, a 400-square-foot sandbox (the entire place is 8,000 square feet), a giant maze, a slide, a two-story fire station, and more. After the kids are done playing visit Barnes & Noble Jr., a great bookstore for kids located at 120 East 86th Street.

● Police Academy Museum (New York City Police Museum)

235 E. 20th Street, 477-9753. Hours: by appointment only, Mon.–Fri. 9–2. Admission: free. **Ages 5–12.**

Not too many people know about this museum, and kids love it. There are firearms, uniforms, and photographs; there is counterfeit money, fingerprinting equipment, and more. You can even look at the mug shots of organized crime members. Kids over seven are usually captivated, especially if they've spent a few years playing cops and robbers.

● Pull Cart Ceramics

31 W. 21st Street between 5th and 6th Avenues, 727-7089. Hours: week-days noon–9, weekends 10–6 (closed weekends in July and Aug.). Admission: $6 per hour plus the cost of the item(s) you decorate. **Ages 5 and up.**

This is a very fun and artistic place. You and your child can pick an item (mug, bowl, or vase) and using glazes (there is help available), decorate the ceramic piece. When you've finished, you normally have to leave the piece there for one week to be fired, then come back and pick it up. But if you are visiting from out of town, mention this, and the staff usually can get the items fired within a day or two. Pull Cart is probably best for children ages five and up, since the time gap between decorating and picking up the object is long enough to be frustrating for younger children.

● Radio City Music Hall

1260 Avenue of the Americas, 632-4041. Hours: Mon.–Sat. 10–5, Sun. 11–5. Tours leave every half hour. Tickets are available on a first-come, first-served basis. Admission: Adults $13.75, children 12 and under $9. **Ages 5 and up.**

If you have the time and are willing to spend a few extra dollars, I would recommend a tour of this famous performing arts center. Take note of the wonderful architecture (the grand foyer has a 24-karat gold-leaf ceiling), marvel at the Mighty Wurlitzer (the world's largest theater organ), and enjoy seeing the workings of the backstage area (kids love this part). If you have even more time (and money), come back in the evening for a live performance. The tours last approximately an hour.

● Riverbank State Park

679 Riverside Drive, 694-3600. Hours: call for hours for specific attraction. Admission: Roller skates rental $2 per person. Call for specific fees for swimming and other activities. **All ages.**

At this very popular place you can swim in one of two pools (one indoor, one outdoor), rollerblade along the river, play basketball in the gymnasium—but the weird thing is, the site is actually built on top of a sewage treatment plant. Sounds strange, but it's true. Nevertheless, you can enjoy the swimming and other recreational activities and also feel perfectly safe since there are plenty of lifeguards and even state police on-site. The park also sponsors concerts in its amphitheater during the summer.

● Rockefeller Center/NBC Studios

30 Rockefeller Plaza, 632-3975. NBC Studios (in G.E. Building): 664-4000. Hours: Rockefeller Center, always open. NBC Studios tour, daily 9:15–5 (tours leave every 15 minutes). Admission: Rockefeller Center, free. NBC Studios, $10. Rockefeller Center, **all ages.** *NBC Studios,* **ages 6 and up.**

The famous Rockefeller Center plaza has shops, an ice skating rink (which is converted to outdoor restaurant seating in the summer), and the famous Christmas tree. If your children are over six years old, then take the tour of the adjacent NBC Studios for an interesting look at the behind-the-scenes workings of a television studio.

● Roosevelt Island Tram

2nd Avenue and 60th Street, 832-4543. Hours: daily, tram leaves every 15 minutes. Admission: $1.50 each way. **Ages 3 and up.**

It may be unusual but try this 10-minute cable car ride which travels at 250 feet above the East River over to Roosevelt Island. When you get there, enjoy that picnic you brought and let the kids run around on one of the playgrounds, or just head right back and for an extra-special treat go to Serendipity 3 for some ice cream (225 E. 60th between 2nd and 3rd Avenues).

● Sony IMAX Theatre

1998 Broadway at 68th Street, 336-5000. Hours: call for show times. Admission: Adults $9, children 12 and under $6. www.sony.com (go to Pictures). **Ages 6 and up.**

To see New York in 3-D is quite something. The films shown here vary from those that provide a real sense of 3-D to others that are just large-screen films. At eight stories high, these are especially large! I would not recommend this for younger children, as some films are quite realistic (and disconcerting). However, for older children who love a heart-pounding experience, these movies are a must-see.

● Sony Wonder Technology Lab

Sony Plaza, 56th and Madison, 833-8100. Hours: Tues.–Sat. 10–6, Sun. noon–6. Admission: free. **Ages 4 and up.**

What a surprise not to have to pay an admission fee, and what a place! Plan to spend at least two hours here; it is hard to leave. Thirty-eight interesting interactive exhibits take visitors through a century of communications history. When you enter, you are required to talk into a computer, have your picture taken digitally, and your voice recorded; then you are given a card that is coded with your name. Each exhibit has an area where you swipe your card; then the computer welcomes you by name and tells you how to proceed with that exhibit. When you are ready to leave, you log out and are given a "Certificate of Achievement" with your picture and names of all the exhibits you visited. Totally fun and engaging.

● South Street Seaport and Museum

12 Fulton Street, on the East River in Lower Manhattan, 748-8600 or 732-7678 (museum recording, 669-9424; museum offices, 669-9400). Museum hours: Apr.–Sept. daily 10–6; Oct.–Mar. Wed.–Mon. 10–5. Museum admission: Adults $6, children $3. www.southstseaport.org/ index.html. **All ages.**

Over 120 shops and food vendors are located in this restored 19th-century seaport district. The museum here features a collection of historic ships and has galleries with changing exhibits. I would heed the advice given to me: avoid all the shops at Pier 17 (they get very crowded and are like mall shops anywhere) and head to Cannon's Walk, Front Street, or Schermerhorn Row. There is a Children's Center at 165 John Street. Stop in at the Visitor's Center on Fulton Street for current information on special events, and to get tickets to the museum and the six historic ships. You can board the ships, and kids really enjoy seeing what it is like below deck and how small the crew's living quarters were. Afterwards, if you feel you need some more adventure, you might take a hike over the Brooklyn Bridge which is close by. Just head over to the walkway entrance on Park Row, and hang on to your hats up there!

● St. Patrick's Cathedral
5th Avenue at 50th Street, 753-2261. Hours: daily 7 A.M.–8 P.M. Admission: free. **All ages.**

Another wonderful Gothic structure in the city of New York? No way! But yes, it's true. Built from 1858 to 1874, this cathedral was designed by James Renwick and is considered the largest Catholic cathedral in the U.S. The exterior is built entirely of white marble. Stop by for an awe-inspiring sight right in the middle of midtown Manhattan.

● Statue of Liberty
Liberty Island, 269-5755 or 363-3200. Hours: Oct.–April daily 9:30– 3:30, May–Sept. daily 9:30–4:30. Admission: free. Ellis Island/Statue of Liberty ferry, leaves from Battery Park, (212) 269-5755, or Liberty State Park in Jersey City, New Jersey, (201) 435-9499. Ferry: Adults $7, children 3–17 $3, children under 3 free. (Note: your ticket includes a stop at Ellis Island.) www.sunp.nyit.edu/Visions/Liberty.html or www.nps.gov/stli/ mainmenu.html. **Ages 5 and up.**

What is a trip to New York City without going to see Lady Liberty? Plan a day trip to visit her and Ellis Island. Climb the 354 steps to the top, if you dare; it will take you two to three hours because of all the other people. Bring lots of bottled water. Or say forget it and take the elevator (at 30 seconds, it's a lot faster). The statue's crown has seven points which symbolize the seven seas and continents. The crown also has 25 windows which symbolize the 25 gemstones found on earth. She is 151 feet tall, her nose is four feet, six inches long, her index finger is eight feet long, and she weighs as much as 45 adult elephants or 225 tons (just to give you a sense of scale). The Statue of Liberty, a gift from France to the U.S. on the occasion of the first centennial of our independence from Britain, was created by Frédéric-Auguste Bartholdi (1834–1904) in 1884. A little-known fact is that the U.S. gave France a sculpture in return. Paul Bartlett (1865–1925) created the *Equestrian Statue of Lafayette* between

1898 and 1908. It used to be located in the courtyard of the Louvre in
Paris, but when I. M. Pei's glass pyramid was installed there in the 1990s,
the statue was moved to the Cours de la Reine, a short distance away
along the Seine. The Statue of Liberty was painstakingly restored in 1986.
You and your family will remember the view from her crown forever.

● Tannen's Magic Studio

6 W. 32nd Street, 239-8383. Hours: Mon.–Fri. 9–5:30, Sat. 9–4. **Ages
3 and up.**

I have added this store at my daughter's request. It is considered
the world's largest magic shop (they have over 8,000 items), so if you
have a kid who is at all fascinated by magic, then I would suggest a visit
here. The store even runs a one-week magic camp. Tannen's has been in
business for more than 60 years and is packed with everything and
anything related to magic. Even the salespeople are magicians. (Really!)

● Whitney Museum of American Art

*9465 Madison Avenue at 75th Street, 570-3600. Hours: Wed., Fri.–Sun.
11–6, Thurs. 1–8. Admission: Adults $8, children under 12 free (free
admission for all Thurs. 6–8). www.echony.com/~whitney.* **Ages 3 and up.**

In 1930, Gertrude Vanderbilt Whitney established her own museum
after the Metropolitan Museum of Art turned down her collection of
artworks. The current building, which looks like an upside-down pyramid, was built between 1963 and 1966 by Marcel Breuer. The Whitney
does not have any permanent exhibits; they are constantly changing, so
if you visit from one year to the next, all the floors will have different
works of art.

● World Trade Center and Observation Deck

*2 World Trade Center, 435-7397. Hours: Memorial Day–Labor Day daily
9:30 A.M.–11:30 P.M.; rest of the year daily 9:30 A.M.–9:30 P.M. Admission: Adults $8, children 6–12 $3, children under 6 free. www.wtc-top.org/.*
Ages 4 and up.

If heights thrill you, then take the elevators up to the 110th floor and
the rooftop observation deck for a very exciting view of Manhattan and
the surrounding area. This is the building that was bombed in 1993, but
don't worry about safety—all is repaired and well secured these days. The
rooftop observation deck is (currently) the highest in the world at just
over a quarter mile high (1,377 feet or 420 meters, to be precise). The
express elevators take only 58 seconds to reach the 107th floor, where, if
going out on the roof is a bit too much for you, you can try the glass-
enclosed observatory. It is just *under* a quarter mile high at 1,310 feet.

Brooklyn

The area code for Brooklyn is 718 unless otherwise noted. For more information on Brooklyn, go to their Web site (www.brooklynx.org/).

● Aquarium for Wildlife Conservation

Surf Avenue at W. 8th Street, 265-3400 (265-FISH). Hours: daily 10–5, summer weekends 10–6. Admission: Adults $7.75, children 2–12 $3.50, children under 2 free. Parking: $6. www.wcs.org/. **All ages.**

Arrive early is the best advice I can give to those planning a visit to this aquarium. Since its renovation was completed in 1994, the museum is better than ever. You'll see interesting ocean mammals such as Beluga whales, and other sea creatures such as giant spider crabs, sea otters, harbor seals, penguins, and seals. The *Sea Cliffs* exhibit re-creates a rocky coast habitat for the penguins, otters, seals, and walruses and features above- and below-water viewing, which is very fun for the kids. The shark tank is also particularly interesting. In the Discovery Tank, children can touch live starfish or even horseshoe crabs if they are willing. On a nice sunny day, enjoy the outdoor snack bar, or eat a picnic lunch on the Oceanic Deck. If it happens to be chilly, stay inside and eat in the ocean-view cafeteria.

Write or call for the aquarium's extensive catalog of adult and family programs.

● Brooklyn Botanical Garden / Brooklyn Museum of Art

Garden: *1000 Washington Avenue at Eastern Parkway, 622-4433. Hours: April–Sept. Tues.–Fri. 8–6, weekends 10–6; Oct.–Mar. Tues.–Fri. 8–4:30, weekends 10–4:30. Admission: Adults $3, children 6–16 $.50, children ages 5 and under free. (Free admission for all on Tues.) www.bbg.org.* **All ages.**
Museum: *200 Eastern Parkway, 638-5000. Hours: Wed.–Sun. 10–5. Arty Facts Program, Sat. and Sun. 11 and 2. Admission: Adults $4, children free. Arty Facts Program, free. Parking: $8. www.brooklynart.org/.* **Ages 4 and up.**

It takes time and a lot of patience to drive to the museum and gardens, but the visit is well worth the effort. The parking lot for both the museum and the botanical garden is on Washington Avenue just behind the museum. It is a convenient and safe place to park, and from there it's easy to take in both the museum and garden in one visit. (If you and your gang have the energy, you can also walk across the street to Prospect Park and Zoo; see separate listing.)

The Brooklyn Museum is the second-largest museum in New York City (450,000 square feet) and is renowned for its extensive collection of

Egyptian art (there's a real mummy which my kids found both gross and intriguing; they asked questions about it all day long). We began on the fifth floor (yes, there really are five floors of art) and worked our way down. I would suggest having some activities planned for children before you start your visit. I ask each of my kids to find a particular object or painting subject (my four-year-old wanted to find paintings of cheetahs) throughout the museum. Another idea is to provide a sketch pad for each child, and let them sketch a favorite work of art. The museum also has a program called Arty Facts, in which children (ages 4–7) and their parents work together to create and learn about art objects. Call for more information regarding programs for older children and for families.

After lunch in the museum café, we headed outdoors for our visit to the botanical garden. The Brooklyn Botanical Garden is an oasis within a metropolis. With over 12,000 different plants from around the world on 52 acres, there is plenty to see and touch and smell here. No food or drink is allowed outside the café area in the gardens and therefore the park is spotless.

We visited the gardens in April, on a day when all the Japanese maples were in bloom. The trees were simply magnificent. The fragrance gardens bloom in the spring with grape hyacinths and traditional hyacinths, lavenders, and other divine-smelling flowers. The entire park is wheelchair accessible—this is a great advantage not only for persons using wheelchairs but for children too. It makes the walking through the park easy for them. My kids enjoyed the gardens more than I imagined they would—they were thrilled to realize they knew some of the flowers, and their excitement turned the visit into an adventure!

Note: The garden gift shop is much too small and cramped to go into with children, especially small children. We also had this crazy idea that we could visit the Brooklyn Children's Museum in the same day, since it is relatively close by, but that really is not possible if you want to have any sanity left at the end of the day.

● Brooklyn Children's Museum
145 Brooklyn Avenue at St. Marks Avenue, 735-4400. Hours: Wed.–Fri. 2–5, weekends 12–5. Admission: Adults and children $3. **All ages.**

The Brooklyn Children's Museum has the distinction of being the world's first children's museum. Founded in 1899, it has recently undergone an extensive $7 million, three-year renovation. The museum offers every kind of program and workshop you can imagine, from Friday evening dance performances to African doll-making to music workshops and storytelling. And while many of more than 200 children's museums in the U.S. are geared towards elementary school age children, the BCM focuses programs on teens as well as the younger set.

The BCM houses a permanent collection of over 25,000 cultural objects from all over the world. One very interesting exhibit is called Ready, Set . . . Sleep—it describes bedtime rituals in different cultures. The Music Studio is a big hit; here kids can play a giant piano or bang on drums. This museum is very popular and can be crowded, so plan to stay a while to make sure you get a chance to see everything. Call for a current schedule of events; exhibits and programs change regularly.

● Coney Island—Astroland Amusement Park

1000 Surf Avenue, Coney Island Chamber of Commerce 266-1234; Astroland 372-0275. Hours: April–mid-June weekends only, mid-June– September daily. Admission: per ride. coneyisland.brooklyn.ny.us/.
All ages.

If you are in Brooklyn, you really should stop in for a visit to the famous Coney Island. It might not be the same place your father or grandfather visited as a child, but there still are plenty of rides including a roller coaster and 15 kiddie rides. The whole area is a bit on the shabby side now, but still brings back memories of another era. You'll have to try some of the rides and eat junk food on the boardwalk (Coney Island is the birthplace of the hot dog, you know). And while you're snacking, I would suggest a visit to 1001 Brighton Beach Avenue for probably the best knishes in New York, at Mrs. Stahl's Knishes. My dad, who grew up in Brooklyn in the 1940s and 1950s, remembers them with affection. Knishes, for those of you not familiar with this very New York delicacy, are a kind of popover filled with mashed potatoes or meat, and boy, are they delicious. You'd better buy a dozen or more and freeze them for later. You'll be glad you did. If you happen to be in the area on January 1st, try to stop by for a visit to watch the annual Polar Bear Club swimmers take a brisk dip into the Atlantic.

Note: The Aquarium for Wildlife Conservation, listed above, is located on Coney Island.

● Nellie Bly Amusement Park

1824 Shore Parkway, 996-4002. Hours: weekdays 12–5, weekends 12–8 Admission: $7 for 10 tickets (most rides cost 2–3 tickets each), $13.50 for 20, $24.50 for 40. **Ages 2 and up.**

If the idea of Coney Island is a little too much for you, try this small (two-acre), old-fashioned amusement park located in the Bay Ridge area of Brooklyn. There are bumper cars and other easy rides such as planes or motorcycles that go in a circle. There are some adult rides, a go-kart raceway, a petting farm, and an arcade. Not too overwhelming, not too crowded. There are food stands, restrooms, and yes, even miniature golf.

● New York City Transit Museum

Moerum Place and Schermerhorn Street, 243-5839. Hours: Tues., Thurs., Fri. 10–4, Wed. 10–6, weekends 12–5. Admission: Adults $3, children $1.50. www.nytransit.com/nytm/. **Ages 4 and up.**

This museum, which opened in 1976, is located in a 1936 subway station, where there are 19 vintage subway cars on display (you can go into the cars and walk around, and even pretend to be a conductor). The museum focuses on the development and history of mass transportation in New York and has nearly 100 years worth of transit artifacts and photographs, as well as an interesting gift shop.

● Prospect Park Wildlife Conservation Center

450 Flatbush Avenue at Prospect Park, 399-7339. Hours: daily 10–5. Admission: Adults $2.50, children 3–12 $.50, children under 3 free. Parking: free on-street parking available on Flatbush Avenue. www.prospectpark.org/ or www.wcs.org/. **All ages.**

This park and zoo is just across the street from the Brooklyn Museum of Art and the Brooklyn Botanical Garden. Built in 1867, this 526-acre park was designed by the landscape architects who designed Central Park, Frederick Law Olmsted and Calvert Vaux. The zoo, which is set on 12 acres within the park, was renovated in 1993; its 160 animals share the park with several other attractions, including six playgrounds, a carousel, and a lake. Just south of the zoo is the large wonderful carousel, originally built in 1912 and recently restored. It is now wheelchair accessible (rides are $.50). Call 965-8999 for more information. You can also rent a pedal boat and enjoy a leisurely ride on the park's 90 acres of water ($10 per hour).

Note: All the zoos listed in this New York City chapter and the aquarium in Brooklyn are members of the Wildlife Conservation Society (WCS).

Queens

The area code for Queens is 718 unless otherwise noted.

● Alley Pond Environmental Center

228–06 Northern Boulevard, Douglaston, 229-4000. Hours: daily, but changes with the seasons, call for current hours. Admission: free (special programs have individual fees). **All ages.**

It's hard to believe but there is actually a working windmill in Queens! It's right here in this 635-acre park where there are also nature trails to hike. The Environmental Center is located at the northern end of Alley Pond Park, near a salt marsh. The center also has a mini-zoo/ aquarium and interactive displays.

● American Museum of the Moving Image

35th Avenue at 36th Street, Astoria, 784-0077. Hours: Tues.–Fri. noon–5, weekends 11–6. Admission: Adults $8, children 5–18 $4. **Ages 9 and up.**

This is the only museum in the U.S. devoted to the history of film, television, video, and digital media. The museum has 13 stations that provide interactive, computer-based, moving-image experiences. There are hands-on video game exhibits as well, which, as you can imagine, are quite a hit. Take a seat in the theater designed by artist Red Grooms and watch some old movies. The museum also has demonstrations of movie special effects and displays of movie memorabilia, including several *Star Trek* outfits. Very cool stuff for older kids and adults!

● Belmont Park and Race Track

Cross Island Parkway, Elmont, exit 26-D, 641-4700. Hours: Wed.–Sun. first race at 1. Admission: depends upon event. General park admission $2, children under 2 free. Breakfast at Belmont, free park admission. **All ages.**

Although Belmont Park is a thoroughbred racetrack geared towards adults, it does offer the Breakfast at Belmont program every weekend and on holidays. These special days include a variety of fun things to do. First take a tram ride around the park, and then enjoy an à la carte breakfast while watching the horses in their morning workout routines. Tours run from 7 A.M.–9:30 A.M., and the breakfast is moderately priced. Belmont Park also has another family program called Family Fun Days held every Sunday. The kids can enjoy such things as riding ponies, petting animals in the petting zoo, getting their faces painted, and watching silly clowns perform. The only fee is the general park admission.

● Isamu Noguchi Garden Museum

3237 Grand Boulevard, Long Island City, 204-7088. Hours: Apr.–Oct. Wed.–Fri. 10–5, weekends 11–6. Admission (suggested contribution): Adults $4, students $2. **All ages.**

Isamu Noguchi (1904–1988) is one of the world's most famous modern sculptors, and in the 1960s he turned his studio into this interest-ing museum, which features over 300 of his sculptures. There are 12 galleries and an outdoor garden designed in the manner of a traditional

Japanese fountain garden *(tsukubai)*. It is a quiet, serene place to take children.

● New York Hall of Science

47-01 111th Street, Flushing Meadows, Corona Park, 699-0005. Hours: Wed.–Sun. 10–5. Admission: Adults $4.50, children ages 4 and up $3, children under 4 free (all visitors free on Wed. and Thurs. 2–5). Parking: $4 in summer. www.nyhallsci.org. **Ages 3 and up.**

The NYH of S is a not-too-crowded hands-on science and technology museum with 160 exhibits, including Seeing Light, Sound Sensations, and the Technology Gallery. There's even a preschool discovery area. Try sliding down one of two slides to see which is faster. Or perhaps you'd like to stand on the Standing Spinner to see what it's like to twirl like an ice skater (yikes). In more than 30,000 square feet of exhibition space, your kids are guaranteed to find something fun and interesting. The museum was renovated in 1996 at a cost of $13 million, and now includes a cafeteria and gift shop. It originally opened in 1964 as a pavilion for the World's Fair. You can walk from here over to the Queens Museum of Art for more adventures.

● Queens Botanical Gardens

43-50 Main Street, Flushing, 886-3800. Hours: Apr.–Oct. Tues.–Fri. 8–6, weekends 8–7; Nov.–Mar. Tues.–Sun. 8–4:30. Admission: free.
All ages.

Right smack in the middle of Queens is this 39-acre park which boasts, among other things, an herb garden, a rose garden, and a Victorian-style wedding garden. If you happen to be in Queens and need a break from all the traffic on the LIE, stop in here for a breather and enjoy yourself for an hour.

● Queens County Farm Museum

73-50 Little Neck Parkway, Floral Park, 347-FARM. Hours: Mon.– Fri. 9–5 outdoor visits only, weekends 10–5 tours of farm house available. Admission: free except on special event days. Hay rides $2 on the weekends.
All ages.

At this historic park you'll find a 47-acre working farm with cows, sheep, lambs, goats, chickens, and turkeys. The farmhouse museum, built in 1772, gives kids a chance to experience what farm life was like more than 200 years ago. The museum offers children's programs in arts and crafts, nature, and farming. The programs are usually geared towards ages

6 through 12 during the summer; educational programs for other age groups are offered throughout the academic year. Call for a schedule of current events, including the county fair and Native American powwow.

● Queens Museum of Art

New York City Building, Flushing Meadows, Corona Park, 592-9700. Hours: Wed.–Fri. 10–5, weekends 12–5. Admission: Adults $3 (suggested donation), children free. **Ages 4 and up.**

If you want to see something really cool, stop in here and check out the Panorama of the City of New York, a 9,000-square-foot model of New York City. It is complete with buildings, bridges, highways, and landmarks, and contains at present almost 900,000 structures built to scale. Flushing Meadows was also the site of the 1939 and 1964 World's Fairs. The Unisphere, a 12-story-high giant steel globe built as a symbol for the 1964 Fair, still stands here today. Call to find out about the special art workshops that take place here on the weekends.

● Queens Wildlife Center

111th Street, Flushing Meadows, Corona Park, 271-1500. Hours: daily 10–5. Admission: Adults $2.50, children 3–12 $.50, children under 3 free. www.wcs.org/. **All ages.**

This recently renovated zoo covers 11 acres of land and features North American species. During the renovation a new children's zoo was created, and the center developed a varied education program that includes an annual sheep-shearing event—kids can decorate paper with real wool, or learn how to spin wool, or do other fun arts and crafts projects. A nice outdoor playground designed for all children, including those with disabilities, rounds out the offerings here.

● Socrates Sculpture Park

Broadway at Vernon Boulevard, on the East River, Long Island City, 956-1819. Hours: daily 10–sunset. Admission: free. **All ages.**

This five-acre outdoor park is one of New York City's 14 designated "pedestrian sites." It was founded in the early 1980s by sculptor Mark di Suvero as an alternative to indoor art galleries. All of the sculpture is hands-on (and feet-on and stand-on), and kids have a blast climbing and scrambling over the works. Occasionally, you can watch sculptors creating new works on-site. The park is now owned by the city and has permanent and changing outdoor sculpture exhibits.

Bronx

For more information on the Bronx, visit their Web site
(www.ilovethebronx.com/).

The area code for the Bronx is 718 unless otherwise noted.

● **Bronx Museum of the Arts**
*1040 Grand Concourse and 165th Street, 681-6000. Hours: Wed. 3–9,
Thurs. and Fri. 10–5, weekends 1–6. Admission: Adults $3 (suggested
donation), children under 12 free if accompanied by an adult.* **Ages 3 and up.**

This museum's focus is on installations of contemporary art from
throughout the world. The public programs office hosts Family Sunday,
which takes place one Sunday per month throughout the year. Families
get a tour of the museum and the exhibits, and attend a creative workshop
afterwards. The fee for this program is $5 per person. Call for additional
information regarding current exhibitions and public programs.

● **Bronx Zoo International Wildlife Conservation Park**
*Fordham Road, Bronx River Parkway, 185th Street and Southern Boulevard,
367-1010. Hours: daily 10–5. Admission: Oct.–Apr. adults $3, children
2–12 $1.50 (all visitors free on Wed.); May–Sept. adults $6.75, children
2–12 $3 (all visitors free on Wed.). Additional fees for rides, parking, and
Children's Zoo. www.wcs.org/.* **All ages.**

We visited the Bronx Zoo on the first warm Sunday in April and it
was crowded, but it wasn't as crowded as it usually gets in the summer.
If you visit the zoo, be prepared! Wear very comfortable shoes or sneakers,
and make sure small children have a stroller, because they'll get tired,
believe me! The park is huge (it's the largest zoo in the U.S.), covering
approximately 265 acres and housing over 4,300 animals.

There are plenty of attractions but there are also many unexpected
costs here. The Zoo Shuttle is a nice way to get around the park but you
have to pay an extra $2 per person. There are additional fees for the
monorail which takes you through Wild Asia and for the Skyfari ride.
Both of these rides are a wonderful way to see the park. The zoo is really
a wonderful zoo, and the animals have wonderful habitats in which
to live.

It's best to visit during the week on the less busy days, but if that's
not possible, then opt for getting there as early as you can. We arrived
about half an hour after the zoo had opened and there was already a long
line to get into the parking area. There are places to buy food, but the
lines tend to get long, and the food is expensive. Bring some sandwiches
if possible, and buy drinks.

Again, we thought we could do too many things in one day. We wanted to visit the nearby botanical gardens also but after four hours at the zoo we (the adults) were wiped out.

● New York Botanical Garden

200th Street and Southern Boulevard, 817-8700. Hours: Tues.–Sun. 10–4. Admission: Garden, adults $3, children 6 and up $1, children 5 and under free (all visitors free Apr.–Oct. Wed. and Sat. 10–12); Conservatory, adults $3.50, children 6–16 $2.50. www.nybg.org/. **All ages.**

The New York Botanical Garden is New York City's oldest (1891) and largest (250 acres). There are 26 specialty gardens here including a rock garden, a rose garden with over 2,500 rose bushes, a fern forest, and a perennial garden, to name just a few. The Enid A. Haupt Conservatory, modeled after the Crystal Palace in London (a large glass building), was built in 1902 and is a magnificent structure to explore in. There is also a Children's Corner and Discovery Room at the botanical garden for children to investigate. The fee for the conservatory is in addition to the admission fee for the garden only.

Staten Island

For more information on Staten Island, visit their Web site (www.si-web. com/nyc/).

The area code for Staten Island is 718 unless otherwise noted.

● Alice Austen House

2 Hylan Boulevard, 816-4506. Hours: Thurs.–Sun. noon–5. Admission: $3 (suggested donation). **Ages 5 and up.**

This house, named Clear Comfort, was the home of the photographer Alice Austen (1866–1930). The small cozy cottage was built in 1710, and she lived here for most of her life. She unfortunately lost all of her money in the stock market crash of 1929, and was forced to move into a poor-house (at age 84). When *Life* magazine published her work a year later, she earned enough to move into a nursing home. Austen left many negatives (she took over 9,000 photographs during her lifetime), and today her home/museum displays changing exhibits of her work. You can get fabulous views of the Statue of Liberty, the Verrazano Bridge, and New York City from the grounds.

● Clay Pits Ponds State Park Preserve

83 Nielsen Avenue at Sharrots Road, 967-1976. Hours: Thurs.–Sun. noon–5. Admission: free. **All ages.**

This is a 260-acre nature preserve with wetlands, hiking trails, and Saturday nature education programs. The park is largely undeveloped, without any playgrounds or ballparks; visitors come here for an enjoyable day hike. The area belonged to a clay mining operation before it became a park in 1980, hence its name.

● Historic Richmond Town

441 Clarke Avenue, 351-1611. Hours: Wed.–Sun. 1–5. Admission: Adults $4, children 6–18 $2.50, children under 6 free. **All ages.**

Twenty-nine buildings, 14 of them open to the public, make up this authentic historic village. Originally founded by Dutch settlers, Richmond Town has the oldest surviving elementary school in the country, dating to circa 1696. The general store dates to 1837, as does the courthouse. There are shops, houses, workshops, and of course, the local tavern. Historic artifacts and toys are on display in the museum. Costumed guides regularly reenact daily life.

● Snug Harbor Cultural Center

1000 Richmond Terrace, 448-2500. Hours: grounds open dawn to dusk, galleries open Wed.–Sun. 12–5. Admission: free ($2 suggested donation for gallery). www.si-web.com/Attractions/SHCC.html. **All ages.**

In the 1830s Scotsman Robert Richard Randall, a reformed pirate, established Snug Harbor, a kind of retirement home for mariners. He built mess halls, meeting halls, and more—28 buildings in all—on an 83-acre site. Today the SHCC is one of the nation's largest ongoing preservation projects. The center offers concerts, exhibits, tours, and educational programs.

● Staten Island Botanical Garden

At the Snug Harbor Cultural Center, 1000 Richmond Terrace, 273-8200. Hours: grounds open daily 8–dusk. Admission: free. **All ages.**

The botanical garden is part of Snug Harbor Cultural Center. There are 15 acres of natural wetland and 13 acres of Victorian landscaping that includes rose, herb, sensory, pond, and annual gardens.

● Staten Island Children's Museum

At the Snug Harbor Cultural Center, 1000 Richmond Terrace, 273-2060. Hours: school year Tues.–Sun. 12–5. Admission: Ages 3 and up $4, children under 2 free. **All ages.**

This is just what every town needs, a small museum with a focus on bugs. Here are exhibits that let kids examine bugs close up. The museum is a nice size for kids to explore freely, and usually there are art installations designed for kids to play in or on. Bring a picnic lunch on a warm afternoon and enjoy yourselves. The main building for Snug Harbor Cultural Center is right next door.

● Staten Island Institute of Arts and Sciences

75 Stuyvesant Place, 727-1135. Hours: Mon.–Sat. 9–5, Sun. noon–5. Admission (suggested donation): Adults $2.50, students $1.50. **Ages 4 and up.**

The Institute of Arts and Sciences was founded in 1881 and is therefore one of New York City's oldest museums. It has a collection of over 2 million objects, including painting, furniture, clothing, crafts, decorative arts, and a natural science collection of more than a half million specimens. You'll find a variety of public programs here including walking tours, lectures, day camps for the kids, and other special events.

● Staten Island Zoo

614 Broadway, 442-3101. Hours: daily 10–4:30. Admission: Adults $3, children 3–12 $2, children under 3 free. **All ages.**

Most children lose it after a few hours or so at a large zoo. This small zoo (eight acres) however, is the perfect size for kids and has mostly indoor exhibits (great on a cold day). Visit the New World Tropical Forest and the zoo's newest addition, the African Savannah. There's a rather large aquarium, with coral fish and even piranhas, and a famous reptile collection complete with lizards and iguanas. On a warm day, enjoy food from the snack bar outdoors, and afterwards treat the kids to a pony ride.

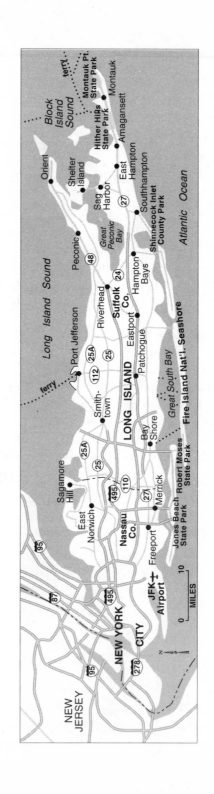

Long Island

LONG ISLAND IS EXACTLY THAT—a *long island,* a 118-mile island
that lies east of Manhattan. It is only 20 miles across at its widest point
and approximately 1,377 square miles. Brooklyn and Queens are geographically part of Long Island, but they are two of the five boroughs that
make up New York City. When people refer to "the island," they are
most likely talking about only Nassau and Suffolk counties.

At the east end, the island splits in two forks. The North Fork is 28
miles long and extends to Orient Point; the South Fork is 44 miles long
and extends to Montauk Point. In-between the two forks are two smaller
islands, Shelter Island and Gardiner Island; the latter is privately owned.
Approximately 25 million people per year visit Long Island for a variety
of activities ranging from swimming, horseback riding, and visiting
historic sites and mansions to strolling along quiet seaside towns, dining
at restaurants, and much more. Long Island has over 100 art museums and
historical sites, 20 art galleries, 16 lighthouses, 18 nature preserves, 2
national parks, 5 arboretums, 11 mansions open to the public, 75 farm
stands and pick-your-own farms, hundreds of miles of beautiful beaches,
and over 4,000 restaurants to get a bite to eat in when you're done with
all the above.

In addition to all the listings included in this chapter, there are
also ferry rides to take, camping possibilities, and lighthouse safaris to
sign up for. For information on ferry services on Long Island, call one of
the following businesses: **Cross Sound Ferry,** 323-2525; **Fire Island
Ferry,** 665-3600; or **Port Jefferson Ferry,** 473-0286 (to Bridgeport,
CT). Many people love to camp at Long Island's many campgrounds; call
1-800-ILOVENY for further details. Or for a truly unique experience try
a safari. Your family will learn about Long Island's rich maritime history.
Safaris can be arranged according to your family's interests. On a safari

you can visit whaling museums or aquariums, take nature walks or just visit the area's lighthouses. Call or write to **Long Island Lighthouse Safaris,** Box 4243, Oak Beach, NY, 11702, 422-4213 for more details.

For a terrific, sturdy map of Long Island, I highly recommend *Streetwise Long Island: Major Roads and Sites from Manhattan to Montauk.* It is available for $5.95 and is plastic-coated so it can be folded and refolded. It is very easy to read and includes major attractions such as parks, wineries, and historical sites. It is available in many bookstores but if you can't find one write to Streetwise Maps Inc., P.O. Box 2219, Amagansett, NY, 11930.

And for the adults, don't forget there are many good wineries (14) on the east end of Long Island. Check the Long Island Visitors Guide Web site at www.licvb.com/liguide/ or call the Visitors Bureau at 1-800-441-4601 for further information.

Tired of malls? Enjoy small-town charm when you try shopping in one of the following Suffolk County villages: Amagansett, Bellport, Bridgehampton, Cold Spring Harbor, East Hampton, Hampton Bays, Montauk, Port Jefferson, Sag Harbor, Southampton, or Westhampton Beach.

All of the sites in this chapter are located in Nassau and Suffolk counties; the area code for both counties is 516. The listings are in alphabetical order by town within each county.

Nassau County

ALBERTSON

● Belmont Park

See listing under Queens in the New York City chapter.

● Clark Botanic Garden

193 I. U. Willets Road, 484-8600. Hours: daily 10–4:30. Admission: free (though it's likely the garden will soon begin to charge a small entrance fee). **All ages.**

The 12 beautiful acres of the Clark Botanic Garden are landscaped with three ponds, lawns, and many types of gardens. Curving paths take you through an iris garden, an herb garden, a rose garden, a rock garden, and several others. Among the special events here are a "Spooky Walk" at Halloween and free concerts on Tuesday evenings during the summer.

CEDARHURST

● Fun Galaxy

591-597 Willow Avenue, 374-1120. Hours: Mon.–Fri. 10–5. Admission: Adults free, children $6.50. **Ages 2–6.**

What kid wouldn't have fun in a 4,500-square-foot indoor playground? Children can jump in ball pits, slide down slides, climb nets, and play Nintendo or take part in a host of other games and rides. This facility is probably best suited for younger children, those in the two-to-six age group. All play areas are on one floor. Those with dietary restrictions will be happy to hear that all food is kosher.

● Kidmazeum

112 Spruce Street, 295-4400. Hours: Tues.–Fri. 11–7, Sat., Sun. 10–8. Call ahead to verify hours; Kidmazeum closes periodically for private children's parties. Admission: Adults free, children $8. Special discount hours Tues.–Thurs. 11–3, children $4. **Ages 1–13.**

This site, designed for ages 1 to 13, has an indoor village and a bilevel crawl-through maze that kids think is absolutely the best thing on earth. There is also a hands-on learning center, cars for your little drivers to pretend-drive, toys to build with, science equipment, computers, musical instruments, a giant sandbox, trampolines, and more. Vending machines and refreshments are available.

Note that there are three levels at this facility, which makes it more difficult to keep an eye on your kids. Also note that kids must wear socks.

COLD SPRING HARBOR

For more information on Cold Spring Harbor, visit their Web site (clio.cshl.org/cshm/index.htm).

● Cold Spring Harbor Fish Hatchery and Aquarium

Main Street (Route 25A), between Rt. 108 and Shore Road, 692-6768. Hours: daily 10–5. Admission: Adults $3, children 5–12 $1.50, children under 5 free. www.okc.com/fish/. **All ages.**

The Cold Spring Harbor Fish Hatchery began operations in 1883. In addition to six outdoor pools where visitors can feed trout, the hatchery also raises turtles and has over 40 aquariums, one of which contains over 30 species of freshwater fish native to New York. My kids loved this site and always ask to go back.

● Cold Spring Harbor Whaling Museum

Main Street (Route 25A), 367-3418. Hours: Memorial Day–Labor Day daily 11–5; Sept.–May Tues.–Sun 11–5. Admission: Adults $2, children 6–12 $1.50, children under 6 free. clio.cshl.org/cshm/whale.htm. **All ages.**

If you have kids interested in anything to do with the sea, then this is the museum for them. Founded in 1936, the museum descibes life in Cold Spring Harbor in its whaling days and displays a fully rigged, 19th-century whaling boat. There are even special exhibits where you can listen to whale calls. Call for current information about special events, which usually take place on Sundays.

● DNA Learning Center

334 Main Street, 367-7240. Hours: Mon.–Fri.10–4, Sat. 12–4. Long Island Discovery Mon.–Fri. at 10, 11, and 1, and Saturdays at 1 and 3. Admission: free. darwin.cshl.org/. **Ages 8 and up.**

The DNA Center is a great place for kids interested in the sciences. It is the nation's first facility dedicated to DNA science education. There is a gallery area with changing exhibits, some of which (it's fair to say) are gross, but kids love them, especially the mannequin pretending to wheel around fake human brains (part of the Story of a Gene exhibit). The *Long Island Discovery* show (produced by Cablevision), a half-hour presentation about the history of Long Island, is also a must-see. It is a multi-image surround-sound presentation that uses 18 slide projectors, 3 video projectors, and 12 speakers to create a dynamic audio-visual experience. Definitely stop in here for a unique afternoon outing. The center is closed some holidays, so call ahead to verify hours.

GARDEN CITY

● Long Island Children's Museum

550 Stewart Avenue, 222-0207. Hours: Wed–Fri. 10–4, weekends 10–5. Admission: Ages 3 and up $4.00, children under 2 free, family membership for one year $40. www.516web.com/museum/licm.html. **All ages.**

This museum is a wonder for children; they'll love permanent exhibits such as *Bubbles, Communication Station, Working on the Railroad,* and others. The number of people allowed in the museum is limited, due to space restrictions, so tickets are sold on a first-come, first-served basis. When the capacity has been reached, timed tickets are sold. No advance sales are possible. No food or strollers are allowed in the museum. Park for free across the street (but please be very careful when crossing, it's a busy street).

GREAT NECK

● Saddle Rock Grist Mill

Grist Mill Lane, 572-0257. Hours: Sun. 1–5. Admission: free. **Ages 3 and up.**

Grist mills normally aren't on kids' lists of things to do, but once they get there they usually find them interesting. Listening to and watching the staff explain the workings of the mill is quite an eye-opener for children, and a perfect opportunity to explain everyday life in past centuries. Saddle Rock Mill is one of the oldest grist mills in the country, dating back to 1702.

HEMPSTEAD

● African-American Museum

110 N. Franklin Street, 572-0730. Hours: Thurs.–Sat. 10–4:45, Sun. 1–4:45. Admission: free. **Ages 3 and up.**

The focus of this museum is on the history of African-Americans on Long Island. Special exhibits are on view from the Smithsonian Institution, the Brooklyn Museum, and other museums nationwide. The birthdays of famous African-Americans are celebrated here, and during the summer, the museum offers workshops for both adults and children.

● Fine Arts Museum of Long Island

295 Fulton Avenue, 481-5700. Hours: Thurs.–Sun. 10–4:30. Admission: Adults $2, children under 12 $1. **Ages 5 and up.**

You'll find more than pieces of fine art here; the museum has a collection of pre-Columbian art, an interactive computer center, a video room, computer-related art exhibits, and international exhibitions.

HICKSVILLE

● Hicksville Gregory Museum

Heitz Place and Bay Avenue, 822-7505. Hours: Tues.–Fri. 9:30–4:30, weekends 1–5. Admission: Adults $3, children 6–14 $1.50, children under 6 free. **Ages 3 and up.**

This small museum boasts a mineral collection of over 10,000 pieces! There are also animal and plant fossil collections, and a butterfly and moth collection that kids love, especially if they are interested in insects and the natural sciences. A rather unique item here is the jail cell which dates to 1915, when this museum was the county courthouse.

● Long Island Reptile Expo and Museum
70 Broadway (Route 107), 931-1500. Hours: Mon.–Thurs., Sat., Sun. 10–6, Fri. 10–9. Admission: Adults $9.95, children $7.95, children under 3 free. **Ages 2 and up**.

If your kids are into reptiles, this is the place to visit. They'll love the petting zoo, live reptile shows, and hands-on exhibits. Over 3,000 reptiles and amphibians are featured. There is also a movie theater, a reptile pet shop and gift shop, and an on-site eatery, called the Snake Bite Café. Be prepared to spend at least two hours here. The museum, which opened in June 1996, covers over 20,000 square feet, and its main objective is to "make education come alive."

JONES BEACH
See listing under Wantaugh.

OCEANSIDE

● Bzircus
2909 Lincoln Avenue, 763-5630 or 1-800-440-5646. Hours: Sun.–Thurs. 11–9, Fri. and Sat. 11–10. Admission: tokens for games or rides vary between $.25 and $1. **Ages 2–12**.

With over 20,000 square feet of space, this indoor family fun center boasts 100 different games, activities, and rides. Kids can jump in a ball pit, slip down slides, and much more. Party rooms are available, and there's a refreshment stand.

OLD BETHPAGE

● Old Bethpage Village Restoration
Round Swamp Road (exit 48S off the LIE), 572-8400. Hours: Mar.–Oct. Wed.–Sun. 10–5; Nov.–Dec. Wed.–Sun. 10–4. (Closed in Jan. and Feb.) Admission: Adults $6, children $3. **Ages 4 and up**.

Experience what life in America was like in the 19th century at this wonderful living history museum. Wander and explore in a 100-acre village complete with furnished homes and stores. Sit on the porch of the hotel and have a root beer. Come into the one-room schoolhouse and practice writing on a slate tablet. Listen to the history provided by guides in historical dress. When you get tired, just sit down on the closest bench and wait for the bus, which circles through the village continually, to come pick you up. Special programs in the past have included cider-making, demonstration 19th-century baseball games, the annual Long

Island Fair (October), and outdoor concerts. Hours sometimes change in December, so call ahead for a schedule.

OLD WESTBURY

● Old Westbury Gardens

Old Westbury Road (exit 39S off the LIE), 333-0048. Hours: Apr.–Oct. daily 10–5; Nov.–Mar. weekends 11–4. Admission: Gardens only, adults $6, children ages 6–12 $3, children under 6 free; house and gardens, adults $10, children 6–12 $6, children under 6 free; special rates for the Christmas season and other special events. **Ages 4 and up.**

Old Westbury Gardens are part of an 88-acre estate built by John S. Phipps in 1906. The estate features a Charles II–style country home, a formal rose garden, a lilac walk, a boxwood garden, several small contemporary gardens, and a thatched cottage. Seasonal events take place throughout the year. From June through August there's a children's reading program for example, and a summer concert series. You'll also find a café and gift shop on-site.

OYSTER BAY

● Planting Fields Arboretum and Coe Hall

Planting Fields Road (exit 41N off the LIE), Arboretum, 922-9201 or Coe Hall, 922-0479. Hours: Arboretum, daily 9–5. Coe Hall Apr.–Sept. daily 12:30–5, first tour at 12:30. Admission: Arboretum, $4 per car. Coe Hall Tours Apr.–Sept., adults $3.50, children 7–12 $1, children 6 and under free. Parking: $3, May 1–Labor Day, holidays, weekends. **Ages 3 and up.**

Planting Fields was designed between 1918 and 1944, by the son and nephew of F. L. Olmsted, one of the landscape architects who planned Central Park in Manhattan. The site includes Coe Hall, a 1920s Tudor Revival mansion, a 409-acre arboretum with formal gardens, a wildflower walk, 40 acres of lawns, 200 acres of woodlands and fields, and a wonderful camellia greenhouse. There are several special programs and a summer concert series called the Friends of the Arts Summer Festival at Planting Fields.

● Raynham Hall Museum

20 W. Main Street, 922-6808. Hours: Tues.–Sun. 1–5. Admission: Adults $2, children ages 6 and up $1, children under 6 free. **Ages 5 and up.**

This museum was once the home of the Townsend family, who were members of George Washington's Culper Spy Ring. The house was built around 1738 and features colonial and Victorian period rooms. Each Christmas season there is a beautiful seasonal exhibit in the Victorian addition (1851) of the house.

● Sagamore Hill National Historic Site

Cove Neck Road (exit 41N off the LIE), 922-4447. Hours: daily 9:30–5, tours leave every half hour. Admission: $5, children free. www.liglobal.com/ t_i/saghill/default.shtml. **Ages 4 and up.**

Sagamore Hill was Theodore Roosevelt's "Summer White House" during his presidency, between 1901 and 1909 (it was built in 1884–85). In 1909, he moved there full-time and stayed until his death in 1919. Now this 23-room Victorian mansion is open for tours daily, and has been since 1966. Children love to see his hunting trophies, and there are wonderful paintings and original furnishings to see as well. There is also a museum and gift shop; the snack bar is open only in the summer.

ROSLYN HARBOR

● Nassau County Museum of Art

1 Museum Drive (off Northern Boulevard), 484-9338. Hours: Tues.–Sun. 11–5. Admission: Adults $4, children $2. **Ages 5 and up.**

The museum was once an elegant neoclassical mansion on the estate of Henry Clay Frick. In the heart of Long Island's historic north shore (the Gold Coast), ten refurbished galleries exhibit works by American and European artists; formal gardens, wildflower walks, and an outdoor sculpture park are also part of this beautiful 145-acre site.

WANTAUGH

● Jones Beach State Park

Accessible by the Meadowbrook Parkway or Wantaugh State Parkway, 785-1600. Hours: dawn to dusk. Admission: Approximately $5 per car (varies per beach). **All ages.**

Jones Beach is one of several famous beaches along the four narrow barrier islands on Long Island's south shore. The first is Long Beach where Atlantic Beach and Lido Beach are located; the second is where you'll find Jones Beach. The third island is Fire Island National Seashore; and the fourth is where Westhampton Beach and the Shinnecock Inlet are located. Jones Beach State Park has much to offer in addition to its world-famous shoreline. Enjoy a two-mile health walk or the four-mile bike path. During the summer, the Jones Beach Theater has a terrific concert series.

For more information call the Long Island Convention and Visitor's Bureau at 1-800-441-4601.

WESTBURY

● Long Island Sports World

51 Frost Street, 333-3091. Hours: Mon.–Fri. 2–10, Sat. 10–10, Sun. 11–10. Admission: Varies per activity. **All 3 and up.**

This facility is the perfect place for your budding athlete to practice his or her favorite sport. Batting cages, a basketball court, and a roller-blading rink, are a few of the venues, and plus there's mini-golf, kiddie rides, and, of course, video games for when they need a break.

Suffolk County

For information specifically on the North Fork of Long Island see: www.northfork.com, which is the Web site for *North Fork Magazine.*

AMAGANSETT

● East Hampton Town Marine Museum

Bluff Road, 267-6544 (or call the East Hampton Historical Society, 324-6850). Hours: Memorial Day–July 1 weekends 10–5; July and Aug. daily 10–5; Sept. and Oct. weekends 10–5. Admission: Adults $4, children 12 and under $2. **Ages 3 and up.**

This museum has three floors of displays that illustrate the history of whaling and fishing on Long Island. There are whaling artifacts and an outdoor trawler for kids to climb on. The museum also has a hands-on discovery room where kids can play with sand, fish bones, shells, and more.

BELLPORT

● Bellport-Brookhaven Historical Complex

31 Bellport Lane (exit 65S LIE), 286-0888. Hours: Memorial Day–Columbus Day Thurs.–Sat. 1–4:30. Admission: Adults $1, children $.50. **Ages 5 and up.**

At this historic site you can find the Post-Cromwell house, built in 1833, which is decorated with period furniture. There is also a barn (it houses a mixed collection of antiques, Native American artifacts, and toys—including 1920s and 1930s Lionel trains) and a blacksmith shop.

CENTERPORT

● Vanderbilt Museum

180 Little Neck Road, 854-5555. Planetarium, 262-STAR. Hours: Tues.–Sun. noon–5. Admission: Adults $5, children under 12 $1. www.webscope.com/vanderbilt. **Ages 4 and up.**

The estate of William Vanderbilt II is located on a beautiful 43-acre site on Long Island's north shore. The mansion is Spanish-Moroccan in style and contains an eclectic mixture of the family's personal collections of stuffed animals and sealife. There is a separate marine museum with additional exhibits. One of the largest planetariums in the United States is also on-site. The planetarium carries a separate fee and you should call ahead since it was closed for restoration when we visited. The Vanderbilt Museum offers a wide variety of summer programs, such as a four-day exploration of the sea and shoreline, a Long Island Sound family eco-cruise, a dinosaur dig, and many others.

COMMACK

● Hoyt Farm Park Preserve

New Highway (just east of Commack Road), 543-7804. Hours: Hoyt House, Memorial Day–Sept. 30, weekends 2–5; Nature Center, Memorial Day–Sept. 30 daily 12–5; Park year-round dawn–dusk. Parking at the center is for Smithtown residents only, but other visitors can park outside the entrance for free. Admission: free. **All ages.**

This 133-acre wildlife preserve includes a nature center, the 18th-century Hoyt house, and a self-guided trail. The nature center has farm animals to see; part of the Hoyt house is open for visitors to view period furniture and artifacts; and the nature trail has 33 stopping points which show all the many wildlife habitats of the area. There are even playgrounds and a ball field on the preserve.

EAST FARMINGDALE

● Adventureland

2245 Route 110, 694-6868. Hours: Apr.–late June and Labor Day–late Oct. weekends 12–5; late June–Labor Day daily noon–11 (Fri. and Sat. noon–midnight); mid-Nov.–mid-Mar. indoor kiddie rides weekends only. Game room and restaurant open all year. Admission: Unlimited rides $15.95, 21 tickets $10.95 (rides are 3–5 tickets each). **All ages.**

Adventureland promotes itself as "Long Island's Amusement Park," and that it is, with video games, rides, cotton candy, hot dogs, and the whole shebang. It has been in business since 1960 and has a total of 24 rides (12 for children under 54 inches), plus an 18-hole mini-golf course, a Ferris wheel, and over 200 other games and attractions. The indoor portion is air-conditioned and has the requisite snack bar.

EAST HAMPTON

For more information about all the Hamptons see www.hamptons.com or for the east end of Long Island more generally, see www.lieast.com.

● Mulford Farm

10 James Lane, 324-6850. Hours: June, Sept., Oct. weekends 10–5; July and Aug. daily 10–5. Admission: Adults $4, children $2. **Ages 4 and up.**

This site is much more than just a farm. It is the historic home of the Mulford family. Not only does it date back to the late 1600s, but it was used continually until 1944 by generations of the same family. Costumed interpreters guide visitors through the farm and give demonstrations of crafts such as butter churning, basket making, and weaving, to name just a few. Rachel's Garden, outdoors, is maintained with typical plants from the 17th century and information is provided on their various medicinal benefits.

● Pollock-Krasner House and Study Center

830 Fireplace Road, 324-4929. Hours: By appointment only (with 1 week advance notice) May–Oct. Thurs.–Sat. 11–4. Admission: Adults $5, children 12 and under free. (Additional costs for lectures and other special events vary.) **Ages 5 and up.**

The former studio and home of the late abstract expressionist painters Jackson Pollock and his wife Lee Krasner, the study center now provides facilities for those doing research on 20th-century American art. The well-known paint-splattered floor on which Pollock created many of his most famous works has been preserved as he left it. Give your child a modern art lesson! Guided tours are available, and special programs include lectures and exhibitions. The center also provides a free workbook on abstract art that has activities for children. Bring a blanket and picnic lunch and enjoy the day on the grounds overlooking Accabonac Creek.

EAST ISLIP

● Empire State Carousel

50 Irish Lane at Brookwood Hall Park, 277-6168. Hours: Sat. 10–4. Admission: free (donations accepted). **All ages.**

Begun in 1984, this incredible hand-carved carousel and its decorations are based on New York history and culture. Among other fanciful objects, the carousel includes two chariot-style pieces—an Erie Canal bargeboat and a scallop shell—as well as two full-sized animals created especially for children in wheelchairs. The carousel features 28 animals, as well as relief portraits of famous New Yorkers such as Teddy Roosevelt, George Gershwin, Walt Whitman, Jackie Robinson, and a host of New York–based folklore characters such as Rip van Winkle, and others.

Note: In the spring of 1998, the carousel is scheduled to increase the hours it's open to the public. Call ahead to verify hours.

● Islip Art Museum

50 Irish Lane at Brookwood Hall Park, 224-5402. Hours: Wed.– Sat. 10–4, Sun. 2–4:30. Admission: free (donations accepted). **Ages 4 and up.**

This museum is housed in the Brookwood Hall mansion and has additional gallery space in the adjacent Carriage House. Brookwood Hall, a 41-room mansion, was built in 1910 and was a private residence until 1942, when it became headquarters for the Orphan Asylum Society of Brooklyn. Between 1965 and 1980 the mansion housed the Islip Art Museum, the Islip Arts Council offices, and the town of Islip's Department of Parks, Recreation, and Cultural Affairs; now it is the site of the museum alone. Although located in an early 20th-century building, the museum's focus is on contemporary art, as well as occasional exhibits featuring fine crafts, folk art, and nonwestern art. There are also workshops for children including their ArtSmart classes, as well as arts and craft classes for adults. Call for current exhibition and workshop information.

Also at this same address is the Empire State Carousel (see previous listing).

FARMINGDALE

● Fun Zone

229 Route 110, 847-0100. Hours: Mon.–Thurs. 11–10, Fri. 11– midnight, Sat. 10–midnight, Sun. 10 A.M.–10 P.M. Admission: pay for tokens ($1 each) or purchase a pay-one-price bracelet—kiddie rides during school year $6.96, summer rate $8.95; all rides during school year $10.95, summer rate $13.95. **Ages 2 and up.**

This indoor amusement park and arcade features a carousel, a dragon ride, a train ride, bumper cars, air hockey, video games, laser tag and more. This facility offers something for every age group—from toddlers to adults. Sometimes a person just needs a place like this to let loose (especially during a long winter when cabin fever has set in).

FIRE ISLAND

● Fire Island National Seashore

289-4810. Hours: National Seashore, daily dawn to dusk; Lighthouse, July and Aug. daily 9:30–5; May–June and Sept.–Dec. weekends 9:30–5. Admission: National Seashore free, beach parking $4 (free with NYS Empire Passport). Lighthouse, $2. www.fireisland.com. **All ages.**

Everyone who visits Long Island needs to plan a trip to the famous Fire Island National Seashore, which encompasses 32 miles of beach. Accessed by the Robert Moses Causeway, the William Floyd Parkway, or by ferry, there are several parking lots to choose from (though in the summer months, lots fill up quickly, especially on the weekends). If you park at the last lot (number two) and take a leisurely half-mile walk, you will end up at the lighthouse which was built in 1858. You can even walk up the 192 steps to the top if you dare! Most people just pack a cooler with lots of drinks, bring a blanket, towels, and sunscreen and enjoy the sand, sun, and surf.

GREENPORT

● East End Seaport Maritime Museum

3rd Street, 477-2100. Hours: May–Sept. 10–6 Wed.–Mon.; Oct.–Dec. Fri.–Sun. 1–5. Admission: Adults $2, children $1. www.greenport.com. **Ages 3 and up.**

The East End Seaport Museum is a storehouse of Long Island maritime artifacts. The tall ship *Regina Maris*, which was built in 1908, is displayed on the wharf. It is one of only two wooden barkentines (a three-masted ship) left in the world and is currently undergoing restoration.

HOLTSVILLE

● Holtsville Park and Ecology Site

249 Buckley Road (exit 63S off the LIE), 758-9664. Hours: daily 9–4. Admission: free. **All ages.**

At this small zoo you can see buffalo, deer, fox, bald eagles, mountain lions, hawks, owls, and turtles, and you can feed farm animals. Many of the animals were brought here because they were injured in the wild; they are here at the park because they wouldn't survive otherwise. You will also find a greenhouse, a picnic area, a playground, and restrooms on-site.

HUNTINGTON

For more information on Huntington, visit their Web site
(www.huntingtonli.org/).

● Heckscher Museum

*Route 25A and Prime Avenue, 351-3250; Heckscher Park, 351-3089.
Hours: Tues.–Fri. 10–5, weekends 1–5. Admission (suggested donation):
Adults $2, children $1.* **Ages 4 and up.**

On display here are works of art from the Heckscher collection—over
800 objects which range from Renaissance European paintings to works
by contemporary American artists. Call ahead for current exhibition
information. You can also stroll over to **Heckscher Park,** where you can
let the kids loose on the playground or if you time it right, hear a concert,
see a musical theater production, or catch a children's show.

● Huntington Arsenal

*425 Park Avenue, 351-3244 (Huntington Town Historian). Hours: Sun.
1–4. Admission: free.* **Ages 5 and up.**

At the only remaining arsenal on Long Island, built around 1740, you
can see lots of Revolutionary War–era artifacts, including weapons and
period furnishings, all shown to you by volunteers in historical dress. Ask
them about what was used to paint the doorways (ox blood and cod oil),
or about other building materials (wooden dowels instead of nails). The
arsenal is an interesting place to stop and get a lesson in American history.

● Kissam House

*434 Park Avenue, 427-7045 (Huntington Historical Society). Hours: By
appointment only, daily 1–4. Admission: Adults $2.50, children under 12
$1, family rate $5.* **Ages 5 and up.**

This house was built in 1795 and today is the location of the
Huntington Historical Society. There are several rooms to view, which
are decorated in the colonial, empire, and federal styles. The museum also
has an outstanding collection of period costumes. In the museum shop,
you can purchase crafts and antiques. For the Huntington Historical
Society see their Web site at: www.huntingtonli.org/hunthistorical/.

KINGS PARK

● Sunken Meadow Park

*North Shore, at the end of Sunken Meadow Parkway (exit 63N off the
LIE), 269-4333. Hours: daily dawn–dusk. Admission: free. Parking: $5.*
All ages.

This beach is a terrific place to take your kids because its on the north shore; there are no large waves so the water isn't as scary for the younger children. The sand is quite rocky though, and water shoes really help keep little feet from getting hurt. There is a wonderful, long board-walk and a snack bar (which also sells beach buckets and shovels if you forget yours). Lifeguards are on duty during the swimming season. If your kids are not tired after swimming and playing on the beach, there are several playgrounds at the park.

LAKE GROVE

● Sports Plus

110 New Moriches Road, 737-2100. Hours: weekdays 10 A.M.–midnight, weekends 10 A.M.–1 A.M. Admission: Pay per activity using tokens; for example, 2 activity tokens ($2) to ride the bumper cars. www.sports-plus.com. **All ages.**

This new facility boasts four acres of sports activities under one roof. Sports Plus features the following: an NHL regulation ice rink, bumper cars, balloon Ferris wheel, 48-lane bowling center, Kids Town, Playmaze, Iwerks Motion Master Theater (ride simulator with movie), 18-hole executive golf course and driving range, virtual reality baseball, birthday party activities, pizza cafe, video games (over 200 of them), Lasertron (laser tag game), a family restaurant and sports bar (called Reunion), and, believe it or not, much more!

MANORVILLE

● Animal Farm Petting Zoo

184A Wading River Road (exit 69S off the LIE), 878-1785. Hours: Apr.–Oct. weekdays 10–5, weekends 10–6. Admission: Adults $10, children 2 and up $7, children under 2 free. **All ages.**

There are plenty of animals to see here including parrots, monkeys, llamas, farm animals, baby animals to pet and feed, rabbits, pigs, and more. The kids will enjoy pony rides, two train rides, and animal and puppet shows. You'll find a picnic area and gift shop here, but bathroom facilities are lacking—only portatoilets as of this writing!

MASTIC BEACH

● Saint George Manor

Neighborhood Road (exit 68S off the LIE, which is Country Road 46 or William Floyd Parkway. Continue for 6.2 miles, turn right on Neighborhood

Road and go one-tenth mile), 475-0327 (trustees of the estate). Hours: May–Oct. Wed.–Sun. 9–5. Admission: free. **Ages 5 and up.**

Saint George Manor is one of the oldest houses on Long Island. Built in approximately 1690, the manor is located on 127 acres, and its interior is decorated with 18th- and 19th-century furnishings. (For those of you who are Suffolk County residents, after your visit to this site you might want to head to the beach at Smith Point County Park for a nice ocean swim. You need a Suffolk County residence permit to visit this beach.)

● William Floyd Estate

245 Park Drive, 399-2030. Hours: Memorial Day–Sept. 30 Fri.–Sun. 11–5; Oct. Sat. and Sun. 11–5. Admission: free. **Ages 5 and up.**

This National Historic Site is the 250-year-old, 613-acre homestead of Long Island's signer of the Declaration of Independence, William Floyd. There are colonial furnishings throughout the 25-room mansion, which was built between 1724 and 1930. Eight generations of the Floyd family lived here until 1976.

MONTAUK

For more information on Montauk, visit their Web site (www.montauk.com).

● Montauk Point Lighthouse

Route 27 (Montauk Highway), Montauk State Park, 668-2544. Hours: Mar.–Oct. daily 10:30–6 (Nov. and Dec. open only on holiday weekends). Admission: Adults $2.50, children $1, children under 6 free. Parking: $3 (free with NYS Empire Passport). **All ages.**

Montauk Point Lighthouse is not only the oldest on Long Island but in the entire state. Constructed in 1796, it was authorized by George Washington in an effort to save lives; many ships were wrecked on the east end of the island. The lighthouse was built by John McComb Jr. for $22,300, a large sum of money at that time. It now stands only 50 feet from the edge of its bluff (down from 297 feet), because of erosion. Visitors at least 41 inches tall can climb the 137 spiral steps to the tower; those who wish to forego that activity can browse in the museum and gift shop.

OAKDALE

● Bayard Cutting Arboretum

Route 27A (Montauk Highway), 581-1002. Hours: Wed–Sun 10–5. Admission: $3 per car or free with NYS Empire Passport. **All ages.**

The first trees in this arboretum were planted by William Bayard Cutting; it now covers 680 acres and is part of the Long Island State Park system. There are five trails, including a wildflower walk and a bird watchers' walk. The grounds are well-manicured, and you can spend a nice afternoon strolling the arboretum. Visitors can also tour the mansion and view several collections—the mounted birds and Native American artifacts are notable. Call or write ahead for information on special events; the Long Island String Quartet often performs here.

PORT JEFFERSON

For more information on Port Jefferson, visit their Web site (www.lieast.com/portjeff.html).

● Mather House Museum

115 Prospect Street, 473-2665. Hours: July and Aug. Tues., Wed., and weekends 1–4; Sept.–June weekends 1–4. Admission: Adults $1, children under 12 free. **Ages 4 and up.**

The Mather House Museum is a complex of four buildings that belonged to the shipbuilder John Mather. The historic buildings include the main house, built in the 1860s, that features marine artifacts and period furnishings; a tool shed; a smaller house called the Craft House; and a barn that features replicas of a country store, a butcher shop, and a barber shop.

● Port Jefferson Steamboat Company

102 W. Broadway, 473-0286. Fees vary depending on day of the week, season, whether you have a car, and whether you purchase round-trip or one-way tickets. (Round-trip fare traveling with a car is $64, ferry ride only one-way $9.) **All ages.**

Take a wonderful hour-and-a-half ferry ride to Bridgeport, Connecticut, either to enjoy the Long Island Sound, continue on to the Bridgeport Zoo, or explore other areas of Connecticut. There is a daily ferry schedule and special daytime tours, moonlight sails, and charter trips. While you're waiting for the ferry, head over to Rocketship Park on Main Street to let the kids climb on the imitation rocketship or play on the swings and slides.

PORT JEFFERSON STATION

● Fun 4 All

200 Wilson Street, 331-9000. Hours: Mon. noon–8, Tues.–Thurs., Sun. 9:30–8., Fri. and Sat. 9:30–9. Admission: Adults and children above age

13 or under age 1 free, children 2–13 $7.99 (2 hours) or $8.99 (all day), children age 1 are half-price. **Ages 1–12.**

This indoor amusement park is open 7 days for children 12 and under with adult supervision. In addition to the crazy ball pit, ladders, rope bridges, and slides, there is also a room for quiet play with toys, books, a chalkboard, or kitchen and carpenter sets. A snack bar is available, as are private party rooms.

RIVERHEAD

● Hallockville Museum Farm
163 Sound Avenue, 298-5292. Hours: Wed.–Sun. 10–4. Admission: Adults $2.50, children $1.50. **Ages 5 and up.**

This museum complex includes original 18th- and 19th-century buildings on a two-and-one-half acre site. Hallock Homestead, one of the buildings here, dates to 1765 and is listed on the National Register of Historic Places. It is one of the oldest working farms on Long Island. Tours of the site are available, and the museum also has craft demonstrations, festivals, and workshops usually held during the summer.

● Riverhead Foundation for Marine Research and Preservation, Aquarium Preview Center
431 E. Main Street (exit 72N off the LIE), 369-9840. Hours: Sat. and Sun 10–5. Admission: Adults $4, children 12 and under $2. **All ages.**

The aquarium was recently moved to this 12,000-square-foot location, which is only an "interim" aquarium, to be used while the foundation constructs its 80,000-square-foot "real" aquarium! When it is complete the new aquarium will feature fresh and saltwater animals from the surrounding waters. Seven areas are currently accessible to the public in this exciting new location, including a 22-foot-long "touch tank" where visitors can see and touch sea creatures. The aquarium sponsors a summer camp in July and August every year, and also runs seasonal whale watch cruises (the cost is approximately $30 per person; each cruise lasts four to seven hours). Write or call ahead for up-to-date information regarding the events at the aquarium as well as the availability and cost of the cruises.

● Splish Splash Water Park
2549 Middle Country Road (Route 25), exit 72W off the LIE, 727-3600. Hours: Memorial Day–Labor Day daily 9:30–6. Admission: $18.95, children under 48 inches tall $14.95, children under 2 free. Parking: $4. **All ages.**

Have a fun water-filled day at 60-acre Splish Splash. Kids love the 18,000-square-foot wave pool that features eight different kinds of waves. There are 16 adult slides, including two which are 30 feet long and definitely high-speed. For those who want to relax, try the 1,300-foot lazy river, which you can float down on inner tubes. For younger children there are three kiddie pools and three young-kid-sized slides. The park also includes two restaurants and a discovery cove that features sea lion shows.

SAG HARBOR

● Sag Harbor Whaling Museum
Main and Garden Streets, 725-0770. Hours: May–Sept. Mon.–Sat. 10–5, Sun. 1–5. Admission: Adults $3, children $1. **Ages 3 and up.**

While geared towards the whaling heritage of Long Island, this museum is also a repository for other interesting artifacts from times past. Miscellaneous marine items, children's toys, and needlework are just some of the items displayed here. Visitors will be amazed at the enormous right whale jaw bones; they have been in this collection for over 100 years. The Sag Harbor Museum is housed in a mansion that dates to 1845.

SEAFORD

● Tackapausha Museum and Preserve
Washington Avenue between Merrick Road and Sunrise Highway, 571-7443. Hours: Tues.–Sat. 10–4, Sun. 1–4. Admission: Adults $1, children 5–12 $.50. **All ages.**

The Tackapausha Museum and Preserve is located on 80 acres in Seaford. Bring the family and enjoy five miles of nature trails. The museum has exhibits of local natural history and has quite a few live animals to see including hawks, owls, snakes, lizards, and fish. At the time of this writing Egyptian fruit bats were being exhibited!

SHELTER ISLAND

● Mashomack Nature Preserve
79 South Ferry Road, 748-1001. Hours: Wed.–Mon. 9–5. Admission (suggested donation): Adults $1.50, children $1. **All ages.**

Accessible by ferry from either Greenport on the north fork or North Haven on the south fork, this 2,000-acre nature preserve is managed by the Nature Conservancy. It consists of woodlands, marshes, freshwater ponds, and plenty of wildlife, including ibis, hummingbirds, fox, harbor seals, and osprey. There is also a gift shop with several small displays. This is a wonderful afternoon excursion. Pack a picnic lunch and enjoy the views.

SOUTHAMPTON

● Parrish Art Museum

25 Job's Lane, 283-2118. Hours: Mon., Thurs.–Sat. 11–5, Sun. 1–5. Admission: Adults $2 (suggested donation). www.thehamptons.com. **Ages 4 and up.**

The Parrish Art Museum is one of the oldest museums in the state having been founded in 1898. It focuses on the works of 19th- and 20th-century American artists and has major works by William Merritt Chase and Fairfield Porter. In addition to paintings, the PAM also boasts an arboretum and a sculpture garden. Call ahead for interesting special programs including lectures, concerts, summer storytelling, and other family entertainment.

SOUTHOLD

● Southold Historical Museum

Main Road, 765-5500. Hours: July and Aug. weekends 1–4. Admission: free (donations accepted). **Ages 5 and up.**

Southold (along with Southampton) was actually the first settlement on Long Island, in 1640. The Southold Historical Museum is located in a Victorian house; it contains an art gallery, collections of toys and dolls, and, of course, period furniture. You can also wander through the Thomas Moore pre–Revolutionary War house, a carriage house, and a blacksmith shop.

● Southold Indian Museum

Main Bay View Road, 765-5577. Hours: Sun. 1:30–4:30. Admission: $1. **Ages 3 and up.**

In addition to having artifacts relating to the Algonquin Indians, the museum is also the home of the Long Island chapter of the New York State Archaeological Association. The museum houses a collection of over 300,000 artifacts, including arrowheads and restored ceramics. The Algonquins were one of the largest groups of Native Americans, comprising over 300 tribes and 50 languages.

ST. JAMES

● St. James General Store

516 Moriches Road, 862-8333. Hours: Mar.–Dec. daily 10–5. Admission: free. **Ages 4 and up.**

The St. James General Store is 139 years old, has its original pot-bellied stove, and still sells penny candy. It is the oldest continuously operating store in the U.S. and has been on the National Register of Historic Places since the 1950s. It's a fun place to poke around, or visit during the free craft demonstrations and fairs with music and children's events.

● Wick's Farm and Garden

445 North Country Road (Route 25A), 584-5727. Hours: Sept. 15–Oct. 31 daily 10–5, Thanksgiving–New Year's Day daily 10–5. **All ages.**

If you are celebrating the holidays on Long Island, visit this farm for its seasonal displays. Come and see the witches and goblins and pick some pumpkins in the fall, or come during the Christmas season to see colonial and Christmas characters on display.

STONY BROOK

● Museums at Stony Brook

1208 Route 25A, Stony Brook, 751-0066. Hours: Sept.–Nov. and Jan.–June Wed.–Sat. 10–5, Sun. 12–5; July, Aug., and Dec. Mon.–Sat. 10–5, Sun. 12–5. Admission: Adults $4, children under 6 free. **Ages 3 and up.**

These museums are truly a treasure on Long Island. They are comprised of several interesting museums: the Margaret M. Blackwell History Museum, the Carriage House, the Art Museum, the Nassakeag One-Room Schoolhouse, the Samuel H. West Blacksmith Shop, and others. The Carriage Museum was the highlight of the visit for my four- and six-year-old children. The museum currently owns approximately 250 carriages, although it can only display fewer than half of them at any one time. They are displayed in an exquisite wheelchair-accessible building, where the first carriage you see is the *Grace Darling Omnibus.* From there you can wander past 18th-century French royal coaches, American stagecoaches (complete with bullet holes), fire-fighting wagons (one we saw was too fancy and heavy to fight fires!), children's wagons, and sleighs. My four-year-old son was so impressed he still remembers the museum and says to me, "Mom, first came carriages and then came cars, right?"

● Stony Brook Grist Mill

Harbor Road, 751-2244. Hours: June–Sept. Wed.–Sun. noon–4:30. Apr. and May, Oct. and Nov. weekends noon–4:30. Admission: Adults $1, children under 12 $.50. **Ages 3 and up.**

The original mill on this site was built in 1699 by Adam Smith. The structure that stands today—which is still one of the oldest grist mills in the country—was built in 1751, after the first one was washed away in a flood. It has recently been completely renovated, and a practicing miller now gives the mill tour. My children were quite captivated by him, especially when he showed how the corn is ground and let them feel the corn at different times during the grinding process.

● Discovery Wetlands Cruise

Shore Road, 751-2244. Hours: Approximately May–Oct., call for a current schedule. Admission: Adults $15, children under 12 $9. Free parking is available at lot near "Boatworks" sign. **Ages 6 and up.**

Take a tour through Stony Brook Harbor on a 35-passenger pontoon boat. On the one-and-one-half hour trip you will learn about the Native American heritage of the area, the wetlands ecosystem, plant and animal life, and more. A naturalist will be on board to guide you through the harbor. Bring binoculars!

WATER MILL

● Water Mill Museum

Old Mill Road, 726-4625. Hours: Memorial Day–mid-Sept. Mon.–Sat. 11–5, Sun. 1–5. Admission: free. **Ages 3 and up.**

This grist mill is Long Island's oldest operating water mill, built in 1644. All children seem fascinated by the workings of a mill; at this mill there are displays of grain grinding tools, as well as a craft shop, special exhibits, and an art gallery.

WEST SAYVILLE

● Long Island Maritime Museum

86 West Avenue, 854-4974. Hours: Wed.–Sat. 10–3, Sun. noon–4. Admission: $2 (suggested donation). **Ages 7 and up.**

As its name suggests, the Maritime Museum offers a range of exhibits having to do with Long Island's sea-related heritage. In addition to several special programs per year, a 19th-century cottage called the William Rudolph Oyster House is open to the public. There is even a workshop where one can watch volunteers restoring old sailing vessels. This facility is most appropriate for kids ages 7 and up.

YAPHANK

● Suffolk County Farm and Education Center

Yaphank Avenue, 852-4608. Hours: daily 9–5. Admission: free. **All ages.**

There's a lot to see and do at this working 300-acre farm—take hay and pony rides, clamber about the playground, pet animals, or check out farm machinery. Several times a year the farm holds special events such as the Annual Pumpkin Festival in October or the Annual Sheep Shearing in May. Call ahead for specific dates for these and other seasonal events.

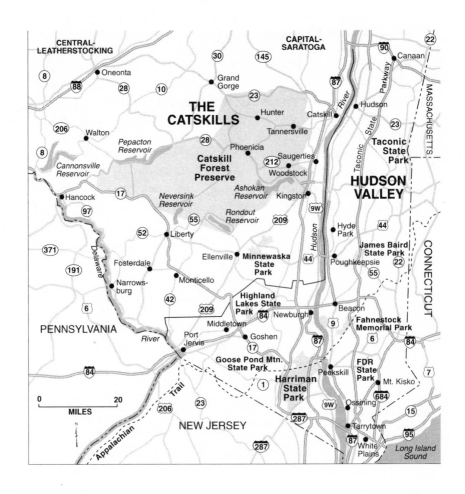

Eastern New York

Hudson Valley Region

Henry Hudson thought he had discovered the water route to the Orient when he came upon the Hudson River in 1609. Instead he is credited with the discovery of the most important waterway in New York State. This area provides visitors with an enormous amount of historical, cultural, and natural sites to explore.

Take a trip to the famous West Point, home of the U.S. Military Academy; Bear Mountain; or perhaps the Roosevelt National Historic Site. Read the book *Legend of Sleepy Hollow* by Washington Irving, and then visit the real town of Sleepy Hollow. (Washington Irving, by the way, was one of the first writers to settle in the Hudson Valley, building a home here in 1835.) Perhaps you can get a quick break from kids' attractions by sampling one of the hundreds of antique shops in the region. For information regarding historic sites in the region call Historic Hudson Valley at (914) 631-8200 or 1-800-448-4007.

For World Wide Web information on Hudson Valley, visit one of the following sites: Hudson Valley Net at www.hvnet.com/, Hudson Link at www.hudsonriver.com, or Hudson Highlands at www.highlands.com/Highlands.html.

The area code for the Hudson Valley is 914 unless otherwise noted.

ANNANDALE-ON-HUDSON

● Montgomery Place
River Road (Route 103), 758-5461. Hours: Wed.–Mon. 10–5. Admission: Adults $6, children 6–17 $3, children under 6 free (grounds pass only $3).
All ages.

Montgomery Place is a classical revival mansion on the 434-acre estate of Janet Livingston Montgomery. She was the widow of General Richard Montgomery, who was killed in the Revolutionary War. The house was built in 1802 and later in the 19th century was transformed into an elegant country estate designed by A. J. Davis. This wonderful site features a waterfall, picnicking area, gardens, trails, hiking, and even pick-your-own raspberries and apples. There are guided tours of the house and grounds every 45 minutes. Call or write ahead for seasonal special events (such as wonderful, romantic twilight garden walks).

BEAR MOUNTAIN STATE PARK
See listing under Harriman.

CARMEL

● Putnam Children's Discovery Center

1 Vink Drive, 227-1535. Hours: Thurs. 10–5. Admission: varies per activity. **Ages 1–16.**

Although this center has limited hours, they do have a lot to offer. Hands-on science activities, birthday parties, computer workshops, toddler play hours, and special summer science programs are all offered here. Call for a current schedule of events and programs.

CLERMONT

● Clermont State Historic Site

Route 9G to 1 Clermont Avenue, 15 miles south of Hudson, (518) 537-4240. Hours: Tues.–Sun. 11–4, Mon. and holidays 10–4. Admission: Adults $3, children 5–12 $1, children under 5 free. **All ages.**

This site is the 485-acre estate of Robert R. Livingston, one of the drafters of the Declaration of Independence. Seven generations of Livingstons lived here up until the 1960s. The home has been restored and is filled with beautiful antiques that may appeal to some older children (my six-year-old daughter loves to see restored homes, but my four-year-old son grows bored and restless quickly). On the grounds are a formal garden, hiking trails, exhibits, and even grills your family can use for a nice afternoon picnic. The view overlooking the Hudson is wonderful. Throughout the year the estate offers various activities on the weekends, including concerts, hayrides, historical plays and reenactments, and much more. Call ahead for a current schedule of events. The site was designated a National Historic Landmark in 1973.

CORNWALL-ON-HUDSON

● Museum of the Hudson Highlands

The Boulevard, 534-7781. Hours: June–Aug. Mon.–Thurs. 11–5, Sat. and Sun. 12–5; Sept.–May Mon.–Thurs. 2–5, Sat. and Sun. 12–5. Admission: $2 per person (suggested donation). **All ages.**

This environmental education center offers much for children of all ages. The museum features photograph and habitat exhibits and natural history displays. Building bluebird nest boxes and making maple syrup and maple candy are just a couple of the many spring and summer environmental workshops that are offered. You can also take a leisurely walk on nearby nature trails. Call or write for an informative brochure listing events and classes.

CROTON-ON-HUDSON

● Van Cortlandt Manor

S. Riverside Avenue off Route 9, 271-8981. Hours: Apr.–Oct. Wed.–Mon. 10–5; Nov. and Dec. weekends only 10–4. Admission: Adults $8, children 6–17 $4, children under 6 free, grounds pass only, $4. **Ages 3 and up.**

When you are visiting the Hudson Valley, you really should try to see many of the historic sites in the area. Van Cortlandt Manor is one such site; it consists of an 18th-century Dutch-English house, a tavern, and a farmer's house. Throughout the year, demonstrations of such things as open-hearth cooking, spinning, and brickmaking (all of which are quite interesting) are held.

FISHKILL

● Splashdown

2200 Route 9, 896-6606. Hours: Memorial Day–Labor Day daily 10–7. Admission: Prices range from $2 to $15 per person. **All ages.**

All kids love water parks, and this one has some fun special attractions such as Polliwog Pond, a play area for smaller children. There's a wave pool, of course, and water slides of all kinds. The attraction that's the most fun is Water Wars, a water balloon game. When you and your group finally get sick of being wet, you can try a game of miniature golf at the park's 18-hole course. For those who love basketball, there's even Hoops USA, a miniature basketball court.

GARRISON-ON-HUDSON

● Boscobel

Route 9D (8 miles north of Bear Mountain Bridge), 265-3638. Hours: Apr.–Oct. Wed.–Mon. 10–5. Admission: Adults $7, children 6–14 $4, children under 6 free; Grounds pass only, adults $4, children $2. www.highlands.com/Museums/Boscobel.html. **Ages 3 and up.**

If you just can't get enough of impressive homes, then you must visit this restored 19th-century Federal-style mansion that, in addition to having wonderful interior furnishings, also has wonderful landscaping complete with an orangerie (greenhouse), an herb garden, and a rose garden. Boscobel was almost destroyed in the 1950s; it was saved by moving it piece by piece to this site 15 miles north of its original location. It was opened to the public in 1961. Purchase tickets for the tour of the house at the Carriage House Reception Center, and while you're there, ask about the concerts held here in the summer.

HARRIMAN

● Bear Mountain State Park/Trailside Museum and Wildlife Center

Bear Mountain State Park (off the Palisades Parkway), 786-2701. Hours: Trailside Museum, daily 9–4:30. Pool, June–Aug. daily 10–6. Admission: Trailside Museum, adults $1, children 6–12 $.50; Parking, $4 on weekends and holidays; Pool, adults $1, children 6–12 $.50. **All ages.**

This small trailside zoo is a perfect place to stop during your travels and take a well-deserved break. Take a walk on the nature trail and the enjoy the magnificent view of the Hudson River. The animals here are those native to New York, such as raccoons, foxes, otters, owls, and black bears. A climb to the top of Perkins Tower will give you an amazing four-state view. In the winter the park opens an ice-skating rink and also features ski-jumping contests; in summer, swimming and boating facilities are available.

HIGHLAND FALLS

● U.S. Military Academy at West Point

Old Storm King Highway (Route 218), 938-2638. Hours: West Point Museum, daily 10:30–4:15. Visitor Center, daily 9–4:45. Admission: free. www.usma.edu/. **Ages 4 and up.**

A visit to the world-famous military academy will provide visitors with a rich history lesson as well as wonderful Hudson River views. George Washington is credited with founding West Point in 1778 as a garrison to protect the Hudson River from the British. The Academy was officially established in 1802 with 10 cadets (today over 4,000 men and women are enrolled annually). Stop in at the Visitor's Center and pick up a map, as there is a lot to see. The West Point Museum has exhibits of flags, weapons, and other military artifacts.

HUDSON

In addition to the attractions listed below, visitors to Hudson can also explore numerous antiques shops along Warren Street.

● American Museum of Fire Fighting

117 Harry Howard Avenue, (518) 828-7695. Hours: daily 9–4:30. Admission: free. **Ages 3 and up.**

My son loves anything that has to do with firefighters and fire trucks, and this museum certainly stands out as a favorite. It has over 21,000 square feet of exhibition space! Equipment dating back to the early 18th century and many different fire fighting–related artifacts are on display. Some of the pieces of equipment are beautiful to look at as objects in and of themselves. The 1846 double-decker hand engine is so detailed and ornate, it's hard to believe it was actually used for fire fighting. There are over two dozen fire trucks on display, and people are usually around to answer kids' fire fighting questions. Call ahead for the special events schedule (most events are held in July).

● Olana

Route 9G, one mile south of the Rip van Winkle Bridge, (518) 828-0135. Hours: Apr.–Oct. Wed.–Sun. 10–4 (the site reopens in Dec. for holiday celebrations). Admission: Adults $3, children 5–11 $1, children under 4 free. 50-minute guided tours begin every 20–30 minutes; tour size is limited and reservations, which can be made up to two weeks in advance, are recommended. **Ages 4 and up.**

This historic site, operated by the New York State Office of Parks, Recreation, and Historic Preservation, is the 250-acre estate of 19th-century artist Frederic Edwin Church (1826–1900). The mansion itself, begun in 1870, is complete with Moorish (Islamic) decor. The grounds were designed with the visitor in mind, to obtain the ultimate view. Olana offers a wide variety of special programs, including a summer arts camp for children 6 through 13, weekend afternoon family fun work-shops, hikes, concerts, and more. Call or write ahead for seasonal schedule of events. If possible, visit Olana during the Christmas season to see the house decorated for a 19th-century celebration.

HYDE PARK

Hyde Park is home to the **Culinary Institute of America** (CIA for short), which operates four award-winning restaurants that are open to the public. For further information and to make reservations call 471-6608. The CIA is closed for part of the summer and at other times during the year, so also call to check the hours of operation.

● Roosevelt-Vanderbilt Museum National Historic Site

519 Albany Post Road, Route 9, Vanderbilt Mansion 229-7770, Roosevelt Home 229-2501, National Park Service and Val-Kill 229-9115. Admission: Vanderbilt Mansion, adults $2, children under 17 free; Roosevelt Home, adults $5, children under 17 free; Val-Kill (Eleanor Roosevelt's cottage), free. Hours: May–Oct. daily 9–5; Nov.–Apr. Sat. and Sun. 9–5. www.nps.gov/ hofr/home.html. **Ages 4 and up.**

The Vanderbilt Mansion is part of a 211-acre estate that includes a fabulous formal Italian Garden. It was designed by the famous architectural firm of McKim, Mead, and White. The house is a 50-room Beaux Arts masterpiece built between 1896 and 1898 for Frederick Vanderbilt, the grandson of Cornelius Vanderbilt, who built the family fortune. The Roosevelt Home is on a 300-acre estate that includes both the Franklin D. Roosevelt Home and the smaller Eleanor Roosevelt cottage. All of the sites are operated by the National Park Service and have walking trails that are part of the Hyde Park Trail system. This is a grand and wonderful place to spend a quiet spring afternoon or to enjoy at the height of summer.

MILAN

● Hudson Valley Raptor Center

RR 1, Route 53 off the Taconic Parkway, South Road, 758-6957. Hours: Apr.–Oct. weekends only 1–4; June–Aug. Fri.–Sun. 1–4. Admission: Adults $7, children under 12 $2.50. **Ages 2 and up.**

Here you can meet all kinds of interesting birds including eagles, falcons, vultures, and owls. The center offers natural history programs and flying demonstrations (flying time is usually 2 P.M.). Please call ahead for the schedule, because hours of operation vary with the season.

MILLBROOK

If you and your kids like antiques stores, Millbrook has over 100 antique shops along Franklin Avenue to explore!

● Innisfree Garden

RR 2, Tyrrel Road, 677-8000. Hours: May–Oct., Wed.–Fri. 10–4, Sat. and Sun. 11–5. Admission: Wed.–Fri. ages 10 and up $1, Sat. and Sun. ages 10 and up $3. **Ages 4 and up.**

Innisfree Garden is a wonderful place to take children. The 200-acre garden has been in the works for over 60 years, its style influenced by Chinese landscape design. Not only are the gardens themselves lovely, but Innisfree also has a 40-acre lake surrounded by cliffs, hills, streams, and waterfalls. It's a wonderful place to bring a picnic. A book was recently published about the garden called *Innisfree: An American Garden,* written by Lester Collins (Timber Press). No dogs are allowed.

● Trevor Zoo

Millbrook School, School Road (off Route 44), 677-3704. Hours: daily 8–5. Admission: $2. **All ages.**

If you are in the area or have perhaps just visited the Innisfree Garden, stop in here to see some 100 animals (50 different species). This small zoo on four acres features birds, mammals, and reptiles. There is a one-mile nature walk nearby that is nice to take on a lovely spring day.

● Wings Castle

RR 1, Bangall Road (one-half mile north of County Route 57, near Millbrook Vineyards), 677-9085. Hours: June 1–Dec. 24, Wed.–Sun. 10–5, reservations encouraged. Admission: Adults $5, children under 12, $3. **Ages 3 and up.**

A visit to this architectural curiosity is certainly worth your while. Peter and Toni Wing, the owners of this building, created their stone castle by salvaging materials from old buildings. Using 80 percent recycled materials, the Wings have combined a variety of architectural styles into a unique residence. Antique birdbaths, for example, are reused as sinks. Bring a picnic lunch to enjoy at this interesting site with great views of historic Hudson Valley.

MONROE

● Museum Village in Orange County

Museum Village Road (exit 129 off Route 17), 782-8247. Hours: late Apr.–June and Sept.–early Dec. Wed.–Fri. 10–2; July and Aug. Wed.–Fri. 11–5 and weekends 11–5. Admission: Adults $8, children 3–15 $5, children under 3 free. **Ages 3 and up.**

As one of the largest living history museums in New York State, Museum Village offers visitors a chance to experience a "real" working 19th-century town. There are over 30 buildings in this complex of homes, shops, and barns. Costumed guides provide an extraordinary amount of information regarding the period and often demonstrate crafts such as candle making (when we visited it was a quiet day and the guide allowed my kids to make and keep their own candles). During the summer the village holds special events on the weekends. Previous events have included a Civil War reenactment; Monroe Centennial Days, which include a children's festival; Christmas festivities; and a fall festival, among others. There is even a local mastodon skeleton on display. Call for a current schedule of events. If you can, plan to visit when there are no school tours scheduled.

MOUNTAINVILLE

● Storm King Art Center

Old Pleasant Hill Road (off NY 32), 534-3115. Hours: Apr.–Nov. daily 11–5:30. Tours available. Admission: Adults $7, children $3, children under 5 free. www.skac.org. **All ages.**

Over 100 works by master artists such as Louise Nevelson, Alexander Calder, Isamu Noguchi, and others adorn 400 acres of hills and fields is this outdoor sculpture park. This kind of park is unusual and allows children to get an up-close view of interesting modern sculpture.

Bring a picnic lunch, enjoy the wonderful views and environment, and let the kids play around some modern art. There are restrooms available and a picnic area. The center also sponsors concerts and storytelling occasionally, so call ahead for a current schedule of events. Pets not allowed.

NYACK

● Hudson Valley Children's Museum
21 Burd Street, Nyack Seaport, 358-2191. Hours: Tues.–Fri. 10–4, Sat. 10–5, Sun. 11–5. Admission: Ages 1 and up $4, children under 1 free. www.Ideo.columbia.edu/HVCM. **Ages 1–12.**

Located in a 5,000-square-foot warehouse, this new children's museum (it opened in 1996) focuses on teaching children about the world around them through interesting, interactive exhibits. Children love the Gadget Garage, where they can use wrenches and hammers on the gears in a stripped-down car. The Young People's Theater, which opened in February 1997, allows children to express themselves on stage with costumes, props, and scenery.

There's something for every child here and you will want to stay several hours.

NORTH TARRYTOWN
See listings under Sleepy Hollow. The town officially changed its name in March 1997.

OLD CHATHAM

● Shaker Museum
88 Shaker Museum Road (off Country Road 13), (518) 794-9100. Hours: May–Oct. Wed.–Mon. 10–5. Admission: Adults $6, children 8–17 $3, children under 8 free, family rate $14. **Ages 4 and up.**

For those interested in history and in exploring other cultures and religions, this museum, which has 24 galleries, presents 200 years of Shaker history. Exhibits display the furniture, tools, machinery and household objects for which the Shakers are known. Also on-site are a library, education center, herb garden, and picnic area. Some special events are held throughout the year; past events have included a strawberry shortcake breakfast, apple harvests, and more.

POUGHKEEPSIE

The name *Poughkeepsie* (pronounced puh-KIP-see) is a Dutch-English derivative of an Indian name for the area meaning "the reed-covered lodge by the little water place." The area was settled in the late 17th century and was actually the state capital in 1777. It is now the Dutchess County seat.

● Mid-Hudson Children's Museum

South Hills Mall, 838 South Road, Route 9, 297-5938. Hours: Tues.–Sun. 11–5. Admission: Ages 2 and up $2.50, children under 2 free. **Ages 2–10.**

This is a nice size hands-on science and art museum. The many interesting stations teach about mirrors and optical illusions, doctors, bubbles, geography, and more. You can have a child's birthday party here or enjoy special exhibits and programs (for example, in spring 1997 kids could see a special dinosaur show or a slide show about snow leopards, or they could take part in a paper-making class).

RHINEBECK

The beautiful small village of Rhinebeck was founded in 1686. It is the home of the Beekman Arms, the oldest inn still operating in the United States. Beekman Arms opened its doors in 1766.

● Old Rhinebeck Aerodome

42 Stone Church Road, 758-8610. Hours: mid-June–mid-Oct., daily 10–5. Admission: Adults $4, children ages 6–12 $2, children under 6 free. (On special show days, adults $10, children 6–12 $5.) www.mainstream.com/ rhinebeck.html. **Ages 3 and up.**

If your kids love cars and/or airplanes, then this is a nice small museum to visit. There are displays of vintage cars and aircraft. On the weekends in summer, there are special air shows. Call for the current schedule of performances.

RYE

● Playland

Playland Parkway (off I-95), 967-2040. Hours: Playland, May–mid-Sept., Tues.–Thurs. and Sun. noon–11, Fri. and Sat. noon–midnight; Pool, Memorial Day–Labor Day, hours same as Playland; Beach, Memorial Day–

Labor Day, hours same as Playland. Admission: Playland, free, purchase tickets for each ride or 36 tickets for $17; Pool, adults $4.50, children under 50 inches tall $1.50; Beach, adults $3.25, children under 50 inches tall $1.50. Parking, weekdays $3, weekends $5. **All ages.**

Playland is probably one of the more interesting amusement parks because it offers much more than your average amusement park: beach access, rides, a children's park, and miniature golf. It's also located within the Edith G. Read Natural Park and Wildlife Sanctuary. Playland was built in 1928 and therefore qualifies as one of the oldest amusement parks in New York state. There are the requisite large thrill-seeking rides, as well as some smaller, less intense rides for younger children. In addition to the rides, there's also a swimming pool to cool off in, or you can even jump into the Long Island Sound. When you have had enough of rides, take the gang on a nice walk along the boardwalk to unleash that excess energy.

SCARSDALE

● Greenburgh Nature Center
Dromore Road, 723-3470. Hours: Nature museum, Sat.–Thurs. 10–dusk; Preserve grounds, daily 10–4. Admission: free. **All ages.**

Those who love the outdoors should take a trip to this 33-acre woodland preserve of trails, ponds, orchards, and gardens. There is even a 21-room manor house open to the public here, and a live animal museum with 140 specimens.

SLEEPY HOLLOW

Due to the popularity of the tours of Philipsburg Manor and the Rockefeller House and Gardens, Historic Hudson Valley, the nonprofit educational organization that manages these and several other historic area residences, advises that you purchase tickets in advance to ensure a place on a tour. Historic Hudson Valley can be reached at (914) 631-8200, or visit their Web site at www.hudsonvalley.org for further details.

● Rockefeller House and Gardens/Kykuit
Pocantico Hills, 631-9491. Hours: Apr.–Oct. Wed.–Mon. 10–5, Nov. and Dec. weekends only 10–4. Tours last 2½ hours (advance ticket purchase recommended). Admission: House and galleries, adults $18, children 6–17 $16, children under 6 free; Garden and sculpture, adults $18, children 6–17 $16, children under 6 free; Combination Kykuit and Philipsburg Manor, adults $22, children 6–17 $20, children under 6 free. (Note: You need to

purchase tickets for Kykuit at Philipsburg Manor, see below.) There is a shuttle between sites. **Ages 4 and up.**

Rockefeller House and Gardens is also known as Kykuit (pronounced kye-kit). Four generations of Rockefellers lived here before the site was opened to the public in 1994. The house and gardens are now property of the National Trust for Historic Preservation. In addition to the history lesson visitors receive, there's a chance to view the house and gardens (the gardens contain many masterpieces of contemporary sculpture including works by Louise Nevelson, Henry Moore, and others), see carriages and vintage automobiles in the coach barn, and take in some wonderful Hudson River views.

● Philipsburg Manor

N. Broadway (Route 9), 631-3992. Hours: Apr.–Oct. Wed.–Mon. 10–5; Nov. and Dec. weekends only 10–4. Admission: Philipburg Manor only, adults $8, children 6–17 $4, children under 6 free. For combination tickets for the Manor and Kykuit, see listing above. Advance ticket purchase recommended for tours. **Ages 4 and up.**

If you visit this site, you should also plan to visit the Van Cortlandt Manor in Croton-on-Hudson, north of here, to round out your education of what life was like in the 18th century. At this early trading center, you'll learn about a water-powered grist mill (which all kids seem to love) and be able to view the stone manor house, as well as visit with the compounds' animals, which include sheep, cows, and oxen. Children will love the costumed guides, who really provide a sense of the past. The manor holds several special Christmas events, such as storytelling, meeting St. Nick, and music and dance performances.

STAATSBURG

● Mills Mansion/Mills-Norrie State Park

Old Post Road between Hyde Park and Rhinebeck on Route 9, 889-8851. Hours: Wed.–Sat. 10–5, Sun. noon–5 (last tour at 4:30). Admission: Adults $3, children 5–12 $1. **Ages 4 and up.**

The Mills Mansion is the Beaux Arts estate of Ogden and Ruth Livingston Mills (designed by Stanford White and built in 1895) and is set on over 1,000 acres. The estate was originally purchased in 1792 by Mrs. Mills's great-grandfather. The mansion is currently undergoing an extensive restoration that is expected to last several years. There are hiking trails with river views and guided tours of the house. On the park grounds is a public 18-hole golf course; the estate also offers camping (reservations are necessary) and picnic facilities. For camping reservations, write to Mills-Norrie State Park, Staatsburg, NY, 12580 for an application.

● Norrie Point Environmental Site and Aquarium Museum

Dutchess Community College, Mills-Norrie State Park, off Route 9, 889-4830. Hours: May–Oct. Mon.–Fri. 8–4, Sat. 11–5, Sun. 1–5; Nov.–Apr. Sat. 11–5, Sun. 1–5. Admission: free. **All ages.**

For a pleasant afternoon trip, visit this museum which not only offers nice hiking trails with wonderful views of the Hudson River, but also features an 8,000-gallon freshwater aquarium.

STANFORDVILLE

● Roseland Ranch Resort

Hunns Lake Road, 1-800-431-8292 or 868-1350. Hours: year-round. **All ages.**

Located on over 1,000 acres and only two hours from New York City, this western-style resort has been in business since 1958. Enjoy unlimited horseback riding; let your kids have fun learning about animals at the petting zoo; swim in the indoor or outdoor pools; or play a variety of outdoor sports (tennis, baseball, and volleyball, for example). There are a lot of different activities to do here, so everyone will be happy, busy, and having fun.

● Wilcox Park

NY 199, 758-6100. Hours: park grounds, daily dawn–dusk; Facilities, Memorial Day–Labor Day. Admission: $3 per car. **All ages.**

A visit to this small park will make your kids very happy. It has a small lake where you can take paddleboats ($3 per half hour) or rowboats ($3 per hour) out for a ride, or you can just play on the sandy beach. Let your older kids play a round of miniature golf ($1 per game), or go for a walk on some of the park's hiking trails. There are restrooms, picnic tables, and a snack bar in season.

SUGAR LOAF

The hamlet of Sugar Loaf is a small community of artists and craftspeople and there are over 60 artist studios, shops, and galleries. Most kids love to spend time looking around the Topsy Turvy Dolls store. A visit to Sugar Loaf will keep you busy for most of the day. You can call ahead for information regarding special tours and events. In mid-October, for example, they hold a three-day fall festival with craft shows, food, and music. The main street of Sugar Loaf is Kings Highway, off Route 17 (exit 127S); for information, call 469-9181.

TARRYTOWN

● Lyndhurst

635 Broadway (Route 9, 1 mile south of Tappan Zee Bridge), 631-4481 or 631-6497. Hours: Apr.–Oct. Tues.–Sun. 10–5; Nov.–Mar. weekends only 10–4. Admission: Adults $9, children 12–17 $3, children under 12 free. www.cmg.hitachi.com/european_art/lyndhurst_home.html. **Ages 3 and up.**

This beautiful Gothic Revival estate, designed by A. J. Davis and built in 1838, is comprised of 14 separate buildings (including a personal bowling alley!). The Carriage House contains the Visitor Center and a good restaurant. Railroad magnate Jay Gould's former home contains period furnishings and a valuable collection of decorative arts. The gardens are truly spectacular and include a wonderful rose garden, a fernery, and a greenhouse over 100 yards long. During the Christmas season, the estate holds a Victorian celebration with music, refreshments, and candlelight tours (reservations are required for these special tours). The site is owned and managed by the National Trust for Historic Preservation.

● Sunnyside

West Sunnyside Lane (off Route 9), 591-8763. Hours: Apr.–Oct. Wed.– Mon. 10–5; Nov. and Dec. weekends only 10–4. Admission: Adults $8, children 6–17 $4, children under 6 free (grounds pass $4). www.hudsonvalley.org/sunny.htm. **Ages 3 and up.**

Washington Irving, the author of *Rip van Winkle* and *The Legend of Sleepy Hollow*, purchased a 17th-century cottage in 1835 and transformed it into this romantic home. At this National Historic Landmark, you can take a hike, bring a picnic lunch, and enjoy the annual storytelling festival held here each summer. Call ahead for the schedule, as dates change from year to year.

TUXEDO

● New York Renaissance Faire

Sterling Forest, P.O. Box 844, Tuxedo, NY 10987, 351-5171. Hours: end of July–mid-September (specific dates for this annual festival vary, so please call or write ahead for a current schedule). Admission: Adults $15, children 3–12 $6. www.renfair.com. **All ages.**

The Renaissance Faire has to be one of the most fun and interesting family events I know of. Not only do children get to go on rides, see live entertainment, watch jousts, and more, they get a history lesson to boot. Pretend the year is 1558, rent a Renaissance-style costume from one of the booths and enjoy yourself in medieval England. There is also an annual Renaissance Festival in Sterling, New York—see the Finger Lakes in the Central Region—and another in Somerset, New Jersey.

WAPPINGERS FALLS

● Stony Kill Environmental Education Center
Route 9D, 831-8780. Hours: Education center, Mon.–Fri. 8:30–4:45, Sat. and Sun. 12–4:30; Grounds, daily dawn–dusk. Admission: free. **All ages.**

Children are innately curious about the world around them, and at this 756-acre education center they have the opportunity to learn about natural history, ecology, wildlife, agriculture, and the outdoors in general. There are extensive trails—bring your own cross-country skis in the winter or try your hand at snowshoeing. Call ahead for current schedule of events, in the past these have included a fall harvest festival and a farm discovery tour.

WEST POINT
See listing for the U.S. Military Academy at West Point under Highland Falls above.

WINGDALE

● Webatuck Craft Village
Webatuck Road (at Route 55), 832-6601. Hours: Jan.–March Fri.–Sun. 10–5; Apr.–Dec. Wed.–Sun. 10–5. Admission: free. **Ages 3 and up.**

It's not often that children (or adults for that matter) get to see the crafts we love actually being created. Here visitors get an up-close view of how glass is blown, how pottery is made, how furniture is built, or how fabric is woven on a loom. Of course, you can purchase these items too, but it sure is fun to watch craftspeople create beautiful objects.

YONKERS

● Hudson River Museum and Andrus Space Transit Planetarium
511 Warburton Avenue, 963-4550. Hours: Wed.–Sun. 12–5. Admission: Museum, adults $3, children 12 and under $1; Planetarium, adults $4,

children 12 and under $2. Call ahead, as the planetarium closes occasionally for school groups. www.mhv.net/~omi/hrmm.htm. **Ages 2 and up.**

Everyone who visits this museum and planetarium will find something to interest them. The museum, located in a Victorian mansion, has exhibits relating to science and art, including several geared towards younger children (which is always a treat to discover at a museum). The planetarium has state-of-the-art equipment and offers a variety of shows, many of which are for specific age groups. Special events are scheduled throughout the year, such as sleepovers under the stars and free night observations. From the museum's Water Color Café you get a wonderful view of the Hudson River.

Catskills Region

Whether you visit the Catskills region in winter, spring, summer, or fall, you will always be pleasantly surprised by the amount of attractions in the area. From skiing to swimming, from hiking to miniature golf, from animal farms to airplanes, there is something to delight each and every family member. The Catskill Game Farm, in operation since 1933, is one of those places kids always remember visiting. If you and your family are interested in the Wild West, stay at one of the several dude ranches in the area, and try your hand at horseback riding. Or for another unique experience, stay overnight at the incredible Mohonk Mountain House, a Swiss-chalet resort with wonderful views and outdoor activities.

The area code for the Catskills is 914 unless otherwise noted.

ARKVILLE

● Delaware and Ulster Rail Ride
Route 28 between Kingston and Oneonta, 1-800-225-4132. Hours: late May–late Oct. weekends and holidays, July and Aug. Wed.–Sun. Departure times are at 11, 12:30, and 3. Admission: rates vary depending on route.
All ages.

Kids will absolutely love taking this train ride where they can see interesting sites, listen to train whistles, and delight in the sounds of a moving train. This old-fashioned train ride gives kids a sense of adventure especially when they host special train rides, including ones with "real" train robberies. The rail company sponsors many themed excursions, including halloween rides and moonlight rides.

CAIRO

● Funtastic Family Fun Park

Route 32, (518) 622-3330. Hours: June–Aug. daily 10–10; spring and fall weekends only 10–10. Admission: pay per ride, 1 ticket $.75, 30 tickets $20, 150 tickets $75. Go-karts, 8 years old or 52 inches tall and up $3 or 4 tickets, children ages 4–7, 3 tickets; mini-golf, 8 years old and up 4 tickets, children under 8, 3 tickets; water wars, 2 tickets; moon bounce, 2 tickets; kiddie swing ride, 2 tickets. **All ages.**

Here is one of those amusement parks that kids under 12 just can't get enough of. Go-karts, miniature golf, an arcade, and a snack bar for popcorn, cotton candy, and other treats, will give your kids plenty to do for a couple of hours. Kids love the moon bounce; all they do is jump up and down in what essentially is a walk-in balloon. Beware, they can do this for hours!

CATSKILL

● Catskill Game Farm

Game Farm Road (off Route 32), (518) 678-9595. Hours: May 1–Oct. 31 daily 9–6. Admission: Adults $13, children 4–11 $9, children 3 and under free. **All ages.**

The Catskill Game Farm is probably one of the more famous sites in New York and one of the oldest game farms in the United States. As soon as you walk through the 1950s style entrance, with its cutout giraffe figures, you know exactly what you're in for. There are over 2,000 species of animals here, plus a petting zoo, so plan to spend a while here. In addition, there's an animal nursery and a bird garden (with a short train ride through it). A playground and an amusement park with rides (and separate fees), make the game farm perfect for young children.

● Clyde Peeling's Reptileland

Route 32, (518) 678-3557. Hours: Memorial Day–Labor Day, daily 10–6; Labor Day–Columbus Day, weekends only 10–6. Admission: Adults $6, children 4–11 $3, childen 3 and under free. **Ages 2 and up.**

Reptiles of all shapes and sizes abound here, with over 60 exhibits of snakes (more than 100 snakes total), lizards, turtles, crocodiles, and more. There are several scheduled shows each day, during which experts answer questions from the audience. An animal trainer even brings out some of the animals for kids to get a closer look at, and to touch if they dare!

EAST DURHAM

● Zoom Flume Water Park

Shady Glen Road (off Route 145), (518) 239-4559. Hours: June–Labor Day weekdays 10–6, weekends 10–7. Admission: Adults $14.95, children 7 and under $12.95 (a pass to the park and picnic areas, without the rides, is available for $3.95). **All ages.**

If you love to get wet, play in the water all day, get other people wet, and just generally be silly, then this is the place for you. Giant water slides tubes, waterfalls, a wild river ride, and more will entertain even the most difficult-to-please child. For others, there is the Moonwalk (a kind of giant balloon you can bounce on—kids absolutely love this and will stand on line forever to do it), a playground (as if all the above isn't enough), nature trails, and more.

EAST MEREDITH

● Hanford Mills Museum

County Road 10 (10 miles east of Oneonta, I-88 to Route 28 to Route 23 to County Road 10), (607) 278-5744. Hours: May–Oct. daily 10–5. Admission: Adults $4, children 5 and up $2.50, children under 5 free. www.norwich.net/catskills/hanford.htm. **Ages 3 and up.**

There are only a handful of grist mills left in the country and here in the village of East Meredith you and your family can find one of them (built in 1846), still working and still powered by water. Fifteen historic buildings on 70 acres make up the museum complex, which is on both the State and National Registers of Historic Places. Daily demonstrations of the machines and the water wheel, in particular, are fun to watch and give visitors a sense of how much went into working at the mill. The museum holds many special events throughout the year; past events have included a Fall Harvest Festival, the Annual Lumberjack Festival (which is usually held in August), and a winter ice harvest, just to name a few. On the Fourth of July, the ice that was harvested in the winter and stored in the ice house is used to make gallons of ice cream. Call or write the museum for current information and schedules of upcoming events. A gift shop and nature trails round out the activities at Hanford Mills.

HIGHLAND

● Rocking Horse Ranch Resort

Routes 44 and 55, 691-2927 or 1-800-647-2624. Hours: year-round. **All ages.**

Considered one of the top family resorts in America, Rocking Horse Ranch has so much to offer families looking for adventure that it would be difficult to list all of the attractions here. Vacation packages include horseback riding, pools, hay rides, court sports, whirlpool spas, sing-alongs, nature hikes, scavenger hunts, a giant playground, kids' programs, a fitness gym, and more! Special getaway packages are available.

HUNTER

● Hunter Mountain Skyride

Route 23A, (518) 263-4223. Hours: Memorial Day–Oct. weekends 11–4:30. Admission: Adults $7, children 6–12 $3.50, children 5 and under $1. www.huntermtn.com. **Ages 3 and up.**

If you visit Hunter Mountain during the summer or fall, you can reap the benefits of this famous New York state ski area by taking a skyride on the lifts to enjoy the breathtaking scenery of the Catskills. Write ahead for a brochure listing the summer and fall festivals your family can attend. You can also call or write for information about skiing at Hunter Mountain in the winter; there are age-appropriate children's programs, and skiers have over 40 runs to choose from.

KERHONKSON

● Pinegrove Dude Ranch Resort

Lower Cherrytown Road, 1-800-926-6520. Hours: year-round. www.pinegrove-ranch.com. **All ages.**

This rustic resort features everything from supervised children's day camps, boating, and fishing to horseback riding and even cattle driving (you can pretend you are in the movie *City Slickers* with Billy Crystal). If horseback riding doesn't appeal to you or your kids, go on a nature hike, play with the animals in the baby animal farm, or try pitching some horseshoes. If it happens to be a rainy day, there are many indoor activities available such as tennis, ping pong, and even indoor mini-golf. The ranch has nightly entertainment including country western bands and family music shows. Special programs and weekend packages are available.

KINGSTON

● Hudson River Maritime Museum

Rondout Waterfront at the foot of Broadway, 338-0071. Hours: May–Oct., Thanksgiving weekend and Christmas through New Year's, Wed.–Mon.

11–5. *Admission: Museum, adults $2, children 6–12 $1, children 5 and under free. Lighthouse, adults $6, children 4–11 $5, children under 4 free.* **Ages 3 and up.**

People interested in boats and shipbuilding will be very interested in this museum which presents the history of the Hudson River in photographs, paintings, models, artifacts, and actual ships and boats. View exhibits of the maritime history of the Hudson River and see the boat collection. You can then take a short boat ride to the historic Rondout Lighthouse. In the summer the museum also offers workshops for children.

● The Rip van Winkle Cruise

Rondout Waterfront at the foot of Broadway, 255-6515. Hours: May–Oct. Tues.–Sun. 11:30 and 2. Admission: Adults $12.50, seniors $11.50, children 4–11 $5.50, children under 4 free. Tickets can be purchased 1 hour before the cruise. **Ages 8 and up.**

This boat provides two-hour Hudson River cruises taking you south to Hyde Park, past lighthouses and mansions and back again. This is a wonderful way to spend a sunny afternoon. The trip might be too long for younger children (my four- and six-year-old children had enough after a one-hour cruise).

● Trolley Museum

89 East Strand, 331-3399. Hours: Memorial Day–Columbus Day weekends and holidays noon–5; July and Aug., daily noon–5. Admission: free (donations accepted). www.mhrcc.org/kingston/kgntroll.html. **Ages 3 and up.**

Visitors to this small museum can enjoy exhibits which evoke a sense of another time. There are subway cars and trolley cars on display and you can also take an old-fashioned trolley ride along the Hudson River. There is no additional fee for this $1\frac{1}{2}$ mile ride, which takes you to a picnic area near the Hudson River. During holidays they have special theme rides such as the Fright Train during Halloween and the Santa run in the beginning of December.

● Volunteer Fireman's Hall and Museum of Kingston

265 Fair Street, 331-4065. Hours: Apr.–Oct. Fri. 11–3, Sat. 10–4; June–Aug. Wed.–Fri. 11–3, Sat. 10–4. Admission: free (donations accepted). **Ages 4 and up.**

Some children just can't get enough of old fire trucks and fire fighting equipment. At this small museum located in a fire station built in 1857, children get an intimate view of antique trucks, fire fighting memorabilia, and beautiful hand-carved furniture.

LIVINGSTON MANOR

● Catskill Fly Fishing Center and Museum

5447 Old Route 17, P.O. Box 1295, 439-4810. Hours: Apr.–Oct. daily 10–4; Nov.–Mar. Tues.–Sat. 10–1. Admission (suggested donation): Adults $3, children under 12 $1. www.catskill.com/flyfish. **Ages 5 and up.**

Fly-fishing is a sport born in the streams of the Catskill Mountains of New York, and this small museum, located on a 35-acre river site, was built to preserve and present the history of fly-fishing. Visit the library, pick up information on environmental education, and take a class or two on fly-fishing and fly-tying. If you are visiting the area in January, check out the **Winter Ice Carnival** (usually the third Sunday). You'll be treated to professional and amateur figure skating shows, snow and ice sculpture contests and more. For more information about the carnival call the Sullivan County Board of Tourism at (914) 256-3083.

NEW PALTZ

● Huguenot Street National Landmark District

Exit 18 off the NYS Thruway (I-87), 255-1889. Hours: May–Oct. Wed.–Sun. 10–4 or by appointment. Tours: Adults: $7, children 7–12 $3.50, children 6 and under free. **All ages.**

Huguenot Street is the oldest street in America that still has several of its original buildings standing. There are six stone houses and a church here, all built between 1692 and 1799. Hiking trails, picnic areas, a gift shop, and a small restaurant complement the historic attraction.

● Mohonk Mountain House and Skytop Observation Tower

1000 Mountain Rest Road, Lake Mohonk (6 miles west of exit 18 off the NYS Thruway, I-87), 255-1000. Hours: year-round. **All ages.**

Lake Mohonk, a beautiful, light green, glacial lake at 1,246 feet above sea level, is home to the magnificent Mohonk Mountain House, an enormous Swiss chalet–style stone mansion, constructed between 1879 and 1910, with over 300 rooms. Located on 2,200 acres, the resort ajoins the 6,300-acre Mohonk Preserve, an ideal place for hiking. Walking along the cliffs near the mansion leads you to the observation tower and a terrific panoramic view. You can visit the area for an overnight stay (very expensive), or just come for a day hike in the summer or a ski in the winter.

PALENVILLE

● Kaaterskill Falls

Route 23A, between Palenville and Haines Falls, Catskill Park, 589-5058. Hours: year-round. **All ages.**

If you are visiting the Catskill region, you should try to budget some extra time to see the highest waterfall in the state, Kaaterskill Falls. At 260 feet, it beats Niagara Falls by almost 100 feet! This is not a place to take really small children (unless you carry them in a child backpack), as you must hike two miles to the falls. My daughter, however, easily hiked the two miles when she was five (she was tired), so judge for yourselves whether to attempt the hike or not, depending on your group. It is definitely well worth the effort if you do decide to go. This was a very popular tourist attraction in the 19th century, and was frequented by painters of the Hudson River School such as Thomas Cole, Asher B. Durand, and Winslow Homer.

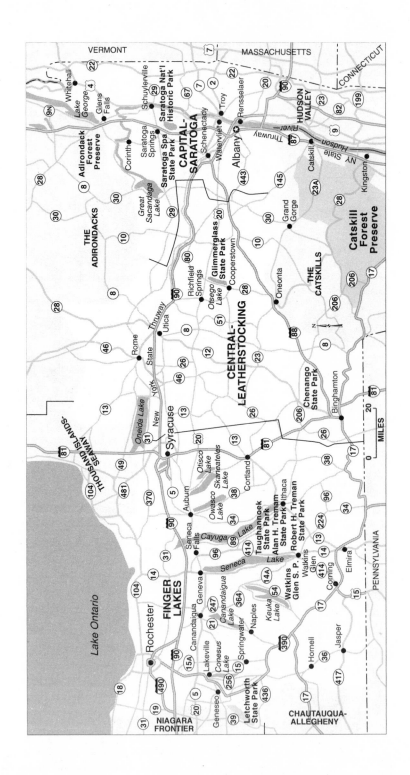

Central New York

Capital-Saratoga Region

Visitors to New York's capital and the surrounding area will find a
region packed with artistic, educational, and historic attractions and a
wealth of outdoor activities to participate in. Albany, the capital city,
has a population of approximately 101,000 people, and is set along the
Hudson River. Originally named Fort Orange by Dutch settlers around
1614, the town was ceded to the English in 1676 and renamed Albany.
Open to the public are the last remaining Dutch house in the area, built
in 1736, and three historic mansions.

Grandma Moses, one of our country's most famous women artists,
lived all her life in upstate New York, in the town of East Bridge, off
Route 67, southeast of Saratoga Springs. And more than 100 years ago in
Cambridge, east of Saratoga Springs, the world-famous pie à la mode was
"invented."

The area code for the Capital-Saratoga region is 518 unless
otherwise noted.

ALBANY

For more information on Albany, visit their Web site (www.albany.org/).

● Albany Institute of History and Art

*125 Washington Avenue, 463-4478. Hours: Wed.–Sun. noon–5. Admission:
Adults $3, children under 12 free (all visitors free Wed.).* **Ages 2 and up.**

There is something for everyone at the Albany Institute, New York
state's oldest museum (it opened in 1791). Installations exhibit works of
art and artifacts from the 15,000-object permanent collection. Most of the
collection relates to the history and culture of the capital–upper Hudson
River Valley region. It includes decorative arts in silver, pewter, ceramics,
and so on, as well as furniture, paintings from the Hudson River School,
and sculpture. Classes, workshops, and lectures take place regularly; the
institute also has an extensive research library.

● Albany Urban Cultural Park and Henry Hudson Planetarium

*25 Quackenbush Square, corner of Broadway and Clinton Avenues,
434-5132. Hours: daily 10–4. Trolley tours: Thurs. and Fri. July–Sept.
Admission: Cultural Park, free; Planetarium, adults $4, children $2;
Guided trolley tours, adults $4, children $2. www.crisny.org/not-for-profit/
albvc/.* **All ages.**

New York has designated Albany as one of 14 Urban Cultural Parks,
located throughout New York state, administered by the State Office of

Parks, Recreation, and Historic Preservation. The program celebrates and preserves regions of historic and cultural significance in the state. Information and exhibits bring to life the history of the city. As part of the Albany Urban Cultural Park, you can find the Henry Hudson Planetarium (open daily for shows), the Albany City Trolley, the Albany Gift Shop, and the Visitor's Center.

● New York State Museum

Empire State Plaza, 474-5877. Hours: daily 10–5. Admission: donations accepted, fees for traveling exhibits. **All ages.**

The State Museum has so much to offer visitors, it is impossible to describe it all. Wander past dioramas that bring to life the history of New York state: a Native American getting ready to kill an elk, an East Side tenement, a Sesame Street set, the Adirondack wilderness. Wonder at the amazing examples of New York gems or enjoy the *Birds of New York* exhibit. Additional exhibits feature furniture, art, historic artifacts, science, technology, and more. Workshops the museum has held for children include Science Lab for Kids, Feathered Friends, Origami, Dig It! Learn About Archaeology, Animals of the Adirondacks, and National Chemistry Day (just to name a few!). There's even a hands-on discovery area for children. Save at least an hour and a half to two hours for your visit here.

BALLSTON SPA

● National Bottle Museum

76 Milton Avenue (Route 50), 885-7589. Hours: June–Sept. daily 10–4; Oct.–May Mon.–Fri. 10–4. Admission: Adults $2, children ages 6–12 $1. **Ages 4 and up.**

For some reason, most children love containers of all kinds, and here they can view over 1,000 of them, from antique bottles to modern glass containers. Videos on glass making provide information on the history of the craft.

PETERSBURG

● Berkshire Bird Paradise and Sanctuary

Red Pond Road, off Country Road 87 (2 miles off Route 2, east of Troy), 279-3801. Hours: May–Oct. daily, 9–6. Admission: Adults $5, children $3. **All ages.**

If you and your child love birds, then this is the place to visit. With more than 2,000 birds from all over the world, including bald and golden eagles as well as rare and exotic birds, you can be sure to see some beautiful specimens. The facility also treats and rehabilitates injured birds. Scenic trails let you get outdoor exercise.

SARATOGA SPRINGS

● Children's Museum of Saratoga Springs

42 Phila Street, 584-5540. Hours: Tues., Wed., Sat. 10–4:30, Thurs., Fri., Sun. noon–4:30. Admission: Ages 3 and up $3, children under 2 free. **Ages 2–10.**

Many interactive exhibits await children here. Among the great things to play with are an interesting toddler-sized cityscape, a pretend fire station complete with model fire truck, a 1930s general store, giant bubbles, and a shadow room. The new *Construction Zone* exhibit has architect's tables, building blocks and Legos, and a stud-wall house where kids can learn about building. Children's workshops include, art, theater, and photography.

● National Museum of Dance

S. Broadway, Route 9, 584-2225. Hours: May–Dec. Tues.–Sun. 10–5. Admission: Adults $3.50, children under 12 $1. **Ages 2 and up.**

The Museum of Dance is the only museum devoted to the history of dance in general and American professional dance in particular. Our daughter is captivated by anything that has to do with dance, and if your child is like that, he or she will love this museum. There are dance studios, a dance-related gift shop, and small café. Starting in 1998, the museum will be open all year. Call for revised hours.

● National Museum of Racing and Thoroughbred Hall of Fame

Union Avenue and Ludlow Street, 584-0400. Hours: Mon.–Sat. 10–4:30, Sun. noon–4:30. Admission: Adults $3, children 5 and up $2, children under 5 free. **Ages 4 and up.**

Many children are interested in horses, and therefore a visit to this museum might need to be on your agenda. There are displays, racing memorabilia, and audio-visual programs. If it's real thoroughbred horse racing you want to see, and you are visiting in August, head down the street to the Saratoga Race Course on Union Avenue (584-6200). Please note, however, that betting is allowed at the race course so it might not be appropriate for children.

● Petrified Sea Gardens

Route 29, 584-7102. Hours: May–Oct. weekends 11–5. Admission: Adults $3, children 6–16 $1.50, children 5 and under free. **Ages 4 and up.**

What kid doesn't like fossils, rocks and minerals? Here children can explore a 500-million-year old reef, glacial remains, and rock crevices. The "gardens" feature a trail where visitors walk on an ancient fossilized dry creek bed. There is also a rock and mineral museum and rock shop, and many children's programs are offered throughout the year.

● Saratoga Spa State Park

Routes 9 and 50, 584-2535 or 587-3330. Hours: daily 8–dusk. Admission: $4 per car in summer only. **All ages.**

This park covers over 2,000 acres, is the home of the Saratoga Springs Performing Arts Center (see separate listing), and is on the National Register of Historic Places. There are mineral springs to enjoy, bathhouses, trails, golf courses, swimming pools, tennis courts, and great places to have a picnic.

● Saratoga Springs Performing Arts Center

Saratoga Spa State Park, Routes 9 and 50, 587-3330. Hours: year-round. Admission: varies according to performance. www.spac.org. **All ages.**

All summer long you can enjoy performances by the New York City Ballet and Opera, the Philadelphia Orchestra, the Newport Jazz Festival, and other terrific artistic groups and individuals. For children, the SSPAC does something terrific, they provide free lawn tickets to children 12 and under if they are accompanied by a paying adult. So on a beautiful summer evening, gather up a blanket and picnic basket, and watch the ballet or listen to the orchestra. Some restrictions apply to the above (and to lawn seating), so be sure to get the specifics when you call for information.

You can also call the Saratoga Springs National Museum of Dance (see above), to reserve a space for your child in one of the behind-the-scenes tours offered at dance matinees.

● Saratoga Springs Urban Cultural Park Visitor Center

297 Broadway, 587-3241. Hours: daily 9–4. **All ages.**

If you are visiting Saratoga Springs, then this is the place to begin your trip. Located in a Beaux Arts trolley station dating to 1915, it is the area's tourist information station. Pick up brochures, view exhibits, and learn about special events.

SCHENECTADY

There are many wonderful places to visit in this quaint small town (pop. 65,500). Schenectady, (pronounced skeh-NECK-ta-dee) was founded in 1661 by the Dutch, and Dutch influence can easily be seen in the architecture of the Stockade District. This area has over 60 buildings built between 1700 and 1850. Parts of the town have undergone some revitalization projects over the years; Jay Street, for example, is now a nice pedestrian mall with shops and cafés.

● Schenectady Museum and Planetarium and Urban Cultural Park Visitor Center

Nott Terrace Heights, 382-7890. Hours: Tues.–Fri. 10–4:30, Sat. and Sun., noon–5. Planetarium shows vary so call for current schedule. Admission: Museum, adults $3, children ages 4–12 $1.50; Museum and planetarium, adults $5, children ages 4–12 $2.50, family rate $15.
All ages.

You'll probably need to plan at least two hours to explore this facility. Exhibits here range from science and art to history and technology. This is in addition to a 93-acre nature preserve that you can enjoy after you've experienced all the interesting things inside.

TROY

To find out about special events in Troy, call the area happenings hotline at 274-TROY.

● Hudson-Mohawk Urban Cultural Park

RiverSpark Visitor Center, at the confluence of the Hudson and Mohawk Rivers, 251 River Street, 270-8667. Hours: Tues.–Fri. 10–5, Sat. 10–4. Admission: free. **All ages.**

As part of the 14-site urban cultural park group, this park has a 26-mile heritage trail that features exhibit areas, 19th-century mill houses, waterfalls, music halls, churches, and more. At the visitor's center you can pick up brochures that outline a self-guided walking tour and provide you with all the information you need about the area.

● Junior Museum

282 5th Avenue, 235-2120. Hours: Wed.–Sun. noon–5. Admission: Adults $3, children $3, children under 2 free. **Ages 2–12.**

How can you go wrong at a hands-on museum with programming geared exclusively towards children? The Junior Museum has something for every child; exhibits range from science, history, and nature, to an 1850s-era log cabin. There's also a gallery where art works by children are often displayed. Located in a 19th-century brick firehouse, the museum also has some live animals such as turtles, lizards, and snakes.

Central Leatherstocking Region

The Leatherstocking region gets its name from the leather leggings or "stockings" worn by the early frontier settlers to the region. James Fenimore Cooper, the 19th-century American writer, immortalized the area in his *Leatherstocking Tales*, describing the life of the frontiersmen of the region. The town of Cooperstown is named after his father, who founded the town in the early 19th century. The Central Leatherstocking region is bordered by two mountain ranges and two bodies of water: the Adirondacks to the north and the Catskills to the south; and the Finger Lakes to the west and the Hudson River to the east. If you and your family are interested in baseball, plan a trip to the famous Baseball Hall of Fame in Cooperstown. But don't stop there, there are many other interesting things to see and do. How about visiting an historic site (the Farmer's Museum in Cooperstown), or maybe music is your thing (the Musical Museum in Deansboro), or perhaps you and your kids would like to practice being geologists (Herkimer Diamond Mines). You'll find that not only does this region have many attractions to visit, but it's also beautiful, and you will enjoy just driving though the area, particularly if you can visit during the fall.

All sites listed are in the 607 area code unless otherwise noted.

BINGHAMTON
Broom County Convention and Visitor Bureau: www.spectra.net/bcc.

● Carousel Museum
Morgan Road at Ross Park, 724-5461. Hours: Memorial Day–Labor Day daily noon–5. Admission: free or one piece of litter! **All ages.**

    The Binghamton area has six restored carousels to enjoy. This one is located in Ross Park, at the same address as the zoo (listed below). Installed in 1920, this carousel has 60 jumping horses sure to delight your children. There is also a playground and picnic area nearby, so bring some snacks, visit the zoo and the Discovery Center (also listed below), and then head to the carousel to relax and have a leisurely picnic.

● Discovery Center of the Southern Tier
60 Morgan Road, 773-8661. Hours: Tues.–Sat. 10–4, Sun. noon–5. Admission: Adults $2.75, children under 3 free, family of 6 or more $12.50. **All ages.**

Hands-on children's museums satisfy every visitor's urge to experience by touching and my kids gave the Discovery Center a thumbs-up almost immediately after we arrived. Here children can pretend to shop with kid-sized grocery carts, and feel what it's like to sit in a plane's cockpit or the driver's seat of a real fire engine. My children spent over two hours here, thoroughly captivated by all the different areas to explore, and did not want to leave (even though they were obviously starving for lunch!). The center also offers various special programs, including School's Out Discovery Camp, programs for children five and under on Wednesday mornings, and many fun weekend programs.

● Roberson Museum and Science Center/Link Planetarium

30 Front Street, 772-0660. Hours: Mon.–Thurs. 10–5, Fri. 10–9, Sat. 10–5, Sun. noon–5. Admission: Adults $4, children 5–18 $3, children 4 and under free (Planetarium $1 extra per person). **All ages.**

The Roberson Museum offers children the opportunity to experience art, history, science, and technology. Part of the museum is located in a turn-of-the-century mansion, and part is in a newer addition. Enjoy the mansion and its period rooms, and then head to the science center where your kids can play with hands-on exhibits. The center also offers a dizzying array of special classes such as puppet-making workshops, painting, sculpture, egg decorating, and ceramics workshops. The Link Planetarium puts on star shows several times per week and also offers planetarium science classes.

● Ross Park Zoo

185 Park Avenue, 724-5461. Hours: Mar.–Oct. daily 10–5. Admission: Adults $3.50, children $2.75, children under 2 free. **All ages.**

Ross Park Zoo is the fifth oldest zoo in the country, set on 75 acres and featuring 200 animals. Highlighted here are white tigers, snow leopards, wolves, and eagles. The terrain is a little hilly so be prepared to push a stroller up a few slopes. Snack bars and a zoo shop complete the picture here.

CAZENOVIA

● Lorenzo State Historic Site

17 Rippleton Road at Routes 13 and 20. (315) 655-3200. Hours: May 15–Oct. 31 Wed.–Sat., 10–5 and Sun. 1–5. **Ages 5 and up.**

Built in 1807, this Federal-style mansion is located on a beautiful site with formal gardens, an arboretum, and a carriage collection. There is a Visitor Center and gift shop, and the site is also open during the Christmas season for special events—call ahead for details.

● Stone Hill Quarry Art Park

3883 Stone Quarry Road, (315) 655-3196. Hours: daily 10–5. Admission: free. **Ages 3 and up.**

Visit this art park each year to see new artwork done by an artist-in-residence. The annual pottery fair is also a treat. Stone Hill Quarry offers workshops and demonstrations, several special family events, and numerous children's art and nature classes.

COOPERSTOWN

For more information on Cooperstown, visit their Web site (www.cooperstown.net).

● American Baseball Archives

99 Main Street, 547-1273. Hours: Apr. 1–May 14, Oct. 27–Nov. 30 weekends only 10–7; May 15–Oct. 21 daily 9–8. Admission: Adults $5.50, children 12 and under $2.50. **Ages 2 and up.**

Not to be confused with the Baseball Hall of Fame, this center houses many attractions, including America's only baseball wax museum. There is an interesting virtual reality pitching exhibit, for those of you who are new-technology inclined, or for a taste of being in an actual ball park, stop in for a hot dog at Shoeless Joe's Baseball Stadium Snack Bar. At the ProImage Photo Studio here, you can get all decked out in an official baseball uniform and have your photo taken.

● Clark Sports Center

Susquehanna Avenue, 547-2800. Hours: May–Oct. Mon.–Sat. 6:30 A.M.– 9 P.M.; Oct.–May Mon.–Fri. 6:30 A.M.–10 P.M., Sat. 6:30 A.M.–9 P.M., Sun. 9–6. Admission: Adults $7 (for weight room, add $5), under 21 $3, children under 18 need a waiver form signed by a parent.

This modern sports, health, and recreation center is open to the public year-round. It has facilities for every kind of fitness activity you could want, including a gym, an indoor track, racquetball and squash courts, lap and diving pools, an eight-lane bowling alley, and a 30-foot climbing wall (which is only available on a limited basis).

● Cooperstown Fun Park

Route 28, 3 miles south of Cooperstown, 547-2767. Hours: Apr., May, and Sept., weekends only noon–9; June–Aug., daily 10 A.M.–11 P.M. Admission: pay per acitivity; go-karts, $3.75 (need to be 54 inches tall);

bumper boats, $3.75 (need to be 45 inches tall); paddle boats, $4 for 20 minutes. **All ages.**

Here's a fun place to take the whole family on a day when you decide to skip all the museums and just enjoy the outdoors. Have a race on the Grand Prix go-kart track, have a blast in the bumper boats, or just relax in the paddle boats. The kids can try out games in the arcade, play a game of mini-golf and more. For those so inclined, the Hamburger Hall of Fame offers every kind of hamburger imaginable.

● Corvette Hall of Fame and Americana Museum

Route 28, 547-4135. Hours: Sept.–Apr. daily 9:30–5; May–Aug. daily 9–9. Admission: Adults $9.95, children 5–13 $6.95, children under 5 free. **Ages 3 and up.**

If you are interested in either cars (Corvettes) or American history, you should find this museum appealing. The museum is a virtual time tunnel with movies, music, and slides carrying you back across the last half century. Displays include pop figures such as Marilyn Monroe, Elvis Presley, and Bruce Springsteen.

● Farmer's Museum and Village Crossroads

Lake Road (Route 80), 547–1400. Hours: Apr., May, and Nov. Tues.– Sun. 10–4; June–Labor Day daily 9–5; Sept–Oct. daily 9–4; Dec. Fri.– Sun. 10–4. Admission: Prices vary. If you purchase a pass for this museum, the Fenimore House, and the Baseball Hall of Fame, you can save 20 percent on admission fees. As of this writing, this special pass is called the "Cooperstown Discovery Pass," cost $22 for adults, $9.50 for children ages 7–15 (children under 7 free). Single tickets, cost $9 per adult for each museum. **All ages.**

This outdoor museum focuses on the way life was in the mid-1800s. Costumed employees work in authentic settings such as at the spinning wheel and loom, in the blacksmith's shop, and at the cabinetmaker's shop. This provides a whole new experience for children, as they get to see and smell and feel what life was like in an earlier era. The museum even has a working farm with live animals. The museum offers a multitude of special programs including Native American storytelling, sheep-shearing demonstrations, a Fourth of July celebration, and many, many others.

● Fenimore House Museum

Lake Road (Route 80), 547-1400. Hours: Apr. and Nov. Tues.–Sun. 10–4; May, Sept., and Oct. daily 10–4; June–Labor Day daily 9–5; Dec. Fri.–Sun. 10–4. Admission: see information in the listing above. www.cooperstown.net/nysha. **Ages 4 and up.**

Just across the street from the Farmer's Museum, you'll find the Fenimore House, an American art museum that has collections of fine art, folk art, historic photographs, and or course, James Fenimore Cooper memorabilia. A new wing houses the Eugene and Clare Thaw collection of Native American Indian art. Enjoy lunch in the museum café overlooking Lake Otsego. Exhibits change regularly; call for a current schedule of exhibitions.

● Lolly Pop Farm and Petting Zoo/Cooperstown Famous Family Campgrounds

Route 28 to County Road 11, 293-7766 or 1-800-959-CAMP. Hours: mid-May–mid-Oct. daily 9–5. Admission: Adults $5, children 3–12 $3, children 2 and under free (admission also free if you are staying at the campground). **All ages.**

Here, children can pet animals and enjoy them up-close in a supervised atmosphere. Twenty-five species of animals—from camels to cougars—and numerous birds in an aviary make up the "livestock" at Lolly Pop Farm. Campers can get pony and hay rides, use the paddle boats on the lake, and play mini-golf.

● National Baseball Hall of Fame and Museum

Main Street at First Street, 547-7200. Hours: May–Sept. daily 9–9; Nov.–Apr. 9–5. Admission: Adults $9.50, children 7–12 $4, children under 7 free. See Farmer's Museum, above, for information about the Cooperstown Discovery Pass. **Ages 2 and up.**

This famous museum was founded in 1939 to honor baseball's stars. Today it has a collection of over 6,000 artifacts displayed in 60,000 square feet of exhibition space. A new permanent exhibit called Pride and Passion is dedicated to the African-American contribution to the sport. Definitely plan a visit here if anyone in your group is a baseball fan.

DEANSBORO

● The Musical Museum

Route 12B, (315) 841-8774. Hours: mid-Apr.–Dec. Thurs.–Sat. 10–3. Admission: please call for current fees. **Ages 4 and up.**

For once in your life, you finally CAN touch the displays, yes, even adults! The Musical Museum encourages visitors to tinker with everything; there are 17 rooms' worth of musical instruments plus a harpsichord music box and a player piano to see, touch, and play.

HERKIMER

● Herkimer Diamond Mines

Road 1 off Route 28 (7 miles north of Herkimer), (315) 891-7355. Hours: Apr.–Nov. daily 9–5. Admission: Adults $6, children 6 and up $5, children under 6 free. **Ages 2 and up.**

Have a hand at being an amateur geologist at this fun site. Most children love to dig for stuff, and here they can dig to their hearts' content and actually find quartz crystals (or "diamonds")! Maybe the most fun part is that they can keep whatever they find. There is also a gem and mineral shop and a restaurant on-site.

HOWES CAVE

● Howe Caverns

Route 7 off I-88 exit 22 (approx. 37 miles from Albany, 105 from Syracuse), 296-8990. Hours: daily 9–6. Admission: Adults $11.50, children 7–12 $6, children under 7 free. **All ages.**

I am sure there are people in your family or travel group who are fascinated by caves, and these caves are 156 feet underground. They are open year-round because of the constant below-the-surface temperature of 52 degrees fahrenheit (12° C). You can take the one-and-one-quarter-hour guided underground tour and enjoy the ride on a flat-bottomed boat on Lake Venus (also underground). When you emerge, take a minute to get used to the light, and have a treat at the restaurant or snack bar. Howe Caverns also offers horseback riding, gemstone mining, and geode cutting.

● Iroquois Indian Museum

Caverns Road, 3 miles from I-88, (518) 296-8949. Hours: Sept.–June Tues.–Sat. 10–5, Sun. noon–5; July and Aug. Mon.–Sat. 10–6, Sun. noon–6. Admission: Adults $5.50, teens 13–17 $4.50, children 7–12 $2.50, children under 7 free. **All ages.**

Let your children learn about the region's Native American heritage with a visit to this museum which helps to serve the continuation of the Iroquois spirit. There are a children's museum; archaeological and historic exhibits; and special events such as storytelling. Take a leisurely walk on one of the hiking trails within the 45-acre nature park. Three times a year Iroquois Festivals are held; food, games, and dance performances keep the celebrations lively. Call for specific dates, fees, and more detailed information.

ONEONTA

● National Soccer Hall of Fame Museum

5-11 Ford Avenue, 432-3351. Hours: June–Sept. daily 9–7:30; Oct.–May 10–3. Admission: Adults $8, children 12 and under $4. www.wpe.com/ ~nshof/. **Ages 4 and up.**

The museum's mission is to promote the sport of soccer and to present the history of soccer in the U.S. This small interim museum has exhibits featuring soccer uniforms, World Cup 1994 memorabilia, and audiovisual displays of soccer games throughout the country. A new museum is in the planning stages, and will be built adjoining the 60-acre sports complex called the Wright National Soccer Campus which has three indoor fields, four state-of-the-art outdoor soccer fields, and a 10,000-seat stadium. If your kid has soccer-mania you will have to stop here for a visit.

● Science Discovery Center of Oneonta

State University College, Physical Science Building, 436-2011. Hours: Sept.–June Thurs.–Sat. 12–4; July and Aug. Mon.–Sat. 12–4. Admission: free (donations welcome). www.oneonta.edu/~scdisc. **All ages.**

Learn about interesting subjects such as matter, motion, sound, electricity, and optics at this hands-on science center that has over 70 exhibits. There is plenty to keep your little ones busy for quite a while, and they will get the beginnings of a science education at the same time.

RICHFIELD SPRINGS

● Petrified Creatures Museum of Natural History

Route 20, 10 miles north of Cooperstown, (315) 858-2868. Hours: Memorial Day–Labor Day Thurs.–Mon. 9–6. Admission: Adults $7, children 6–12 $4, children under 6 free. **Ages 3 and up.**

What are petrified creatures? Fossils, of course! In addition to digging for fossils and learning about them afterwards, visitors to this museum can bring fossils home to show their friends and teachers. The public is allowed to excavate and keep what they find in a rock outcrop which is approximately 500 feet wide by 1,000 feet long. Staff members demonstrate how to dig for fossils. The museum claims that no one goes home without a fossil! There are even life-size dinosaurs on display, as well as a hands-on discovery center and a science and education center.

ROME

● Erie Canal Village

5789 New London Road, (315) 337-3999. Hours: mid-May through Labor Day. Admission: Adults $6, children 4–17 $4, children 3 and under free. Boat and train ride, ages 4 and up $3. **All ages.**

Living history museums teach children (and adults) about the past. This village, located near the site where engineers began to construct the Erie Canal in 1817, has all the parts of an actual 19th-century town, complete with homes, a tavern, a church, a schoolhouse, and a blacksmith's shop. Most of the buildings are historic and were moved here from other locations. A collection of horse-drawn carriages and other vehicles is also on view. Call ahead for information regarding seasonal events, particularly those held during Halloween and Christmas. A special summer history education program for children is also great fun and extremely popular.

● Fort Rickey Children's Discovery Zoo

5135 Rome–New London Road, Routes 46 and 49, (315) 336-1930. Hours: mid-May–mid-June, weekends only 10–6; mid-June–Labor Day daily 10–6. Admission: Ages 2 and up $6, children under 2 free. **All ages.**

This zoo is perfect for young children: it's not too big, yet there are plenty of animals to look at and other fun things to do. The zoo has a large petting and feeding area that kids love. When they get done enjoying the animals, kids can head over to the soft-play area and crawl through tubes and tunnels and mazes, or go over to the new water-play area where there are fountains and waterfalls they can splash in (don't forget to bring extra clothes and towels). A snack bar and a picnic area on-site provide for refueling.

● Fort Stanwix National Monument

112 East Park Street, (315) 336-2090 or 336-2092. Hours: Apr.–Dec. daily 9–5. Admission: Adults $2.50, children 16 and under free. www.nps.gov/fost/. **All ages.**

No matter how many forts kids visit, they always seem to love them. Here, costumed guides provide information, by offering tours and answering questions, regarding this reconstructed Revolutionary War fort. The original fort was built in 1758 by the British, but by 1781 it had been leveled and the city of Rome was being built atop it. In 1935, the area was declared a National Monument. After three blocks' worth of buildings were torn down and the site was excavated in the late 1960s, the fort was rebuilt on its original foundations. The fort opened to the public in 1976, just in time for the Bicentennial celebrations. During the last weekend in July, the Syracuse Symphony Orchestra performs the *1812 Overture,* and the fort supplies the authentic sights and sounds of muskets, cannon fire, and fireworks. At Christmas, the fort is decorated and lit throughout with candles.

UTICA

● Children's Museum of History, Natural History, and Science

311 Main Street, (315) 724-6129. Hours: Tues.–Sat. 10–4:30, Sun. noon–4:30. Admission: $2.50. **All ages.**

At this museum, children can play at various exhibits, see the Iroquois longhouse, and check out the fun dinosaur dioramas. There is even a play space just for children under five. Children can create artwork in the craft area, and then head upstairs to investigate the insect zoo.

● Munson-Williams-Proctor Institute, Museum of Art

310 Genesee Street, (315) 797-0000. Hours: Tues.–Sat. 10–5, Sun. 1–5. Admission: free. **Ages 4 and up.**

Famed architect Philip Johnson designed this museum in 1960. The collection features 18th-, 19th-, and 20th-century American and European artists such as Pablo Picasso, Salvador Dali, and Charles Burchfield.

● Utica Zoo

Steele Hill Road, (315) 738-0472. Hours: daily 10–5. Admission: Adults $3.95, children 2–12 $2.25, children under 2 free. www.cybervillage.com/uticazoo/. **All ages.**

This is another good-sized zoo, not too large to be overwhelming. It features reptiles, birds, a red panda, a Siberian tiger, a snow leopard, buffalo, goats, ducks, and more. There's also a small petting zoo and daily sea lions feedings each day at noon and 3 P.M.

Finger Lakes Region

The Finger Lakes region of New York is known for its unique landscape and attractions. There are 11 Finger Lakes—6 major lakes and 5 smaller ones—all formed by glaciers. Although the Finger Lakes region is the United States' second largest wine-producing region, I have left out any mention of the many wineries because the focus of the book is places to go with children. If you enjoy good wine, though, do try to visit one of the more than 50 world-famous wineries during your stay in the area. You can ask at any Convention and Visitors Bureau for a brochure listing wine tours of the Finger Lakes or write the Finger Lakes Association, 309 Lake Street, Penn Yan, NY, 14527, or call for the Finger Lakes brochure at 1-800-KIT-4-FUN. You can also get information through their Web site at www.embark.com/FingerLakes.

Please note that Letchworth State Park is listed in the Niagara Frontier region, under Castile. The park crosses into the Finger Lakes region, but for all practical purposes it is in the Niagara Frontier region of the state.

The area code for the Finger Lakes region is 607 unless otherwise noted.

AUBURN

● Harriet Tubman Home

180 South Street, (315) 252-2081. Hours: Tues.–Fri. 11–4, Sat. by appointment only. Admission: free (donations accepted). **Ages 4 and up.**

Born a slave in Maryland around 1820, Harriet Tubman escaped to New York and rescued over 300 slaves by way of the Underground Railroad. Her home, where she lived until her death in 1913, is now open to the public. Here you can view a videotape describing her life and accomplishments. A guided tour is available.

● William H. Seward House

33 South Street, (315) 252-1283. Hours: Apr.–Dec. Tues.–Sat. 1–4. Admission: Adults $3, children 12–18, $2.50, children under 12 free. **Ages 4 and up.**

William Henry Seward (1801–72) was the governor of New York, a state senator, the secretary of state under Presidents Lincoln and Johnson, a strong anti-slavery advocate, and a leading figure in the deal to purchase Alaska. His house was turned over to the state after the death of his grandson, and is now a National Historic Landmark. The house was built in 1816–17, and 16 rooms are open to the public. Visitors can see Seward's uniform, the special gold-leaf furniture used on special occasions, and famous paintings by 19th-century artists such as Emanuel Leutze, Thomas Cole, and others.

BALDWINSVILLE

● Beaver Lake Nature Center

8477 East Mud Lake Road, 20 miles northwest of Syracuse, (315) 638-2519. Hours: daily dawn–dusk. Admission: $1 per car. **All ages.**

If you and your family love the outdoors, the 600-acre Beaver Lake Nature Center can be enjoyed in all seasons. In addition to nine miles of hiking trails there is also a bog boardwalk, a lake observation tower, a visitor's center with changing exhibits, spotting scopes at notable observation areas, and lots more. In winter, borrow some snowshoes or go cross-country skiing; in spring enjoy the thousands of wildflowers; in summer paddle a canoe across the lake; in fall marvel at the magnificent fall foliage. Write ahead for information regarding workshops and special events for families, and ask for a sample copy of the *Beaver Tales* newsletter. A subscription comes with family membership to Beaver Lake. In 1997, the family membership was $28.

CANANDAIGUA

● Bristol Mountain Sky Rides

5662 Route 64, (716) 374-6000. Hours: Sept. and Oct. Sat. and Sun. noon–4. Admission: Price varies each year; under $5 per person. **All ages.**

Enjoy the fall foliage in all its splendor from this fantastic vantage point. Ride a triple chairlift for a mile, up 1,200 vertical feet, for an incredible view at 2,200 feet. You can then either ride the chairlift back down, or enjoy a beautiful two-mile hike down along a ski trail. In the winter, the mountain becomes a ski resort, complete with, lounge, cafeteria, and nursery.

● *Canandaigua Lady* Paddlewheel/Steamboat

169 Lakeshore Drive, (716) 394-5365. Hours: May–Oct. Tues.–Sun. Admission: price varies depending on length and type of excursion. **All ages.**

Sometimes it's fun to just sit back and take in the scenery, and a few hours aboard a replica 19th-century paddlewheel boat, perhaps including a light lunch, is the perfect way to do just that. The scenery is, in this case, one of the Finger Lakes. Canandaigua Lake is one of the six largest Finger Lakes. If you plan on visiting the area in the fall, take the annual fall foliage cruise and enjoy regional wine and food.

● Granger Homestead and Carriage Museum

295 N. Main Street, (716) 394-1472. Hours: May, Sept., and Oct. Tues.– Fri. 1–5; June–Aug. Tues.–Sun. 1–5. Admission: Adults $4, children over 6 $1, children under 6 free. **Ages 4 and up.**

Gideon Granger (1767–1822) was postmaster general under Presidents Thomas Jefferson and James Madison. He built this federal-style home in 1816, and many of the pieces of furniture on display today are original to the house. Another interesting part of a visit here is the

Carriage Museum. Over 50 horse-drawn carriages are on exhibit, and children are often fascinated by these examples of our ancestors' mode of transportation. Each September a Civil War reenactment takes place on the homestead grounds.

● Sonnenberg Gardens

151 Charlotte Street, (716) 394-4922. Hours: May–Oct. daily 9:30–5:30. Admission: Grounds, adults $6.50, children 6–16 $2.50, children under 6 free; Mansion, adults $1, children 6–16 $.50, children under 6 free. **Ages 4 and up.**

Sonnenberg is the 40-room, summer mansion built in 1887 for Frederick Ferris and Mary Clark Thompson. The architecture is an eclectic blend of Queen Anne, Tudor, and Richardson Romanesque styles. Mrs. Thompson's heir sold the 50-acre estate to the federal government in 1930, and in 1973 the estate began to be restored. There are nine formal gardens to explore, including the Italian garden, the rose garden, and the Japanese garden. More than 20,000 annuals and 2,600 rose bushes grow on the grounds accented by waterfalls, caverns, and more. There are many special events throughout the year, including a spooky Haunted Garden for Halloween, the wonderful Festival of Lights during the Christmas season, periodic concerts and picnics, and even a visit from the Easter Bunny.

CORNING

● Corning Glass Center

151 Centerway (off Route 170), 974-2000. Hours: daily 9–5, July and Aug. until 8. Admission: Adults $7, children 6–17 $5, children under 6 free, family rate $16. www.corningglasscenter.com. **Ages 3 and up.**

My children loved this museum. At every turn I heard, "Oooh, Mom, look at this," and "Wow, is this really glass?" After you have looked at every conceivable beautiful glass object dating from 1500 B.C. to the present, you can wander down to the Steuben Factory to watch artists create glass works right before your eyes. This is a special treat, as it is always fascinating to watch an object being made from molten glass. In the Hall of Science and Industry, marvel at one of the largest pieces of glass ever made. Of course, there are also shops featuring glass items ranging from wine glasses to bowls to earrings.

If you are visiting the region, this is one attraction you should not miss.

● Rockwell Museum

111 Cedar Street, (607) 937-5386. Hours: Mon.–Sat., 9–5, Sun. 12–5. Admission: Adults $4, children 6–17 $2, children under 6 free. www.stny.lrun.com/rockwellmuseum. **Ages 4 and up.**

Housed in a Romanesque Revival house built in 1893 and located in the Market Street Historic District in Corning, this museum displays the collections of the Rockwell family, which includes American western art, Steuben glass, and antique toys.

There is a lot to see at this museum, but the paintings of the American West are likely to capture your children's attention almost immediately.

Market Street is a terrific street to stroll down: buy some ice cream, enjoy the restored 19th-century architecture, explore an antique shop, or linger in a one-of-a-kind boutique.

CORTLAND

● 1890 House Museum—Center for Victorian Art

37 Tompkins Street (Route 13), 756-7551. Hours: Tues.–Sun. 1–4. Admission: Adults $3.50, children under 12 free. **Ages 3 and up.**

This massive limestone castle, built in an eclectic chateauesque style for the Wickwire family, was designed by architect Samuel Reed. The famous J. B. Tiffany and Company consulted on the interior design. There are over 30 rooms complete with towers and turrets, which children love to explore.

The Wickwires lived here for over 80 years, and in 1974 the building was designated a historic house museum.

ELBRIDGE

● Carpenter's Brook Fish Hatchery

Route 321 (off Route 5, west of Syracuse), (315) 689-9367. Hours: daily dawn to dusk. Admission: free. **All ages.**

I don't know why exactly but it seems that most kids love fish hatcheries. Children love to watch the swimming fish and all the commotion it raises when the fish are fed.

Special programs here include children's fishing derbies, a 16-by-24-foot kids' fish pool, and hatchery tours. Kids can feed the trout in the outdoor ponds, which they love to do and which is really fun to watch.

ELMIRA

● Arnot Art Museum

235 Lake Street, 734-3697. Hours: Tues.–Sat. 10–5, Sun. 1–5. Admission: Tues.–Fri. Adults $2, children over 6 $.50, children under 6 free; Sat. and Sun. free for all. **Ages 4 and up.**

The Arnot Art Museum, founded in 1913, is located in a neo-classical mansion built in 1833 by John Arnot. On display are 17th- to 19th-century European and American paintings and sculpture. Works of art by famous masters such as Lorrain, Breughel, Breton, Millet, and Courbet are featured. In addition to works by European masters, there are smaller collections of Oriental, Egyptian, pre-Columbian, and Native American art.

● The Mark Twain Study and the Mark Twain Exhibit

Elmira College at the Center for Mark Twain Studies, 1 Park Place, 735-1941. Hours: mid-June–Labor Day Mon.–Sat. 9–5, Sun. 12–5; rest of the year by appointment only. Admission: free. **Ages 9 and up.**

Famous author Mark Twain (Samuel Clemens) spent over twenty summers writing in this small study now located on the Elmira College campus. He and his family are buried in the nearby Woodlawn Cemetery. Mark Twain wrote this about this room: "It is the loveliest study you ever saw. It is octagonal, with a peaked roof, each face filled with a spacious window . . . . It is a cozy nest and just room in it for a sofa, table, and three or four chairs . . . imagine the luxury of it." In Hamilton Hall visit the exhibits about his life and work featuring photographs, paintings, writings, and other memorabilia.

● National Soaring Museum and Gliderport

Harris Hill, 51 Soaring Hill Drive (off Route 17 exits 48 or 56 between Elmira and Corning), 734-3128. Hours: daily 10–5. Admission: Adults $4, children 7–17 $2.50, children 7 and under free. **Ages 3 and up.**

I must admit I wondered whether kids would like this place, but when we visited my fears were dispelled. They don't just like this place, they love it! At the Glideport you can sit back and watch gliders move through the air as quiet as the wind, or if you dare, you can take a trip in one yourself. The museum is also interesting for children. Here they can see the only full-scale replica of Orville Wright's *Glider #5,* which soared for over nine minutes in 1911, and sit in a display glider to see what it feels like to be in a sailplane. There are many other planes to look at on display as well. (The museum is geared towards children ages 7 and up).

Don't think your fun ends here though. After you leave, head down the hill going east, and you will find yourselves at **Harris Hill Park,** a small family amusement park, complete with old-fashioned rides, cotton candy, batting cages, miniature golf, and more (there is even an Olympic-sized swimming pool). The park was almost as much fun as the Soaring Museum, especially since we found it by accident.

GENEVA

● Prouty-Chew Museum
543 S. Main Street, (315) 789-5151. Hours: Tues.–Fri. 10–noon, 1– 4:30, Sat. 1:30–4:30. Admission: free (donations accepted). **Ages 4 and up.**

The Prouty-Chew Museum is in a federal-style home built in 1829 by Charles Butler, an attorney from Geneva. The house was purchased by the Prouty family and renovated between 1850 and 1870. In 1960, the Chew family gave the house to the Geneva Historical Society and it was subsequently renovated with area 19th-century furnishings. There are changing art and history exhibits, and visitors can tour the house and its period rooms. The museum has also established a research library where you can search for information about your ancestors or learn more about local architecture. Special events are usually held in the summer and fall and during the Christmas holiday. Call or write for current information.

● Rose Hill Mansion
Route 96A (off NYS Thruway exits 41 or 42 south), (315) 789-3848. Hours: May–Oct. Mon.–Sat. 10–4, Sun. 1–5. Admission: Adults $3, children 10–18 $2, children under 10 free. **Ages 5 and up.**

In 1839, General William Kerley Strong built this wonderful Greek Revival mansion which is now a National Historic Landmark. Strong lived here for only four years; when his wife passed away he moved. He sold the house to Robert Swan who developed a tile drainage system to help his crops grow and became a prosperous farmer. The 21-room house is furnished in an empire style and many of the pieces are original to the Swan family.

ITHACA

● Buttermilk Falls State Park
Route 13S, 273-5761. Hours: daily dawn–dusk. Admission: $5 per car or NYS Empire Passport. **All ages.**

If you've never experienced the fun of swimming at the base of a waterfall, then you should definitely plan a visit here. The swimming area is designated at the bottom of the falls. Two glens and 10 waterfalls are part of what this 750-acre park has to offer. Bring a picnic lunch and plan on several hours here to enjoy yourselves. There are also hiking trails, places to fish, and playgrounds to keep your group entertained. Lifeguards are on duty in the summer, and vending machines and a bathhouse are available.

● Cayuga Nature Center

1420 Taughannock Boulevard, 273-6260. Hours: Mon.–Fri. 8–4, Sat. and Sun. 12–4, trails always open. Admission: free (Sun. afternoon Discovery Programs $3 person). www.fcinet.com/cnc. **All ages.**

The Cayuga nature preserve, on over 125 acres, was founded in 1975 and provides outdoor and environmental education programs for all ages. A wide variety of classes are offered, including evening stargazing sessions, canoe trips, and Sunday afternoon programs for families. Take a hike on five miles of trails, or tap into the center's extensive programming. The nature center's main building has snakes, turtles, and doves, plus a hawk and a fox. To find out more call for a current schedule of classes and programs.

● Cornell Plantations

Botanical Gardens, Arboretum, and Natural Areas, One Plantation Road, 255-3020. Hours: Apr.–Oct. dawn–dusk. Admission: free. **All ages.**

The Plantations offer many ways to explore nature—one of our favorite places to spend a quiet afternoon, especially in nice weather, is the 200-acre arboretum complete with pond, ducks, and easy walking trails.

Across the road is the wildflower garden, which has gentle paths leading you through the plantings. The herb garden is nearby and is fun to visit to learn about a variety of plants and herbs. The plantations' Garden Gift Shop is located here. Stop in for an herb plant, or pick up a great poster or T-shirt.

● Herbert F. Johnson Museum of Art

Cornell University campus, 255-6464. Hours: Tues.–Sun. 10–5. Admission: free. www.museum.cornell.edu. **Ages 3 and up.**

Designed by world-famous architect I. M. Pei, this museum opened in 1973. In addition to providing wonderful art to view, the museum also provides the best view of Cayuga Lake and Ithaca. Asian art, 19th- and 20th-century American art and graphic arts form the bulk of the museum's collection, though works by old masters, 19th-century French Impressionists, and many others are also on display. Children love the museum not only for the painting and sculpture, but also for the magnificent views, and the interior circular staircase (it's fun). Throughout the year the museum offers a variety of public programs, including children's programs, lectures, and dance and music performances.

● Paleontological Research Institution

1259 Trumansburg Road, 273-6623. Hours: Mon.–Fri. 9–5. Admission: free (donations welcome). **Ages 3 and up.**

If your kids love fossils, they will love this place. Founded in 1932, the PRI has over 1 million specimens in its collection. The number of visitors the institution can handle is limited and therefore it is recommended that you call before you plan to visit.

● Robert H. Treman State Park

Route 327 (off Route 13S), 273-3440. Hours: daily dawn–dusk. Admission: $5 per car or NYS Empire Passport. **All ages.**

Like Buttermilk Falls State Park in Ithaca (listed above), Treman Park has a good old-fashioned swimming area. There really is nothing like swimming in cold creek water on a hot summer day. There are hiking trails here, picnic areas, refreshment stand, and playgrounds for your four-season enjoyment. (You can cross-country ski here in the winter.)

● Sciencenter

601 First Street, 272-0600. Hours: Tues.–Sat. 10–5, Sun. 12–5. Admission: Adults $4.50, children 4–12 $3.50, children 3 and under free. sciencenter.org. **All ages.**

The Sciencenter opened in 1993 and it has been busy ever since. Children are fascinated by the exhibits, which are on two floors and include a discovery/play area outside. There are hands-on activity areas throughout the center, and kids continually go from one area to another and back again. One of the most interesting exhibits is the room-sized camera, where you can walk in and adjust the lens to see how a camera works. The two-story audio kinetic sculpture is truly a wonder; you'll find yourself staring at it for a long time.

Note: If you are a member of a science museum already, you might qualify for free admission. Check with your local science museum and request the list of reciprocal centers.

● Taughannock Falls State Park

See listing under Trumansburg for information.

Taughannock Falls is the most famous waterfall in the area, and one which most people (even Ithacans) think is in Ithaca, but officially it is in Trumansburg. See the full listing there.

JAMESVILLE

● Pratt's Falls Park

Pratt's Falls Road (southeast of Syracuse), (315) 682-5934. Hours: daily dawn–dusk. Admission: $1 per car. **All ages.**

This park has over 300 acres to explore, complete with scenic hiking trails that lead to a 137-foot waterfall. Younger children need to be supervised on the trails. Bring a picnic and enjoy yourselves.

MORAVIA

● Fillmore Glen State Park

Route 38, 1 mile south of the town of Moravia, (315) 497-0130. Hours: daily dawn–dusk, gorge trails closed in winter. Admission: free. **All ages.**

Fillmore Glen is named for the 13th president of the United States, Millard Fillmore, who was born in a log cabin near the park in 1800. A replica of this cabin now stands within the park grounds. The park itself is over 900 acres of beautiful forests, streams, and plant and animal life. The park and trails are wonderful, especially on hot, humid summer days. On the gorge trail, eight bridges cross over a stream that provides a welcome cool breeze. Bring your bathing suit and you can take a dip in the park's natural pool, then have a relaxing picnic at one of the many picnic areas.

MUMFORD

● Genesee Country Museum

Flint Hill Road, 20 miles southwest of Rochester, (716) 538-6822. Hours: Museum, May and June, Sept. and Oct. Tues.–Fri. 10–4; July and Aug. Tues.–Sun. and holidays 10–5; Nature Center, Nov.–Apr. Thurs.–Sun. 10–4. Admission (includes Gallery of Sporting Art and Nature Center): Adults $10, children 4–16 $6, children under 4 free. **All ages.**

The name of this site might lead you to think it is just another local history museum but think again. Not only does the Genesee Museum have one of the largest collections of sporting and wildlife art in the U.S., a sculpture garden and a carriage museum, but it also has a beautiful nature center and an extensive historic 19th-century village. The nature center offers over five miles of nature trails, a water garden, children's nature classes, family nature walks, and more. It is a wonderful place to explore in any season (you can cross-country ski on the hiking trails in the winter). The nature center also has 10 re-created historic gardens that trace the traditions of gardening in the Genesee Valley. The elaborate historic village incorporates 57 restored and furnished buildings, including shops, schools, churches, and residences. A free trolley travels throughout the village; get on and off wherever you'd like. Beautiful gardens, interesting architecture, and a fun history lesson will keep your children entertained for the day. Call or write ahead for special events. One recent year, for example, included concerts, a Fourth of July celebration, a Civil War history encampment, a fun and games week, garden symposiums, and other interesting activities.

NAPLES

● Cumming Nature Center

Gulick Road, (716) 374-6160. Hours: Wed.–Sun. 9–5. Admission: Adults $4, children in grades K–12 $1.50, children under 5 free. **All ages.**

Have a wonderful day hiking the six miles of trails on over 900 acres. The Visitors Center has exhibits and seasonal displays, and children's programs all summer long. On site is a pioneer cabin, from the 1790s and a re-created farming homestead. Call the Rochester Museum and Science Center, which manages the nature center, or call the number listed above for complete program information.

NORTH CHILI

● Victorian Doll Museum and Chili Doll Museum

4332 Buffalo Road, (716) 247-0130. Hours: Feb.–Dec. Tues.–Sat. 10–4:30. Admission: Adults $2, children 3–12 $1. **Ages 2 and up.**

Thousands of pairs of eyes stare back at visitors through floor-to-ceiling glass cases. Linda Greenfield started collecting dolls when she was eight years old and hasn't stopped yet. Not only are there hundreds upon hundreds of dolls to marvel at, but if you have your own antique doll, Linda can appraise and repair it for you. Appointments are needed for the appraisals.

OWEGO

● Tioga Gardens

Route 17C, 687-5522. Hours: daily 8:30–6, Sun. 11–5. Admission: free. **All ages.**

If you love plants, visit this conservatory which sits on two acres complete with a Japanese garden, lily ponds, and a greenhouse filled with exotic plants, herbs, and wildflowers. There is also a small gift shop on-site.

● Tioga Scenic Railroad

25 Delphine Street, 687-6786. Hours: Memorial Day–Oct. Sat. and Sun., train leaves at noon and 3 P.M. Admission: Adults $7, children 4–11 $5, children 3 and under ride free. Call ahead for reservations. **All ages.**

Take a journey back in time aboard this historic train. Take a special meal excursion and enjoy lunch or dinner, or take the regular nonmeal trip—either way you cruise through the landscape between Owego and Newark Valley (essentially along Route 38) in restored early 1900s railroad cars. In summer, you can enjoy the late 1880s open-air car. The regular (nonmeal) trips are approximately two hours round trip (22 miles). Tell the kids they get a treat when you return to the Owego Depot; there's an ice cream shop on-site. Write ahead for a schedule of special train rides; in one recent year the railroad offered an Easter Bunny Express, a Mother's Day dinner, a Halloween Express, and a New Year's Eve dinner excursion (among many others).

ROCHESTER

● George Eastman House

International Museum of Photography and Film, 900 East Avenue, (716) 271-3361. Hours: Tues.–Sat. 10–4:30, Sun. 1–4:30. Admission: Adults $6.50, children 5–12 $2.50, children 4 and under free. **Ages 2 and up.**

This world-renowned museum is a treat for young and old alike and for all those with any interest in photography. George Eastman (1854–1932), founded the Kodak company. (He created the word Kodak himself because it could be spoken in all languages.) Eastman wanted to make the then-cumbersome photographic process easier to use and so, in 1888, developed the first portable box camera. Ten years later, he was a millionaire. In 1905, he completed this 35,000-square-foot house; it is now a National Historic Landmark. Considered colonial revival in style, the house has 37 rooms, 13 baths, 9 fireplaces, and 5 greenhouses. After a nationwide search, over 85 percent of the original furniture has been recovered and is back on display. The interior of the house is absolutely magnificent; children love to see the chandeliers and all the animal trophy heads. The gardens are just as wonderful, and spring is one of the best times to view them. In 1989, a new building was added to the property to house the museum's large and growing collection of over half a million photographs and negatives and other photo-related memorabilia. Over 8,000 photographers are represented in the collection.

● Memorial Art Gallery
500 University Avenue, (716) 473-7720. Hours: Tues. Noon–9, Wed.– Fri. 10–4, Sat. 10–5, Sun. noon–5. Admission: Adults $5, children 6–19 $3, children 5 and under free. **Ages 3 and up.**

If you are visiting Rochester, stop in for a visit to this museum which is a perfect size for children. Expose them to world-famous artists such as Monet, Matisse, and Cassatt, or wander around in the indoor sculpture garden. The entire collection of over 9,000 objects spans more than 5,000 years.

● Rochester Museum and Science Center
657 East Avenue, (716) 271-4320. Hours: Mon.–Sat. 9–5, Sun. and holidays noon–5. Admission: Adults $6, children in grades K–12 $3, children under 5 free. **All ages.**

A kid could literally stay here for days and have plenty to do. This center is considered the area's most comprehensive museum of regional archaeology, geology, and natural science. In addition to innovative exhibits such as the Seneca Iroqouis Native American display, the museum also has a theater, a planetarium, a 900-acre environmental education center in Naples, and more. They have so much to offer it is definitely worth your while to plan ahead and call for a current schedule of events.

● Seabreeze Park/Raging Rivers Water Park
4600 Culver Road on Lake Ontario (off I-590 N), (716) 323-1900. Hours: May 1–June 15, Sat. and Sun. noon–10; late June–Labor Day Sun.–Thurs. noon–10, Fri. and Sat. noon–11. Admission: Adults $13.95, children under 48 inches tall $9.95, children 2 and under free. **All ages.**

This amusement park provides a lot of fun stuff for children. There are waterslides, tube slides, a huge loop roller coaster, and more. There is even an antique wooden carousel for younger children. Over 75 different attractions, food, games, and entertainment complete Seabreeze's offerings. No glass containers are allowed into the park.

● Seneca Park Zoo
2222 St. Paul Boulevard, Seneca Park, (716) 266-6846. Hours: daily 10– 5. Admission: Ages 16 and up $4, children 5–15 $2, children under 2 free. **All ages.**

This is a perfect-sized zoo for kids, not too big, not too small. See polar bears, elephants, sea lions, penguins, and many other interesting animals. At the Discovery Center, you'll learn about insects, and you can also see seals swimming while you look at them close-up through a glass wall. The entire zoo can be managed on foot and is stroller/wheelchair accessible.

● Strong Museum

One Manhattan Square, (716) 263-2700. Hours: Mon.–Sat. 10–5, Sun. 1–5. Admission: Adults $5, children 3–16 $3, children under 3 free. **All ages.**

Strong Museum has such a wide variety of exhibits that everyone will enjoy wandering around for several hours. Everyday objects are on display, including items such as tools, sporting goods, home furnishings, and more. Kids love to try on clothes from other eras (this is my daughter's favorite thing in the world to do), and while they explore the exhibits with objects from the past, they gain a sense of the life of their ancestors. There's also have a gift shop and café, and the museum sponsors special programs for children. On Tuesdays and Wednesdays a tots program offers a series of performances ranging from storytelling and juggling, to dancing and music. Several new exhibits have opened recently; the first is a miniature supermarket geared towards children nine and under; another is a TV news studio where children can make a videotape of themselves; the last is a life-sized Sesame Street where kids can "walk onto" the street and play with props.

● Susan B. Anthony House

17 Madison Street, (716) 235-6124. Hours: Thurs.–Sat. 1–4. Admission: Adults $2.50, children under 12 $.50. **Ages 4 and up.**

Upstate New York is the birthplace of the women's rights movement in the United States, and here we can see the residence of one of the founders of the movement. Susan B. Anthony lived here for 40 years, during which time she wrote her famous *History of Women's Suffrage* and was arrested for voting in 1872.

ROMULUS

● Misty Meadow Farm

2828 Vineyard Road, (607) 869-9243. Hours: late June–Labor Day Tues.–Sat. 10:30–4, Sun. noon–4; Labor Day–Columbus Day, weekends only 10:30–4. Admission: Adults $4, children 3–11 $3, children under 2 free (prices include everything except lunch). **All ages.**

Located on the west side of Cayuga Lake, Misty Meadow is a 160-acre working farm where 1,000 pigs and other animals are raised each year. Here children can meet, hold, and feed baby farm animals such as ducklings, chicks, piglets, calves, and lambs. If they want to roughhouse let them jump around in the century-old hay barn or ride in the haywagon (provided they don't have asthma of course). In the summer, enjoy the sunflower maze and pick-your-own sunflowers. When you're all hungry, head to the farm kitchen where you can have farm-raised BBQ pork or burgers (meatless dishes are also available); kids get to choose from their own menu. End your visit with a piece of fresh-baked pie, and perhaps a stroll over to the farm shop where handcrafted items are for sale. Call ahead for special events, which take place on Saturdays during the summer.

SENECA FALLS

Seneca Falls is known as the Home of Women's Rights. The first Women's Rights Convention was held here in 1848, led by Elizabeth Stanton.

● Elizabeth Cady Stanton Home

32 Washington Street, (315) 568-2991. Hours: May–Oct. daily 1–5 (tours begin at 2 P.M.; please register in advance), Nov.–April by appointment only. Admission: free. **Ages 4 and up.**

The home of one of the founders of the Women's Rights Movement is a terrific place to take children, especially those who might be working on American history topics in school. Her restored home, built in 1836, is open for tours, and is filled with period furniture and memorabilia.

● National Women's Hall of Fame

76 Falls Street, (315) 568-8060. Hours: May–Oct., Wed.–Sat. 10–4, Sun. noon–4; Nov.–Apr. Wed.–Sat. 10–4, Sun. 1–4. Admission: Adults $3, children $1.50, children 5 and under free ($7 maximum per family). **Ages 4 and up.**

This museum honors the contributions and achievements of American women. Artifacts relating to Elizabeth Stanton, Susan B. Anthony, Emily Dickinson, Helen Keller, Rosa Parks, and 131 other women are currently on display in varying exhibits.

● Women's Rights National Historic Park and Visitors Center

136 Falls Street, (315) 568-2991 (National Park Service). Hours: daily 9–5. Admission: free. **Ages 4 and up.**

The park was built to present to the public the history of the women's rights movement through films, exhibits, and lectures. Several times a year the park holds special events relating to women's rights. It has 19 life-sized statues of some of the people who attended the first Women's Rights Convention in 1848. In 1995, the three-story visitors center was opened, and here you can request a special tour of Seneca Falls. Call for current information and dates.

SKANEATELES

● T. C. Timber
4407 Jordan Road, (315) 685-6660. Hours: Sat. 10–1. **All ages.**

Although I generally have not listed stores in this book, I will list this one because it is such a great place for kids and because the town of Skaneateles (pronounced "skinny-atlas") is such a delight to visit. T. C. Timber is one of the largest producers of wooden toys in the country, and you can find excellent deals on trains, puzzles, blocks, beads, and lots more. Skaneateles itself offers quaint shops and stately older homes to look at. Stop in for a cup of coffee and a pastry at the Framboise Café and then head down to the lake, which at 863 feet above sea level, is the highest of all the Finger Lakes.

STERLING

● Renaissance Festival
15431 Farden Road, (800) 879-4446. Hours: late June–mid-Aug., weekends only 10–7. Admission: prices change each year, call ahead for current information (1997 price was $12. 99). **All ages.**

New York State is lucky enough to host two Renaissance Festivals; this one in the northern Finger Lakes region, and another in Tuxedo, in the Hudson Valley region. If you attend the fair in Tuxedo the year there is 1558; here in Sterling, it is 1585 (although both are Renaissance England). You really should dig out your fancy costumes and wear them here. If you don't have any, costumes are available for rent (for children and adults). The Sterling festival features a full-time professional actors' group that makes rounds throughout the day, speaking in dialect and pretending to be a wide variety of people. There is plenty of food; entertainment, rides, and theatrical performances abound—the legendary Shakespeare himself even makes an appearance. My children had an absolutely wonderful time and did not want to leave although we had been there for over five hours. (After we left we took a short drive to Fair

Haven Beach State Park on Lake Ontario, where the kids enjoyed playing in the sand and the water, and I had a chance to relax in the sun.)

SYRACUSE

For more information on Syracuse, go to their Web site (www.syracuse.com) or call the 24-hour events line (1-800-234-4797) for current events.

● Burnet Park Zoo

1 Conservation Place (off South Wilbur Avenue), (315) 435-8511. Hours: daily 10–4:30. Admission: Adults $5, children ages 5–14 $2, children 4 and under free, family rate $12. **All ages.**

This has to be one of best zoos I've ever visited, for the simple reason that it is the perfect size to take children to, even the youngest ones. All the exhibits and zoo services are stroller- and wheelchair-accessible. The zoo is very easy to navigate: you progress in more or less an oval and return to where you started. There are no difficult hills to navigate, and because of its size children do not get wiped out (like they do at the Bronx Zoo and other larger zoos). There are over 1,000 animals and since the zoo is open year-round, you can see many of them in their winter coats, or watch them grazing in fields of wildflowers in the spring. One of the kids' favorite areas is the lion exhibit, where floor-to-ceiling (thick) glass is all that separates you from the lions. On one visit, the male lion came right up to the glass and roared—it was quite a scene. The aviary is really something special, as are the outdoor areas where bears and other animals live. When you finish your tour of the zoo, you'll end up at the restaurant area, which is right next to the elephants. Sometimes the elephants like to swim in their pool and this is just a wonderful sight.

Note: If you are planning to visit a lot of zoos in a year, consider purchasing a family membership. For $39, you get free admission to this and 100 other zoos nationwide.

● Erie Canal Museum

318 Erie Boulevard (Route 5) at Montgomery Street, (315) 471-0593. Hours: daily 10–5. Admission: free (donations appreciated). **Ages 3 and up.**

The Erie Canal is an important part of the history of New York state, and the Erie Canal Museum is the best place to learn about the canal's history. Here visitors can board an actual 65-foot passenger cargo boat and really get a sense of life during the 19th-century on the Erie Canal. The museum also features history exhibits and rooms which are decorated in the style of the period. For information on tour boats or renting your own boat on the canal, call (518) 436-2983. The Erie Canal is 348 miles long and 12 to 14 feet deep; if you're considering renting a boat, there is a 10 mph speed limit, and the season runs May through November.

● Everson Museum of Art

410 Harrison Street, (315) 474-6064. Hours: Tues.–Fri. 12–5, Sat. 10–5, Sun. 12–5. Admission: $2 (suggested donation). **Ages 3 and up.**

I. M. Pei, the famous 20th-century architect, designed this museum in 1968. It features 10 galleries on three levels and houses the Syracuse China Center for Ceramics, which has one of the largest collections of American ceramics in the country. American painting, sculpture, and graphics are also on display in the galleries. During the Christmas season, as part of the week-long Holiday Festival of Trees, over 100 decorated Christmas trees are displayed in the upper galleries of the museum.

● Milton J. Rubenstein Museum of Science and Technology (MOST)

500 S. Franklin Street, Armory Square, (315) 425-9068. Hours: daily 10–5. Admission: Adults $4.50, children 2–11 $3.50. **All ages.**

Science museums are to children as water is to a fish. At this nicely planned hands-on museum, it seems as if children can't stay in one place very long, because as soon as they look around, another area captures their attention. The Planetarium offers shows several times a day, and even has special showings for children under four. In addition to the myriad exhibits, the staff also holds live demonstrations, either displaying exotic live animals or doing science experiments. Recently, the museum opened the Bristol Omnitheater, a domed IMAX theater that will give your kids a thrill.

● Sainte Marie among the Iroquois

Onondaga Lake Parkway (Route 370), (315) 453-6767. Hours: Visitor Center, Tues.–Sun. 10–5. Admission: Adults $3.50, children 5–14 $1.50, children under 5 free, family rate $10. **All ages.**

Be transported back to the year 1657 at this living history museum. The name of the museum comes from the time when French Jesuit missionaries and Canadian explorers met the Native American Iroquois who had already been living in the region for hundreds of years. Costumed interpreters help visitors get a sense of the life all these people led over three centuries ago. Some of the special events offered are family activity days (Sunday Fundays), toy and craft making, and even themed sleepovers.

● Salt Museum

Onondaga Lake Parkway (Route 370), (315) 453-6767. Hours: May–Oct. Tues.–Sun. noon–5. Admission: Adults $.50, children under 15 free. **Ages 4 and up.**

Syracuse earned the name "Salt City" in the 19th century when it was the country's leading salt manufacturer. Self-guided exhibits in this small museum include original and restored equipment used to make salt, a salt-workers' neighborhood, and re-created craft shops. The museum is located less than a quarter mile away from the museum, Sainte Marie Among the Iroquois. The Salt Museum is located in Onondaga Lake Park, which has a great children's playground. (Both the Salt Museum and Sainte Marie are located in the town of Liverpool but since it is right on the Syracuse boundary, I have listed them here for convenience.)

TRUMANSBURG

● Taughannock Falls State Park

Route 89, 387-6739. Hours: daily dawn–dusk. Admission: $5 per car or NYS Empire Passport. **All ages.**

Taughannock Falls is one of the most famous attractions in the Finger Lakes region. The falls plunge 215 feet (50 feet more than Niagara Falls), and the rock walls surrounding them reach up 400 feet. You can stop at a parking area for an overview looking across the gorge, or park in the lot off Route 89 and hike the easy one-mile hike to the base of the falls. Across the road (Route 89) from the parking lot is the developed area of the park, which features swimming in Cayuga Lake, a concession stand and picnic areas. A summer concert series takes place here on Friday evenings.

TULLY

● Song Mountain Alpine Slide

3 miles west of I-81, exit 14, (315) 696-5711. Hours: June 15–Labor Day Mon.–Fri. 11–5, Sat. and Sun. 11–7. Admission: Adults, all-day pass $13, three-hour pass $10, children under 5 free with an adult. **All ages.**

Even though Song Mountain may be a ski area in Cortland County by winter, in the summer it is transformed into a winding 3,000-foot alpine slide, where you slide on plastic sleds. If that's not enough, try the water slide, the go-karts, or the 18-hole miniature golf course. Call for information regarding summer concert programs.

WATKINS GLEN

● Captain Bill's Seneca Lake Cruises

1 N. Franklin Street, 535-4541. Hours: May–Oct. daily 9 A.M.–11 P.M. Admission: Adults $7.50 (without meals), children ages 2–12 $3. Meal cruises range between $21.50 and $35.50 per person. **All ages.**

If you visit the Watkins Glen area, take an enjoyable 10-mile Seneca Lake cruise. Choose either a 50-minute sightseeing cruise or a longer three-hour dinner excursion. It is a wonderful way to relax as you take in the lake landscape and look at the stately homes that are built along the lakeshore.

● Farm Sanctuary

3100 Aikens Road, 583-2225. Hours: May, Sept., and Oct. weekends only 10–4; June–Aug. Wed.–Sun. 10–4. Admission: Adults $2, children 4–12 $1, children under 3 free. **All ages.**

In addition to being a 175-acre working farm that children can visit to learn about farm animals, the Farm Sanctuary is also a farm-animal shelter for hundreds of rescued pigs, turkeys, goats, and others. Feed some sheep, check out the visitor center, or buy a treat from the country gift shop.

● Seneca Grand Prix–Family Fun Center

2374 Route 414, 535-7981. Hours: June–Aug. daily 1–11; May and Sept. weekends only 1–10. Admission: pay per ride, go-karts $4 (need to be 54 inches tall), bumper boats $4 (need to be 42 inches tall), mini-golf $4.50 per game. (If there is no answer at the listed number, try the Watkins Glen Chamber of Commerce at 1-800-607-4552.) **All ages.**

If you happen to be visiting the area and your kids are going nuts, take them to this family amusement center to let some energy loose. There are go-karts, bumper boats, an arcade, miniature golf, and a refreshment stand.

● Watkins Glen State Park

At the south end of Seneca Lake, 535-4511. Hours: mid-May–mid-Oct. 8–dusk. Admission: park, free; parking $5 per car. **All ages.**

You really must visit this park—it has 19 waterfalls, and the one-and-one-half-mile-long gorge (three miles if you hike both ways), stretches from the village's main street deep into a rock-walled canyon. If you only feel like hiking one way, a shuttle bus is available for a nominal fee during the summer to take you back to the mouth of the gorge. Nearby, Seneca Harbor Park also has a nice 300-foot fishing pier that is good for a stroll and a view of Seneca Lake.

WEEDSPORT

Weedsport hosts the Cayuga County Fair, usually in the second week of July. Call (607) 834-6606 for more information.

● D. I. R. T. Motorsport Hall of Fame and Classic Car Museum

Route 31, Cayuga County Fairgrounds, (315) 834-6667. Hours: Apr.– Labor Day Mon.–Sat. 10–5, Sun. 12–7; Sept.–Dec. Mon.–Fri. 10–5, weekends 11–4. Admission: $4. **Ages 4 and up.**

For those car lovers of yours, here are dozens of classic cars on display, including a 1929 Dodge Roadster, a 1957 Chevy, a Fleetwood, and many more. For the adults in your group, there's even a car finders network that helps people buy and sell classic vehicles. Race car fans won't feel left out either; the museum has stock car memorabilia to see. And the place wouldn't be complete without a classic car gift shop, of course!

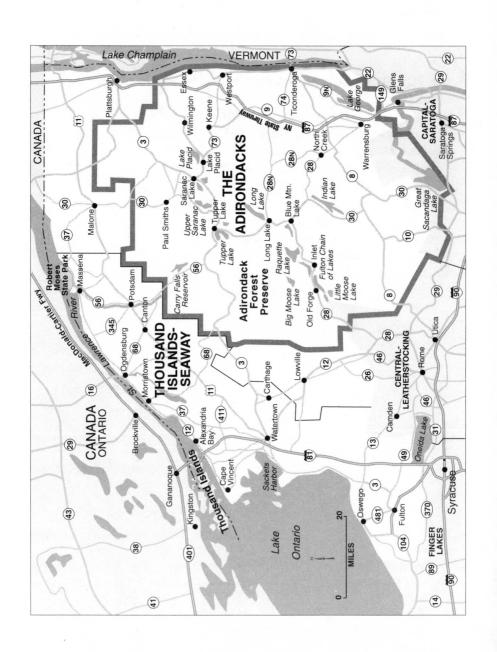

Northern New York

Adirondacks Region

If you were planning to visit the Adirondacks in the winter of 1997, you would have had to deal with an incredible blizzard—90 inches of snow in one weekend (that's the usual average for an entire season)! It sounds unbelievable, but it's true. Most of the time, however, the region is accessible in all seasons. All kinds of activities await you here: skiing, snowmobiling, hiking, golfing, swimming, sailing, camping, and whitewater rafting are just a few of the fun outdoor things to do. The Adirondack Mountain region comprises an area of over 6 million acres of both public and private land (this is larger than the state of Massachusetts, by the way). Mt. Marcy is the tallest peak in the state, reaching an impressive 5,344 feet. For additional information visit the region's Web site at www.adirondacks.org/.

The area code for the Adirondacks Region is 518 unless otherwise noted.

AUSABLE CHASM

● Ausable Chasm
Route 9 (exit 34 or 35 off I-87), 834-7454 or 1-800-537-1211. Hours: Memorial Day–Columbus Day daily 9:30–4:30. Admission: Walking tour $9. **All ages.**

This tourist site is one of the oldest in the United States, having opened in 1870. The incredible Ausable Chasm is a one-and-one-half-mile gorge with 200-foot sandstone cliffs that are probably over 500 million years old! You can take a half-mile walk through the chasm and marvel at the water and cliffs. When you return from your tour, you can let the kids play on the playground and have a picnic lunch. (You used to be able to take a half-mile boat ride through the chasm but in the past two years bad floods have raised water levels too high and destroyed several bridges. Call ahead for up-to-date information regarding park conditions).

BLUE MOUNTAIN LAKE

● Adirondack Lakes Center for the Arts
Routes 28 and 30, 352-7715. Hours: Mon.–Fri. 9–4. Admission: varies per program, between $8 (for kids summer programs) to $250 (for adult boat building classes). **All ages.**

The ALCA opened in 1967 and since then has provided visitors diverse exhibitions, concerts, theater performances, and adult workshops.

Programs for children include dance, music, and wonderful arts and crafts projects. Definitely call ahead for current programming schedule and information.

● Adirondack Museum

Route 30 (exits 28 or 37 off I-87), 352-7311. Hours: Memorial Day– mid-Oct. daily 9:30–5:30. Admission: Adults $10, children ages 7–16 $6. **All ages.**

This unique museum is a must for anyone visiting the region. Exhibits allow visitors to experience Adirondack life and get a sense of the history of the region in the process. See the hermit's camp and then, for contrast, inspect an elegant railroad car. Twenty-two exhibit buildings on over 30 acres provide a rich amount of information regarding the region's history of logging, farming, and mining, as well as its art and crafts.

Most people are familiar with the region's famous Adirondack Chair, which can be seen on porches and lawns all over the country, and which is displayed here with a history of its creation. Marvel at the 50 horse-drawn carriages on display and then take in the view of Blue Mountain Lake. Take a stroll along the nature path and enjoy the beautiful plantings in the scenic surroundings. Plan on at least three to four hours for this visit, and try to come in good weather so that you can enjoy the entire facility (it tends to get crowded on rainy days). Refreshments are available at the restaurant (with a terrific view, as you might expect). Call for current information regarding special events such as music and storytelling performances.

ELIZABETHTOWN

● Adirondack History Center (Essex County Historical Society)

Route 9, Court Street, 873-6466. Hours: mid-May–mid-Oct. Mon.–Sat. 9–5, Sun. 1–5. Admission: Adults $3.50, children 6–18 $1.50. **Ages 3 and up.**

A visit to this museum will delight you. There's a beautiful perennial garden to explore outdoors, but there is also a terrific stagecoach to see (which always fascinates kids), a doll room, and several exhibits that portray pioneer life. The pioneer exhibits are especially interesting because they include a sound and light show. The museum also has a neat forest fire observation tower (58 feet high) that can be climbed for an incredible view.

GLENS FALLS

● The Hyde Collection

161 Warren Street, 792-1761. Hours: Apr. 30–Dec. 31 Tues.–Sun. 10–5; Jan. 1–Apr. 29 Wed.–Sun. 12–5. Admission: free. **Ages 3 and up.**

This wonderful collection of old masters and American works of art is housed in an Italian Renaissance-style villa. Charlotte Pruyn Hyde (1867–1963) founded the collection in 1952 to benefit the Glens Falls community. Notable in this collection are works by Botticelli, da Vinci, Rembrandt, Renoir, van Gogh, and Picasso, among many others. The Hyde Collection provides visitors a way to enjoy art in a beautiful, serene atmosphere without having to fight crowds of people at every turn. The museum offers several interesting children's programs, including art hunts and summer art workshops; call for information.

LAKE GEORGE

Lake George is an exquisite place to visit. Although the area is now brimming with theme parks and wax museums, you can still take pleasure in the scenic 32-mile long lake with over 200 islands. I highly recommend taking a summer cruise on the lake, if you can. Call the **Lake George Steamboat Company** at 1-800-533-BOAT for a complete schedule.

● Great Escape and Splashwater Kingdom Fun Park

Route 9 (between exits 19 and 20), 792-3500. Hours: Memorial Day–Labor Day 9:30–6. Admission: Adults and children 48 inches and up $22.99, children under 48 inches $16.99, children 2 and under free. 2-day passes are also available for $29.99 and $23.99. **All ages.**

This is one of New York state's largest theme parks, with over 100 wet and dry rides, including a 500,000 gallon wave pool, and a crazy roller coaster which loops forwards and then (as if that's not enough), backwards! There are restaurants, picnic areas, and a snack bar. For your younger ones, there are several tame rides a bit farther away from the screaming older kids. The park also has circus and cabaret performances daily. This attraction is very popular and gets crowded on hot summer days.

● Magic Forest Family Fun Park

Route 9, 668-2448. Hours: Memorial Day–late June weekends only 9:30–6; late June–Labor Day daily 9:30–6. Admission: Adults $11.95, children 1 and up $9.95. **Ages 2–9.**

Magic Forest is designed for younger children and therefore the scene is a bit more laid-back than at other amusement parks. Younger children aren't intimidated by older children, and can feel more playful here. The park features 25 rides, a fairy tale area, and other attractions for younger children.

● Shepard Park

Canada Street. Call the Lake George Chamber of Commerce for information at 1-800-365-1050. Hours: daily dawn–dusk. Admission: free (fees vary for performances during the summer). **All ages.**

This is a nice, relatively small family beach and recreation area, and if you are visiting Lake George you will probably wind up here at some point (or you should). There's a dock and diving board in a roped off swimming area, and during the summer the park offers plenty of entertainment including fireworks and music performances.

LAKE PLACID

For more information on Lake Placid, go to their Web site (www.lakeplacid.com).

● Around the World in 18 Holes

183 Saranac Avenue, 523-9065. Hours: May–Oct. 10 A.M.–11 P.M. (weather permitting). Admission: Adults $4.50, children 11 and under $3.50. **Ages 3 and up.**

When you've had enough of historic sites and museums for the day and would like to do something for pure fun, try this 18-hole miniature golf game, where each hole is decorated with items from a different country (so you also get a little geography lesson to boot).

● Lake Placid Center for the Arts

Saranac Avenue, 523-2512. Hours: Mon.–Fri. 10–5, weekends 1–5. Admission: varies per event. **Ages 3 and up.**

This arts facility, which serves as the summer institute for the Parson School of Design, is a bustling place in the summer, with all kinds of performances including dance, jazz, and classical music concerts, (the intimate theater holds 300 people), as well as an impressive series of exhibitions throughout the year. If you are planning to stay for a while in either July or August, check out the weekday morning program for kids called Young and Fun.

● Lake Placid Marina & Tour Boat Cruises

Mirror Lake Drive, 523-9704. Hours: boats leave 3 times a day, circa 10:30, 2:30, and 4. Admission: Adults $6, children 3 and up $4, children under 3 free. **Ages 3 and up.**

With this tour, you can be sure to enjoy yourself no matter what the weather, because the boat is enclosed. In one hour you can cruise 16 miles and listen to information about the lake and area wildlife, as well as about the homes that dot the shoreline. Call for a current schedule.

● Lake Placid Olympic Center

523-1655. Olympic Center tours: July–Sept. 10–3, tours leave on the hour. Adults $4, children 7–12, $2. Olympic Center public skating rink: mid-June–Aug. Mon.–Fri. 8 P.M.–9:30 P.M. Adults $4, children 7–12 $3, skate rentals $3. **Ages 3 and up.**

Explore the site of the 1932 and 1980 Winter Olympics to your heart's content. There is so much to see here that it will be hard to do everything, but you can certainly give it a shot! Several of the major attractions at the Olympic Center are listed separately below, but you can also call the Olympic Tourism Office at 1-800-462-6236 or 523-1655 for more detailed information. Admission is free, except during special performances and tours.

On the site of the 1980 Olympics ice arena, there are three rinks where you can watch all kinds of performances on ice: figure skating, hockey, and speed skating. If you and your group are so inclined, you can take a guided tour which will provide you with an in-depth look at the facilities. Or perhaps you'd rather take a spin on the ice on the Olympic Center public skating rink, where for $4 you can find out for yourself how amazingly difficult it is to look graceful on the ice. If you'd rather watch the pros, they perform on Saturday evenings from early July through mid-August.

● Olympic Ski Jumping Complex

523-2202. Hours: mid-May–mid.-Oct daily 9–4. Admission: Complex only, adults $3, children 7–12 $2, children under 7 free; Complex, chairlift, and elevator, adults $7, children ages 7–12 $4, children under 7 free. **All ages.**

Believe it or not, skiers train all summer on this 90-meter hill which has a special porcelain- and plastic-covered landing hill. The skiers fit their skis into ceramic grooves and "ski" down, landing on the cushioned surface. (I'm not sure, though, how this really works or how the athletes escape injury!) Kids love riding the chairlift up the hill and taking the elevator to the SkyDeck for the great view from the top of the 120-meter tower. At the complex, you can also watch freestyle-ski athletes perform incredible twists and flips before landing in the giant 750,000 gallon pool.

● 1932 and 1980 Winter Olympic Museum

523-1655. Hours: late May–mid-Oct. daily 10–5. Admission: Adults $3, children $1. **Ages 3 and up.**

At this particular Olympic museum, videos, memorabilia, and historical information bring to life the excitement of these two Olympic games. Using sport-events simulators, pretend you are skiing a slalom race, or view displays of sports equipment used by different athletes over the years.

● Whiteface Mountain Chairlift Skyride

946-2223. Hours: mid-June–mid-Oct. daily 9–4. Admission: Adults: $7, children 7–12 $4, children under 7 free. **Ages 3 and up.**

What a wonderful way to experience the mountains! Have a seat in the chairlift and ride up to the top of the 3,600-foot peak where you can enjoy a picnic amidst incredible views from the observation deck. You can either take the lift down again or enjoy an easy two-mile hike along waterfalls and streams.

NORTH HUDSON

● Frontier Town

Blue Ridge Road (exit 29 off I-87), 532-7181. Hours: late June–Labor Day daily 9:30–5. Admission: Adults $17.95, children 3–12 $14.95. **Ages 3 and up.**

Head into the Wild West in the Adirondacks. A visit here even starts off fun, because you'll take a steam train ride from the parking area to the actual attraction. Here you'll find stagecoach rides, Indian pow-wows, and a pioneer village. There are restaurants, snack bars, and picnic areas at Frontier Town and camping nearby. Call for information about special events.

NORTH RIVER

● Garnet Mine Tours/Gore Mountain Mineral Shop

Barton Mines Road (exit 23 off I-87), 251-2706. Hours: late June–Labor Day Mon.–Sat. 9–5, Sun. 11–5; Labor Day–Columbus Day Sat. 9:30–5, Sun. 11–5. Admission: Adults $4, children $3. **Ages 6–13.**

Most children love rocks and crystals, and at this mine and shop, they can explore to their hearts' content. This is considered to be the world's largest garnet mine; visitors can take a tour of the open pit mine or watch a gem-cutting demonstration. Just viewing the rock exhibit area will be enough to keep you interested for a while. You can even search for stones yourself, but if you want to take them with you, you have to pay for them.

OLD FORGE

● Adirondack Scenic Railroad

Route 28, 1 mile south of Old Forge, (315) 369-6290. Hours: May–Oct. daily, train leaves every 1½ hours (but times vary year to year so call ahead for the current schedule). Admission: Adults $6, children 2–12 $4. **All ages.**

Our family was staying in the Old Forge area for a Thanksgiving retreat, and we took this train ride on our last day there. The kids got a visit from Santa—he visited with all the children on the train during the ride. Do dress warmly—the temperature was in the teens the day we rode the train and it is not heated (as far as we could tell!). The railroad holds several holiday-related trips in season: Mother's Day and Father's Day trips, a Halloween Express, and of course, the Santa Claus Special.

● Enchanted Forest Water Safari

Route 28, (315) 369-6145. Hours: Memorial Day–Labor Day daily 9:30–6. Admission: Adults $16.50, children 2–11 $14.50, children under 2 free. **All ages.**

With 60 acres of park, 23 water slides, 14 amusement rides, bumper cars, a Moon Walk, and more, Enchanted Forest is guaranteed to wear your kids out. There is an area for smaller children (which is good since this place can get quite overwhelming for little ones), that has storybook characters such as Cinderella and Snow White. They also have changing rooms and coin lockers available, and strollers are supplied at no charge.

PAUL SMITH'S

● Adirondack Park and Visitor Interpretive Center

Route 30 (1 mile north of intersection with Route 86), 327-3000. Hours: daily 9–5. Admission: free. **All ages.**

Perhaps the best time to visit here is in August, during the wildlife festival. At the same time, you can also have fun in the terrific butterfly house. In addition, there are trails to hike, a 60-acre marsh to explore, and exhibits that provide information about the natural history of the Adirondacks. Outside the visitors center is a pleasant play area for children. If you visit during the winter season, the park is open for cross-country skiing. For more information on fun things to do in the area, call and request two helpful brochures: *Day Hikes and Paddles for Families with Children* and *Family Camping Itineraries in the Adirondack Park.*

POTTERSVILLE

● Natural Stone Bridge and Cave

Route 9 (exit 26 off I-87), 494-283. Hours: Memorial Day–Columbus Day, daily 9–dusk. Admission: Adults $8, children 6–12 $4, children under 6 free. **All ages.**

This natural wonder area features a massive stone arch, waterfalls, and caves, not to mention trout fishing, picnic areas, geode-cutting demonstrations, and more. Wear good walking shoes and take a hike through this beautiful area. Pack a picnic and enjoy the day.

QUEENSBURY

● Skateland and Aqua Adventure Waterslide

Route 9, 792-8989. Hours: Skateland, daily 11–6; Waterslide, Memorial Day–Labor Day, daily 11–6. Admission: $9.50 (includes free indoor roller skating); Kiddie pool $4 per child; Go-karts $3.50. **All ages.**

Climb the 31-foot tower and head down one of two giant waterslides. Or if your children are small, let them have fun in the kiddie pool play area. Relax and have lunch at one of the many picnic tables. There is a snack bar open during the summer season. In addition, the park has an indoor roller-skating rink, and go-karts.

● Spanky's Fun Place

Route 9, 761-0449. Hours: Wed. and Thurs. 10–5, Fri. and Sat. 10–6, Sun. 10–5. Admission: Adults free, children 1–12 $4.50. **Ages 1–12.**

OK, OK. Not another indoor amusement place. Yes, but this one has areas good for smaller children who might be a bit too young for some of the larger amusement parks or water parks. Tubes, tunnels, ball pit, and a separate toddler room are available. Probably the most favorite thing to do here is to take the free train ride around the complex (indoors). Also at this same location on Friday and Saturday nights from 7 to midnight, the place gets transformed into JAMS (Junior Adult Music Scene), a music and dancing club for teenagers 13 through 18. There is a $4 cover charge and no alcohol is served.

TICONDEROGA

● Fort Ticonderoga

Route 74 (exit 28 off I-87), 585-2821. Hours: May and June, Sept. and Oct. daily 9–5; July and Aug. daily 9–6. Admission: Adults $8, children 7–12 $6, children under 7 free. **All ages.**

Constructed by the French in 1755 under the name Fort Carillon, Fort Ticonderoga was taken first by the British and then, in 1775, by the colonists. Restored in 1908, the fort has the distinction of being the country's first restored historic site. Many New York school children take field trips to this site, and the author is no exception. I still can remember visiting here and being totally awed by the place. It sits on Crown Point overlooking Lake Champlain, and throughout the summer there are demonstrations, battle reenactments, marches, and more. There is a snack bar on-site but perhaps bringing a picnic lunch would be best, in order to sit and take in the wonderful view of the lake.

WILMINGTON

● High Falls Gorge
Route 86, 946-2278. Hours: mid-May–June, Sept.–mid-Oct. daily 9–4:15; July and Aug. daily 8:30–4:45. Admission: Adults $5.50, teens 12–17 $3.50, children ages 4–11 $1.50, children under 4 free. **All ages.**

You have to visit this incredible natural wonder, where three waterfalls plunge 700 feet between ancient granite cliffs. Bridges and paths lead you on a self-guided hike in this beautiful gorge (which takes about 45 minutes). Bring a picnic lunch and enjoy it next to the Ausable River, or visit the restaurant. Take a minute to look around in the gift and rock shop. The gorge and the rest of the site are wheelchair accessible. Wilmington is only 10 minutes driving distance from Lake Placid.

● Santa's Workshop, North Pole
Route 431, 946-2211 or 1-800-488-9853. Hours: mid-June–mid-Oct. daily 9:30–4. Admission: Adults $11.95, children 3–17 $7.95, children under 3 free. www.north-pole.ny.us. **All ages.**

If your child has ever written a letter to Santa, this is most likely where it ends up. At the North Pole, of course (in New York!). Open since 1949, this attraction is the oldest theme park in the United States. Younger children love this place, as they get to visit with Santa, his friends, and live (yes, real) reindeer. There are children's rides, an animal park, and live shows. Santa's Workshop is 12 miles east of Lake Placid.

● Whiteface Mountain Veterans' Memorial Highway
3 miles west of Route 431, 946-2223 or 523-1655. Hours: late-June– Labor Day daily 9–6; mid-May–late June and Labor Day–mid-Oct. 9–4. Admission: vehicle fee of $8 for the driver and car and $4 for each passenger (maximum vehicle fee of $25). **All ages.**

Take a drive (not in winter) on six miles of road reaching up to 4,867 feet! There is a parking area near the summit of Whiteface Mountain from where the views are spectacular. On a clear day you can easily see for 100 miles. From the parking lot, you can hike the .2 mile trail to the top for that 360-degree view, or board the in-mountain elevator.

Thousand Islands—Seaway

The Thousand Islands region (yes, this is where the salad dressing originated, around the turn of the century) comprises the area around the convergence of the St. Lawrence River and Lake Ontario. This region is almost equally shared by the United States and Canada. In New York, it begins slightly south of Oswego and continues up the northwest portion of the state to Massena. The areas which make up the Thousand Islands region are Jefferson County in New York, southeastern Ontario in Canada, the St. Lawrence River, and eastern Lake Ontario. The name of this region is not an exaggeration—in actuality the St. Lawrence has over 1,800 islands! The St. Lawrence International Bridge, built in 1938, provides easy access between the two countries. The American span is 4,500 feet in length; the Canadian span, 3,300 feet. Both sides have pedestrian walkways that provide visitors a wonderful view of the St. Lawrence River and its islands. The entire bridge was built by a crew made up largely of Mohawk Indians. Native Americans of the region called the Thousand Islands *man-i-to-anna* which translates to "the garden-place of the Great Spirit." Certainly a visit is necessary to see if this is true for you. For additional information, visit the region's Web sites at www.1000islands.com or www.thousandislands.com.

Visitors to the Thousand Islands–Seaway can enjoy many other activities not listed below. The region is world-renowned for its excellent fishing—Oswego is known as the Salmon Capital of the Northeast! Or perhaps you would like to take a helicopter ride over the Thousand Islands (call Thousand Islands Helicopter Tours in Alexandria Bay, 482-5722), or take a boat tour of the islands. Uncle Sam's Boat Tours (which you use to get to Boldt Castle in Alexandria Bay) offers long trips through the islands. There are over 30 golf courses in the area, if that is your preference for the day (obtain a copy of local visitors' guides for more specific information). For those of you who are a little more adventurous (or have older children), there are also whitewater rafting trips available in the Watertown area (14 major rapids within an eight-mile stretch of river). Call Hudson River Rafting Company in Watertown for more information at 1-800-888-RAFT. In winter, don't forget all the downhill skiing in the

area, as well. For more information about that, call the Watertown
Chamber of Commerce at (315) 788-4400. And last but not least, you can
get a wonderful view of the Thousand Islands themselves from the 1000
Islands Skydeck located between the spans of the Thousand Islands
International Bridge. With three observation decks rising 400 feet above
the St. Lawrence River, an ice cream shop, a souvenir shop, and a currency
exchange desk, at this convenient stopping point you might be able to
accomplish several things at once.

■ United States

The area code for the U.S. Thousand Islands region is 315 unless
otherwise noted.

ALEXANDRIA BAY

Every June, Alexandria Bay hosts a weekend of activities just for kids
called the Kidrific Weekend. There are children's activities galore,
a parade, magicians, pony rides, and lots more fun. Call the Alexandria
Bay Chamber of Commerce for current information at (315) 482-9531
or 1-800-541-2110.

● Alex Bay 500 Go-Karts

*Route 12 (quarter mile north of the Thousand Islands Bridge), 482-2021.
Hours: May–Sept. daily 10 A.M.–11:00 P.M. Admission: 1 lap $3, 4 laps
$10 (need to be at least 16 and 54 inches tall; all those under 10 and 54
inches tall, can ride free with an adult 16 years and older).* **Ages 4 and up.**

For your older kids and their friends, this might be the most exciting
place in the Thousand Islands. This site features more than a mile of
asphalt track with over 40 go-karts to rent. It is also fully lit for night-
time driving fun! If you and your kids get tired of driving, there are over
50 games available in the arcade.

● Aqua Zoo

*Route 12N, exit 50N, 482-5771. Hours: Memorial Day–Labor Day
daily 10–9; Labor Day–May weekends only 10–6. Admission: Adults $4,
children 12 and under $3.50, children under 36 inches tall $2.50, children
under 2 free.* **All ages.**

This zoo (or underwater museum as it is called), is one of the newer
attractions to the region and features water-related animals such as
alligators, sea horses, sharks, and many tropical fish. There are 20 large
exhibits that use approximately 15,000 gallons of water and include a
shark petting area! The sea creatures exhibit has anemones, crabs, and
other creatures kids are encouraged to touch.

● Boldt Castle

Heart Island, only accessible by boat, P.O. Box 428, 482-2501 or 1-800-8-
ISLAND. Uncle Sam Boat Tours, 1-800-ALEXBAY. Hours: May–Oct.
daily 10–6. Admission: Boat, adults $6, children 12 and under $3. Boldt
Castle, adults $3.25, children 6–12 $1.75. Note: both Uncle Sam Boat
Tours and Boldt Castle indicate that fares are subject to change without notice.
All ages.

Boldt Castle is truly a wonderful place to visit. Its story begins with
a real-life fairy tale of a man who wanted to build a beautiful, magnificent
castle as a present for his wife. In the early 1900s, George C. Boldt
(millionaire proprietor of the Waldorf Astoria) planned a castle with
more than 120 rooms, a built-in swimming pool, a separate yacht house,
a clock tower, and even a playhouse with its own two-lane bowling alley.
He had already invested over $2 million (an enormous sum of money at
the beginning of the century) when his wife died unexpectedly and he
decided to halt all work on the castle. It was in terrible condition (it sat
unfinished and unattended for 73 years) when funds were raised to begin
restoration in 1977. Since the 1980s visitors have been able to tour the
mansion and grounds and experience the grandeur of the site. For the
most part the building has been preserved exactly as it was left in 1904
(some areas of the mansion have begun to be restored/finished). There are
several exhibition areas with photographs of the Boldts and the construction of the original building. My children loved the mansion, and being
able to see the stages of a building in progress was interesting, but the
fairy tale aspect of the castle was the most enchanting (especially to my
six-year-old daughter!).

● Bonnie Castle Greens Miniature Golf Course & All Weather Driving Range

Route 12, 482-5128. Hours: approximately May–Sept. (depending on the
weather) opens at 9 A.M., closing times vary. Admission: Golf, 18 holes
$5.25, 36 holes $7.95; Batting cage, $1 for 15 balls. **Ages 4 and up.**

If your kids love miniature golf, they'll love this 36-hole miniature
golf course. When they get tired of that there are batting cages, a video
game room, a gift shop and an information center.

● Mazeland Gardens and Discovery Center

Collins Landing Road, right next to the Thousand Islands Bridge, 482-
LOST. Hours: May 15–Labor Day daily 10–7. Admission: Adults $6,
children 5–15 $4, children under 5 free. **Ages 3 and up.**

Mazeland offers families a challenge and a fun way to get some
exercise. This is the largest garden maze in North America. There are

five mazes to navigate through and some of them are quite tricky. Most of the mazes are made out of tall bushes, although one is made out of screens (if you get lost in this one, you can just crawl underneath to get out). Visitors are given a piece of paper with a blank box for a rubber stamp. The stamp is hidden somewhere within each maze! When you finally find the stamp in the maze, you stamp your paper, ring the bell and then try to find your way out again (not as easy as it sounds!). Our kids loved this place and almost one year later, still remember it and want to go back again.

Be prepared for walking! There is a small shop that sells souvenirs and drinks, and there are plenty of picnic tables to sit and relax at after you've navigated a couple of mazes. Across the street is the Alexandria Bay Visitor's Center—very convenient.

● Minnia Anthony Common Nature Center

Wellesley Island State Park, exit 51 off I-81 (4 miles west of Alexandria Bay), 482-2479. Hours: July and Aug. Mon.–Sat. 8:30–8:30, Sun. 10– 4:30; Sept.–June Mon.–Sat. 8:30–4:30, Sun. 10–4:30. Admission: $5 per car in summer only, free other seasons. **All ages.**

This island in-between Alexandria Bay and Canada is a beautiful place to take a summer bird walk or a hike within this 600-acre wildlife sanctuary. The nature center offers canoeing programs, guided hikes, and other nature-related activities, demonstrations and slide lectures. In winter, the trails turn into seven miles of groomed cross-country ski trails. Several trails for the disabled and a small museum round out this park's attractions.

And while you're on Wellesley Island, explore the Thousand Island's Park for an architectural treat. There are hundreds of Victorian houses to view. For more information, call 482-7700.

CAPE VINCENT

● Cape Vincent Fisheries Station–Aquarium

Broadway, 654-2147. Hours: May–Oct. daily 9–5. Admission: free. **All ages.**

This aquarium has exhibits featuring the fish of Lake Ontario and the St. Lawrence River. There are five large tanks to view and fishing facilities are nearby. This location is also the office of the NYS Department of Environmental Conservation. The building is wheelchair-accessible. Outdoors, there are picnic tables and grills available for public use.

CLAYTON

For more information on Clayton, visit their Web site (www.gisco. net/ Jefferson/Clayton/).

● The Antique Boat Museum

750 Mary Street, 686-4104. Hours: mid-May–mid-Oct. daily 9–5. Admission: Adults $6, children 6–17 $2. www.thousandislands.com/abm. **Ages 4 and up.**

This small museum houses one of the largest collections of recreational boats in the world. It has several exhibit areas that highlight the history of life along the St. Lawrence River. The museum also offers boat-building classes, as well as several workshops for children and families. Sessions for 1997 were available for 4- to 8-year-olds and for 9- to 13-year-olds at a cost of $5 per class. In previous years, classes have included learning about fossils, seaplanes, drums, ships, and herons. The grounds themselves are beautifully situated; bring a picnic and enjoy the view.

● Clayton Recreation Park and Arena

East Line Road (off Route 12), 686-4310 or 686-3282. Hours: daily dawn–dusk. Admission: free. **All ages.**

Here you can find all kinds of outdoor recreational activities to keep your gang busy. They have everything from an Olympic-sized outdoor swimming pool to tennis courts, a basketball court, a softball field, an exercise trail and playgrounds, as well as an outdoor covered pavilion for a family picnic or family reunion.

● American Handweaving Museum and Thousand Islands Craft School

314 John Street, 686-4123. Hours: May–Oct. Mon.–Fri. 9–4. Admission: free. **Ages 3 and up.**

For those of you interested in arts and crafts generally, and textiles in particular, this is a very nice (if small) museum to visit. It features North American handwoven textiles, jewelry, and pottery. There is also a textile library and gift shop on the premises. Courses in weaving, pottery, jewelry-making, painting, and other arts and crafts are offered.

MASSENA

● Eisenhower Lock

180 Andrews Street (off Route 37), 764-3213. Hours: daily 9–9. Admission: free. **All ages.**

From the viewing deck, visitors to the lock can watch ships being lifted or lowered 42 feet into the lock chamber. Kids find this fascinating, and it is impressive watching the working of the lock. An interpretive center and picnic tables make this a pleasant place for an afternoon visit.

● **St. Lawrence–FDR Power Project Visitor's Center**
Barnhart Island (off Route 131), 764-0226 or 1-800-262-6972. Hours: Memorial Day–Labor Day daily 9:30–6; Labor Day–Columbus Day daily 9–4:30; Columbus Day–Memorial Day Mon.–Fri. 9–4:30. Admission: free. **All ages.**

There is plenty to enjoy here with your family and friends. There are hands-on exhibits on energy, electricity, and the natural world; you can even watch the plant operators at the controls! There are also films, multi-media exhibits, and an audio-visual terrain map of the region. Get a view of the power dam and the surrounding area from the observation deck 116 feet above the river.

NATURAL BRIDGE

● **Natural Bridge Caverns**
Route 3, 644-4810. Hours: June–Sept. daily 9–5. Admission: Adults $5, children 5 and up $3, children under 4 free. **All ages.**

These caverns are truly a wonder to behold. You can take a flat-bottomed boat ride through this natural formation, which was carved by the Indian River millions of years ago. The cavern had been blocked by debris, but was finally cleared out in the 1930s by a crew of workers, and eventually was opened for boat rides.

OGDENSBURG

● **Frederic Remington Art Museum**
303 Washington Street, 393-2425. Hours: May–Oct. Mon.–Sat. 9–5, Sun. 1–5; Nov.–Apr. Wed.–Sat.11–5, Sun. 1–5. Admission: Adults $4, ages 6–22 $3. www.northnet.org/broncho/. **Ages 3 and up.**

In 1997, the Frederic Remington Art Museum reopened after a $2.5 million expansion and renovation. Remington (1861–1909), although born in Canton, New York, was one of the principal painters of the American West. He traveled out west extensively, to research subjects, sketch, and take many photographs (photography was a new invention at that time). Although he had a home in New Rochelle, New York, and a studio in Ridgefield, Connecticut (which is reconstructed at this site), this museum was opened in the house his widow, Eva, lived in after he died. If you love paintings and sculpture of Native American subjects, cowboys, and soldiers, or if you are just interested in this time in history, this is the perfect museum to visit.

OSWEGO

If you happen to be in the area in August, don't miss the Oswego Harborfest, a three-day celebration featuring musical performances, arts and crafts, tall ships, and fireworks over the harbor. For information about this and other Oswego events, check the Internet at www.oswego.com.

● Fort Ontario

E. 7th Street, 343-4711. Hours: mid-May–Oct. Wed.–Sat. 10–5, Sun. 1–5. Admission: Adults $3, children under 12 $1. **All ages.**

This state historic site, fortified in 1755 and once owned by the British and then the French, has been in U.S. possession since 1796. Costumed guides give demonstrations, including rifle and artillery drills, for visitors. Visit the site for the wonderful views of Oswego Harbor and Lake Ontario, in addition to its historical significance.

● Richardson-Bates House Museum

135 E. Third Street, 343-1342. Hours: Apr.–Dec. Tues.–Fri. 10–5, weekends 1–5; Jan.–Mar. Tues.–Fri. 10–5. Admission: Adults $2, children $.50. **Ages 5 and up.**

This beautiful Italian villa is listed on the National Register of Historic Places. Five period rooms have been refurbished, with many original furnishings, according to photographs taken around 1890. There are also permanent and changing exhibits relating to the history of the city of Oswego.

SACKETS HARBOR

The village of Sackets Harbor was the center of military activity for northern New York during the War of 1812, and was the headquarters for the U.S. Navy. During that time it was also a major shipbuilding center. Because of the town's historical significance it is part of the Urban Cultural Park system, the program that preserves the state's historic sites. Visit them on the Internet at www.1000islands.com/Sacketsharbor/Sackets.htm (you'll hear Tchaikovsky's *1812 Overture* when you download the site!).

● Old McDonald's Children's Village

North Harbor Road (off Route 81), 583-5737. Hours: May–mid-June daily 10–5; June–Labor Day daily 10–8; Labor Day–Sept. weekdays 10–5, weekends 10–6. Admission: $4. **All ages.**

This 1,200-acre working dairy and crop farm is also presented as a small animal village with over 100 different animals. Old McDonald's has been entertaining children and families since 1986. All visitors can pet the baby animals or visit the "adults" (animals), in the "Grown-up Neighborhood." Pony rides and hay rides are available for an extra $1 per ride. The reindeer exhibit opened in 1997. Kids are usually fascinated by these animals and are surprised they don't look like Rudolf! There is also a craft shop on site. This is a fun and friendly place to take children.

● Sackets Harbor Battlefield State Historic Site

505 W. Washington Street, 646-3634. Hours: mid-May–Oct. Wed.–Sat. 10–5, Sun. 1–5. Admission: Adults $3, children $1. **Ages 4 and up.**

Aspects of the War of 1812 are preserved in this historic site, which features a restored 1850 navy yard and military exhibits in the furnished historic house museum (the commandant's home, built in 1849). Every summer Sackets Harbor holds the Can-Am Festival, to honor the military history of the area. For further information about the festival call the Sackets Harbor Visitors Center at 646-2321.

● Sacket Mansion and Urban Cultural Park Visitors Center

W. Main Street, 646-2321. Hours: July–Labor Day Mon.–Sat. 10–4, Sun. noon–4; Labor Day–Christmas Wed.–Sat. 10–2; all other times by appointment. Admission: free. **Ages 4 and up.**

Visit the Williamsburg of the North—all 156 historic buildings in the village were built during the 19th century. Augustus Sacket founded the village in 1801; his mansion, now the location of the Visitors Center, was built in 1802 and served as both an officer's headquarters and a temporary hospital during the war. The site has exhibits which help to illustrate the town's role in the War of 1812, and a video provides an overview of the battle.

WATERTOWN

● Jefferson County Historical Society Museum

228 Washington Street, 782-3491. Hours: May–Nov. Tues.–Fri. 10–5, Sat. noon–5; Dec.–Apr. Tues.–Fri. 10–5. Admission: Adults $2 (suggested donation). **Ages 5 and up.**

The former home of Edwin and Olive Paddock (he was a banker) is now open to the public, and here visitors can explore this 19th-century Victorian mansion. The facade gives the impression of a Swiss chalet. Inside, you'll find the displays from the permanent collection, which includes original portraits, Victorian furnishings, and more. Outside there are beautiful gardens, and during the summer carriages and antique fire fighting equipment are displayed.

● Sci-Tech Center of Northern New York

154 Stone Street, 788-1340. Hours: Tues.–Sat. 10–4. Admission: Adults $3, children 3–18 $2, family rate $10. **Ages 2 and up.**

This hands-on museum is designed to interest children of all ages in the sciences. There are over 40 exhibits including a smelling garden, a shadow room (which all kids love). Special programs are offered for kids, usually on Saturdays and over school holidays. The store offers a variety of science-related toys as well.

● Thompson Park Zoo and Conservancy

Route 3 (off State Street), 782-6180. Hours: daily 10–5. Admission: Adults $3, children 4–12 $1.50, children under 4 free, family rate $10. **All ages.**

After a two-year renovation project between 1992 and 1994, the zoo reopened with naturalistic habitats for animals including cougar, lynx, wolf, and elk. The zoo's focus is on wildlife native to northeastern North America. There is also a children's zoo, which includes a petting area and pony and camel rides, as well as a wonderful play area which is open from early spring through late fall. (In addition to all this fun stuff, surrounding the zoo is Thompson Park, where you will find picnic areas, a swimming pool, exercise course, and walking trails.)

WELLESLEY ISLAND

See Alexandria Bay for listings.

■ Southeastern Ontario, Canada

The area code for the Canadian portion of the Thousand Islands region is 613 unless otherwise noted.

BROCKVILLE

For information regarding Brockville contact the Tourism Office at 342-8772 or visit them on the World Wide Web at www.kosone.com/brockville.

● Fulford Place

287 King Street, 498-3003. Hours: June–mid-Oct. Wed.–Sun. 11–4; mid-Oct.–May 31 Sat. and Sun. 11–4. Admission: Adults $4, children under 12 free, family rate $10. **Ages 4 and up.**

Between 1899 and 1900, Senator George Taylor Fulford built this enormous 20,000-square-foot Edwardian mansion. All the furniture in it was purchased in 1900 in New York City; all the woodwork was done in Canada. Three floors are open to the public; guided tours of the home take approximately 50 minutes. Mr. Fulford built his fortune manufacturing a cure-all remedy called Pink Pills for Pale People. This little iron pill supposedly cured everything from a toothache to that little pain behind the left knee.

GANANOQUE

Each summer in August, the town of Gananoque holds its annual Festival of the Islands—a 10-day celebration with concerts, fireworks, historical reenactments, boat races, and more. For more information call the Chamber of Commerce at 1-800-561-1595 or on the Internet go to www.canlink.com/gan/.

KINGSTON

In addition to the attractions below, Kingston also runs a summer theater from June through September. For current information on the season's performances call the Grand Theatre at 530-2050 or 1-800-615-5666. For those of you who want a more physical activity, call the Kingston Diving Centre for scuba diving charters at 634-8464. On the weekends during the summer, Kingston also has very nice farmers' and antique markets behind City Hall. Call the Kingston Tourism Information Office at 548-4415 for a free visitor's guide.

● Agnes Etherington Art Centre

University Avenue at Queen's Crescent, 545-2190. Hours: Tues.–Fri. 10–5, Sat. and Sun. 1–5. Admission: free. **Ages 4 and up.**

For the art lovers in your group, visit this museum, which has seven galleries of changing exhibits of contemporary and historical art. The museum opened as a small gallery in 1957; today it has one of Canada's most comprehensive collections of Canadian art, as well as large collections of African and Inuit art. The museum offers a wide variety of public programs, including artists' talks, family events, and concerts. The art centre is actually part of the former home of Agnes Etherington (1880–

1954), the museum's benefactor. She was a lifelong resident of Kingston, and one of the principal organizers of the arts community in the early part of this century. She was the first president of the Kingston Art and Music Club in 1927. During her lifetime, her home was open to visiting musicians and artists, and as she wanted that tradition to continue, her home has become the Agnes Etherington Art Centre.

● Bellevue House National Historic Site

35 Centre Street, 545-8666. Hours: Apr.–May 31 and Labor Day–Oct. 31 daily 10–5; June–Labor Day daily 9–6. Admission: Adults $2.75, children 6 and up $1.40, children under 6 free. **Ages 3 and up.**

This Italianate villa was the home of Sir John A. Macdonald, Canada's first prime minister. The house, gardens, and orchard have been restored in the style of the 1840s, which is when he lived here. Staff members in period costume are on hand in the summer to provide interpretive tours for visitors. For those who are interested, there is also a visitors center where the life and career of Mr. Macdonald are described.

● Confederation Tour Trolley

209 Ontario Street (across from City Hall), 548-4453. Hours: mid-May–Sept. daily 10–7, tours leave every hour on the hour. Admission: Adults $8, seniors and students $6, children under 6 free. **All ages.**

Take a leisurely 50-minute trolley tour and enjoy historic Kingston. You'll view the beautiful waterfront, the forts and museums, and more. This short ride provides a nice overview of the history and architecture of the city.

● International Ice Hockey Federation Museum

York and Alfred Streets, 544-2355. Hours: mid-June–mid-Sept. daily 10–5. Admission: Adults $2, family rate $4, children under 13 free. **Ages 3 and up.**

If someone in your family plays or watches ice hockey, then a visit to this museum may be in order. Exhibits of trophies, memorabilia, photographs, skates, and more highlight the sport and its history.

● Kingston Archaeological Centre

370 King Street West, 542-3483. Hours: Mon.–Fri. 9–4 (or by appointment). Admission: free (donations appreciated). **Ages 3 and up.**

This facility houses an interesting interpretive area which chronicles the 8,000-year history of the Kingston area. There are maps and local artifacts, in addition to a research library available to the public.

● Kingston Family Fun World

McDoo's Lane (north of 401), 530-2707. Hours: Mon.–Thurs. 11–11, Fri. and Sat. 11–midnight, Sun. 11–10. Admission: Miniature golf, adults $4, children $3; go-karts $3.75 for 6 laps. **All ages.**

This is a family recreational area featuring miniature golf, go-kart, two drive-in movie theaters, and more. Please call for information regarding the film showings and schedule.

● Marine Museum of the Great Lakes at Kingston

55 Ontario Street, 542-2261. Hours: May–Dec. daily 10–5; Jan.–Apr. Mon.–Fri. 10–4. Admission: Adults $3.95, family rate $8.75, children under 6 free. (Note: they also have a combined rate with the Pump House Steam Museum if you'd like to do both in one day.) www.MarMus.ca. **Ages 2 and up.**

At this interesting museum you'll see the *Alexander Henry*, a 3,000 ton ice-breaker moored here. (The ship also serves as a bed-and-breakfast from late spring to early fall.) Exhibits highlight the history of the Great Lakes region. There is also a book and gift shop on the premises, in addition to a library/archive. The museum has special exhibitions on occasion; in 1998 there will be an exhibition on shipwrecks. The museum offers tours in English, French, German, Japanese, and Spanish.

● Pump House Steam Museum

23 Ontario Street, 542-2261. Hours: May–Labor Day, daily 10–5. Admission: Adults $3.75, family rate $8.50, children under 6 free. See the Marine Museum, above, for information on a combined rate. **Ages 2 and up.**

This Victorian building, built in 1849, is Kingston's first water pumping station. Children of all ages will be awed by the sight of the monster engines with seven-to-nine-ton flywheels. There are also steam engines and models, and an O-gauge model train.

MORRISBURG

● Fort Henry

Right outside Kingston, St. Lawrence Parks, RR 1, Morrisburg, 1-800-437-2233 (in both the U.S. and Canada). Hours: mid-May–mid-Sept. daily 10–5. Admission: Adults $8.75, children 5–16 $4.65, family rate $23.70 including tax. e-mail: ft-henry@adan.kingston.net. **All ages.**

This restored fort, originally a port of defense during the War of 1812, provides a glimpse into life during the war. Visitors can take a tour with a costumed guide (ours played the wife of a low-ranked soldier).

Tour the barracks and mess halls, and the dining and living quarters of the captains and generals. Experience a typical classroom for the children of the soldiers. A Military Muster Parade in which children get to wear military uniforms and practice being in a military march is a regular event here (the kids love this!).

● Prehistoric World

Just west of Upper Canada Village (off Route 2), 543-2503. Hours: May 25–Labor Day daily 10–4. Admission: Adults $6, children 4–15 $4, children under 4 free. **All ages.**

This attraction features over 50 full-size reproductions of dinosaurs and other prehistoric animals displayed in an open forest setting along a nature trail. Not only can children touch and climb on these sculptures, but they can also watch others being constructed. Upper Canada Village (see below) is only five minutes away by car.

● Upper Canada Village

Highway 401, exit 758, off Route 2, 1-800-437-2233. Hours: mid-May–mid-Oct. daily 9:30–5. Admission: Adults $12.50, children 5–12 $6, children under 5 free, family rate $29. **All ages.**

Experience life in the 1860s at this reconstruction of a riverfront community complete with 40 buildings including mills, factories, homes with beautiful gardens, a bakery, general store, schoolhouse, and more. At this living history museum, costumed interpreters take visitors through the village and answer questions as well as provide demonstrations along the way. In July and August the museum puts together a children's activity center where kids can play 1860s games. At the village store you can buy some fresh-baked bread and other village-made souvenirs.

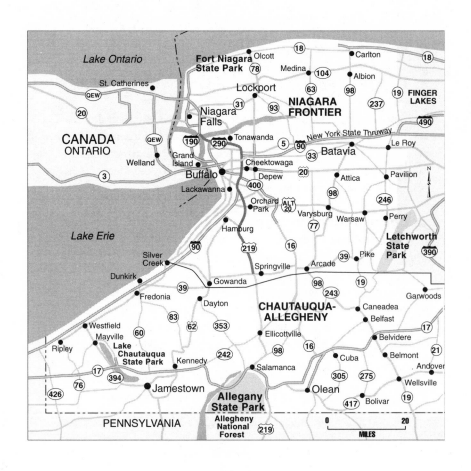

Western New York

WHEN MANY PEOPLE THINK of the western portion of New York state, they immediately think of one thing: Niagara Falls. While this is one of the major tourist attractions in this area (it draws over 10 million visitors a year), there are many other places families can enjoy while exploring western New York, which comprises two regions, the Niagara Frontier in the northwest corner of the state and the Chautauqua-Allegheny region in the southwest corner.

One sightseeing adventure your family might like to undertake, particularly if you are traveling by motor home, is the 454-mile Seaway Trail, which begins at the border of Ohio and Pennsylvania on Lake Erie and continues up the west coast of New York state, alongside Lake Ontario, to the Canadian border. If you have the energy and will, you can continue your tour of the region by crossing the border into Canada, and head south towards Toronto along Canada's Heritage Highway. For information regarding sights in Pennsylvania, contact the Erie Area Convention and Visitors' Bureau at (814) 454-7191 or the New York regional visitors' bureau in the areas you will be visiting. On the Internet, visit the Seaway Trail Web site at www.seawaytrail.com/.

Niagra Frontier Region

Niagara Falls is an incredible natural wonder that everyone should see at least once. They were discovered by the ancestors of the Seneca Indians over 2,000 years ago. The Niagara Frontier region has many other attractions, however, so you should plan to take the time to see a few other sites, such as the Albright-Knox Museum in Buffalo, the Herschell Carousel Museum in N. Tonawanda, or even the Jell-O Museum in Leroy. For more information on the Niagara Frontier region, visit the Internet at iloveny.state.ny.us/iloveny/nf.html.

All area codes in this region are 716 unless otherwise noted.

ALABAMA

● Iroquois National Wildlife Refuge

Route 77 (8 miles north of I-90), 948-5445. Hours: Refuge, mid-July–mid-Mar. daily dawn–dusk; Headquarters, Mon.–Fri. 8–4, weekends 9–5. Admission: free. **All ages.**

Get out your binoculars and hiking boots and have a blast exploring this 11,000-acre wildlife refuge. Bring along your camera too, because along the hiking trails are photography blinds (hidden viewing areas), where you might be able to take some pictures of waterfowl. Recently the refuge had a very interesting feature at the visitors center: a live broadcast of the nest of a bald eagle. Workers mounted a video camera in a tree above an eagle nest during the winter and, at this writing, two bald eagle eggs were in the nest waiting to hatch. The visitors center has maps and information about the refuge.

AMHERST

● Amherst Museum

3755 Tonawanda Creek Road (off I-90), 689-1440. Hours: May–Oct. Tues.–Fri. 9:30–4:30, weekends 12:30–4:30; Nov.–Apr. Tues.–Fri. 9:30–4:30. Admission: Adults $2, children 5–12 $1, family rate $5.50. Special events have an additional fee. **Ages 2 and up.**

Although this museum isn't a living history museum per se, there are 10 restored 19th-century buildings on this 35-acre site. Indoor exhibits feature period costumes, photographs, and other artifacts. There is also a children's discovery room, which has some wonderful attractions including Grandmother's Attic, a pioneer log cabin, and a 19th-century school room. In the Gallery of the Senses, reproduction artifacts can be handled by children; all the labels are also written in braille.

BUFFALO

For more information on Buffalo, visit their Web site
(www.buffalocvb.org/).

● Albright-Knox Art Gallery

1285 Elmwood Avenue, 882-8700. Hours: Tues.–Sat. 11–5, Sun. 12–5. Admission: Adults $4, children under 12 free, family rate $8, free Sat. 11– 1. Free parking in the back of the gallery. **All ages.**

One of the finest art galleries in the United States, the Albright-Knox is housed in a beautiful Greek Revival building and is a wonderful place to expose children to the arts. The gallery (a museum, really) has an outstanding collection of modern and contemporary art, with works by 19th-century French Impressionists Monet and Renoir, as well as 20th-century artists such as Picasso and Andy Warhol. In addition to modern art, the gallery also has collections of painting and sculpture dating back to 3000 B.C.E. Children are particularly intrigued by artist Lucas Samaras's *Mirror Room,* a three-dimensional sculpture that children can enter and experience. The gallery's size is not overwhelming and small children can easily handle a visit. There are a restaurant and gift shop on-site.

● Buffalo and Erie County Botanical Gardens

2655 South Park (at McKinley Parkway), 828-1040. Hours: daily 9–4. Admission: donations appreciated. **All ages.**

What a wonderful place to visit—particularly in the middle of a bleak winter! Fruit trees, orchids, and many other varieties of flowers can be seen and smelled at this beautiful conservatory and 12 greenhouses which were built in the late 1890s.

● Buffalo Fire Museum

1850 William Street, 892-8400. Hours: Sat. 10–4 or by appointment. Admission: free. **Ages 3 and up.**

My son is fascinated by anything that has to do with firefighters, and for those of you who have young ones with the same interest, this small museum, run by the Buffalo Fire Historical Society, should be included in your visit to Buffalo. View their antique equipment (which includes a 1907 horse-drawn steamer) and exhibits that highlight Buffalo's past firefighters. Children can also participate in hands-on activities such as the 1800 Bucket Brigade.

● Buffalo Museum of Science

1020 Humboldt Parkway, 896-5200. Hours: Tues.–Sun. 10–5. Admission: Adults $5.25, children ages 3–17 $3. (If you are a member of one of almost

200 science museums in the U.S. you are probably entitled to free admission to the BMS). **Ages 2 and up.**

Children have an inherent interest in science, and this museum will foster that interest in a multitude of areas. Four floors of exhibits will keep your children (and you) occupied for hours. Just when you think it's time to leave, your gang will discover something else and be enthralled all over again. They can explore the mysteries of the oceans, the wonders of dinosaurs, or the secrets of ancient civilizations. They can learn about the weather, rain forests, and what our future environment may be like. There is a small children's discovery room, as well. In fall and winter, the Kellogg Observatory (stars) is open; and in summer the solar observatory is open, both on Friday evenings from dusk until 9:30 (weather permitting, of course). If you are planning to be in the area for a while, the museum also offers children's classes and various family programs throughout the year. Knowledgeable staff and guest scientists are available to answer questions and provide more information, and there is a museum gift shop on-site for the end of your visit. The museum manages the Tifft Nature Preserve in Buffalo (see the listing below).

● Buffalo Zoological Gardens

300 Parkside Avenue, 837-3900. Hours: spring/summer daily 10–5; fall/winter daily 10–4. Admission: Adults $6, children 4–16 $3, children under 4 free. Parking: $3. **All ages.**

There is something for everyone to enjoy at the 23-acre site of our nation's third-oldest zoo. Over 1,300 animals live here at the zoo, including a one-horned Indian rhinoceros, a rare white tiger, lowland gorillas, and all the members of a very large reptile zoo. The children's zoo is a terrific place for your younger ones to get up close to the animals. The zoo recently renovated its lion and tiger areas, and these animals now enjoy a more natural habitat. Carousel and train rides are also available in season, and these provide a perfect opportunity to sit and relax for a minute, before your kids run you ragged to the next attraction! (Bordering the zoo and grounds is **Delaware Park,** designed by Frederick Law Olmsted, the landscape architect of New York City's Central Park. Here you and your family can rent a paddleboat, have a picnic lunch, ride bikes, or just relax.)

● Martin's Fantasy Island

2400 Grand Island Boulevard (on Grand Island), 773-7591. Hours: May 6–June 23, Fri.–Sun. (variable hours, call ahead); late June–Labor Day daily 11:30–8:30. Admission: Adults $14.95, children under 48 inches tall $11.95, children under 2 free. **All ages.**

Need another theme park to visit? If so, try this 80-acre, family-oriented park with rides, a water park, a children's petting zoo, miniature golf, paddleboats, a western town, and rides for younger children.

● Pedaling History—The Burgwardt Bicycle Museum

3943 North Buffalo Road (off Route 20 in Orchard Park), 662-3853. Hours: Apr. 2–Jan. 14 Mon.–Sat. 11–5, Sun. 1:30–5; Jan. 15–Apr. 1 Fri., Sat., Mon., 11–5, Sun. 1:30–5. Admission: Adults $4.50, children 7–15 $2.50, family rate $12.50. **Ages 3 and up.**

If bicycling is your thing (or rather, your kids' thing), this collection of 300 bicycles and memorabilia dating from between 1817 and 1990 is the place to visit. It is the only all-bicycle museum in the U.S. and has one of the world's largest collections of antique bikes. Various exhibits illustrate the history of this vehicle and provide interesting insights into the development of something most of us take for granted. The Floating Marine Bicycle from the 1880s is very cool!

● Theodore Roosevelt Inaugural National Historic Site (Wilcox Mansion)

641 Delaware Avenue, 884-0095. Hours: Jan.–Mar. Mon.–Fri. 9–5, Sun. 12–5; Apr.–Dec. Mon.–Fri. 9–5, Sat. and Sun. 12–5. Admission: Adults $3, children 6–14 $1, family rate $6.50. **Ages 5 and up.**

President Roosevelt was inaugurated at this site on September 14, 1901, after the assassination of President McKinley. The mansion, a Greek Revival built in 1838, provides a tangible piece of history for visitors who tour the restored rooms and explore the beautiful gardens. For middle school or high school students who are studying American history, this site will provide a lively evocation of the past. Call ahead for information about special events such as the Victorian Christmas celebration.

● Tifft Nature Preserve

1020 Humboldt Parkway or Fuhrmann Boulevard, 896-5200. Hours: Grounds, daily during daylight hours; Visitors center, Tues.–Sun. 9–5. Admission: free (donations are appreciated). **All ages.**

Located approximately three miles from the center of downtown Buffalo, this 264-acre preserve offers visitors a chance to enjoy nature within sight of a large city! Take a hike on five-and-one-half miles of nature trails, or do some bird-watching. Take some photographs of the wildflower garden or of the 75-acre cattail marsh. If you visit during the winter months, try snowshoeing or cross-country skiing. There is something for everyone to enjoy here, especially after days of visiting all the other sites in the region.

CASTILE

● Letchworth State Park

Route 19A, Park, 493-3600; Glen Iris Inn, 493-2622. Hours: daily, dawn–dusk. Admission: $5 per car or NYS Empire Passport. **All ages.**

Even if you are just quickly passing through this region, try to schedule a stop at Letchworth State Park which comprises over 14,000 acres. The Genesee River Gorge, within the park, is a 17-mile long, 600-foot-deep gorge with three waterfalls; the scenic roads have several overlook areas. It is a wonderful place to visit in all seasons: in summer for special nature programs, canoeing, tubing, whitewater rafting, and more; in winter, for the wonderful views of ice-laden cliffs.

Overlooking the middle waterfall, the Glen Iris Inn serves meals and has 15 guest rooms for overnight accommodations in the former home of William Pryor Letchworth. If it is a bit too fancy for you, the inn also manages five concession stands throughout the park for ice cream and sodas.

DARIEN CENTER

● Darien Lake Theme Park and Camping Resorts

Route 77 (exit 48A off I-90), 599-4646 or 1-800-5-DARIEN outside of New York state. Camping reservations, 599-2211. Hours: May and Sept. weekends only 10:30–9; mid-June–Labor Day daily 10:30–10. Admission: Adults $19.99, children under 48 inches tall $14.99, children under 2 free. Prices include all wet and dry rides. (If you see a Tops Market along the way, you can usually buy discounted tickets there.) www.darienlake.com. **All ages.**

Darien Lake is not only a theme park with over 100 wet and dry rides and attractions (new in 1997 is Crocodile Isle, a million-gallon wave pool), three world-class roller coasters (the newest one called Mind Eraser where riders are suspended from the track while their legs and feet dangle—yikes!), and Adventureland for smaller kids, but a resort with 2,000-site campgrounds, RV rentals, and a performing arts center! Darien Lake is New York state's largest entertainment complex, on over 164 acres.

Every evening the park has a fireworks and laser show. There are plenty of places to get food and refreshments throughout the park, including four sit-down restaurants. Call for information regarding summer events.

EAST AURORA

● Explore & More

430 Main Street, 655-5131. Hours: Wed–Sat. 10–4. Admission: Adults $2, children 1–12 $3, children under 1 free. **Ages 7 and under.**

This new museum is geared towards children from birth to seven years old. Here they are encouraged to touch, experiment, discover, play, and learn. For babies under one year old, there are textures to feel, shapes to sort, soft building blocks, and a quiet reading room. Hands-on exhibits include a building center, science and nature projects, and performing arts activities. Call or write for special workshops and after-school programs.

● Toy Town Museum

636 Girard Avenue, 687-5151. Hours: Mon.–Sat. 10–4. Admission: free (donations accepted). **Ages 7 and up.**

Toy Town Museum is the perfect place for kids ages 7 and up. In addition to being a learning center for children, it is a museum dedicated to the history of toys, Fisher-Price toys in particular. The permanent collection features Fisher-Price toys dating from 1931 to the present, and the museum includes a theater, exhibition areas, ToyWorks, and a museum store. ToyWorks is a play area where children can learn about how toys work through hands-on experience. A very special event called ToyFest takes place each year (in 1997 it was held August 23 and 24), which celebrates toys in general and attracts thousands of visitors. The event features an outdoor play area, storytellers, a parade, children's theater performances, and much more. Each year, Fisher-Price creates a special toy in limited quantities especially for the festival. Please call or write ahead for information on current exhibits and other special events (such as a recent exhibit on Raggedy Ann and Andy).

LEROY

● LeRoy House and Jell-O Museum

23 Main Street (exit 47 off I-90), 768-7433. Hours: LeRoy House, Tues.– Fri. 10–4 , Sun. 2–4; Jell-O Museum, June–Labor Day daily 10–4. Admission: LeRoy House, free; Jell-O Museum, Adults $3, children $1. **Ages 2 and up.**

For those of you who love Jell-O, you'll be interested to know that it was invented here in LeRoy, New York (in the eastern portion of the Niagara Frontier), in 1897. And if your interest is really piqued, you'll have to stop in for a visit at the LeRoy House, a historic museum which is now the home of the Leroy Historical Society (the house was built in 1822). In the rear is the Academy Building, where you'll find changing exhibits highlighting Jell-O memorabilia. Who can resist? They even have an interactive kitchen for youngsters.

LEWISTON

● Artpark
S. 4th Street, 1-800-659-PARK. Hours: daily dawn–dusk. Admission: Varies per performance and activity. Parking: $4 per car July–Aug.
All ages.

Artpark is a lovely 200-acre park along the Niagara River Gorge that boasts recreational facilities (nature trails and picnic areas), as well as a 2,300-seat theater and arts complex. Call for further information on current performances. The town of Lewiston has the distinction of being the site of the original Niagara Falls some 12,000 years ago. (Erosion caused the falls to shift to their current location.) The city is also known for being the site of the invention of the cocktail.

NIAGARA FALLS, NEW YORK

If you feel like visiting the Niagara Falls area on the spur of the moment, call the Niagara Falls 24-hour events hotline for current information at (716) 285-8711, call the visitors center at (716) 278-1796, or visit their Web site at www.nfcvb.com/.

● Aquarium of Niagara
Whirlpool Street at Pine Avenue, 278-3575. Hours: Memorial Day–Labor Day daily 9–7; rest of the year 9–5. Admission: Adults $6.25, children ages 4–12 $4.25, children 3 and under free. **All ages.**

Who doesn't like aquariums? Most kids are intrigued by creatures of the sea and will be especially enthralled here by over 150 species in more than 50 exhibit areas. The sharks, sea lions, dolphins, and seals are the most popular. The aquarium has special dolphin shows several times a day that are a blast for kids—especially when the dolphins jump high up in the air and splash the spectators!

● Niagara Falls/Niagara Reservation Park
Prospect Park, 278-1796. Hours: daily 8 A.M.–10 P.M. Admission: Visitors center, free; View Mobile, adults $4.50, children 6–12 $3.50.
All ages.

Opened in 1885, Niagara Reservation Park is the oldest state park in New York. This 400-acre park, which contains the falls, also has a visitors center where you can pick up detailed information about the region and park. One option for visitors is to hop aboard the View Mobile, a bus which holds about 70 people and takes them on a three-to-four-mile trip around the park. This is especially nice if you and your kids are tired, or if your kids are too small for the Cave of the Winds Trip. The other convenient feature of this ride is that you can get off anywhere along the way, sightsee for a while, and board another bus later.

● Cave of the Winds Trip

Goat Island, 278-1730. Hours: May–mid-Oct. daily 9–8, tours leave every half hour. Admission: Adults $5.50, children ages 6–12 $5, children under 6 free. Note: To go on the tour children must be over 42 inches tall and be able to walk unassisted. **Ages 4 and up.**

The Cave of the Winds Trip leaves from Goat Island, which separates the American and Canadian falls and is accessible by foot or a vehicle bridge. Goat Island has wonderful views of the river and falls, and you can even walk from it over a bridge onto Three Sisters Island, which is actually in the middle of the rapids! The Cave of the Winds Trip is quite spectacular. You walk up very close to the falls (within 25 feet!) and then take an elevator 175 feet down to where you can view the falls from between the cave rocks. The American Falls are 184 feet high!

● Maid of the Mist

Prospect Point, at the Observation Tower, 284-8897 or 284-4233. Hours: May–Oct. daily 9–8 (tours leave every 15 minutes). Admission: Adults $8, children ages 6–12 $4.50. $.50 fee for the tower elevator. **Ages 4 and up.**

For a real thrill, take a boat tour of Niagara Falls. The admission fee includes waterproof clothing which you definitely will need because you come within 25 feet of the falls! There is nothing quite like the feel of the spray coming from this immense waterfall.

● Niagara Power Project Visitor Center

4 1/2 miles north of the falls on US 104 or off the Robert Moses Parkway, 285-3211. Hours: July 1–Labor Day daily 9–6; rest of the year daily 10–5. Admission: free. **Ages 3 and up.**

The Niagara Project's observation and information building offers views of the river and gorge. Working models and other exhibits explain power plant functions. For the art lovers in your group, there is a mural painted by the American artist Thomas Hart Benton inside.

● Niagara's Wax Museum of History

303 Prospect Street, 285-1271. Hours: May 15–Oct. 15 daily 9 A.M.–11 P.M.; Oct. 16–May 14 daily 11–5. Admission: Adults $4.95, teens 13–17 $3.95, children 6–12 $2.95. **All ages.**

Wax figures are fascinating to kids, and these which depict figures from the Niagara Frontier region's historical past, provide kids with an educational experience in addition to being fun. There are scenes of Native Americans in longhouses, soldiers from Old Fort Niagara, and even a display of Abraham Lincoln (who once visited Niagara Falls) getting his haircut.

● Wintergarden

Rainbow Boulevard, 285-8007. Hours: daily 9 A.M.–11 P.M. Admission: free. **All ages.**

When the winter blahs get you down, take a trip to see this beautiful structure, a glass-enclosed tropical paradise! Featuring winding paths, platforms, and a three-story glass elevator, visitors can view tropical and desert plants, waterfalls, and over 5,000 trees. Secluded rest areas provide wonderful places to stop and take in the sights and smells (before heading back outdoors to subzero weather if you happen to visit in January!).

NIAGARA FALLS, CANADA

On the Canadian side of Niagara Falls there are just as many places to visit (if not more), as on the New York side, and you can actually get a better view of the falls from the Canadian side. The Canadian or Horseshoe Falls are 176 feet high, slightly less than the American side. The first person to go over the falls (in 1901) was a woman named Annie Taylor. The New York and Canadian Niagara Region attracts over 16 million visitors per year, so plan your trip here accordingly. A sampling of some of the Canadian attractions are listed below. Give a call to the Canadian Tourist Office for more detailed information about this side of the falls at (905) 356-6061 or visit them on the Internet at www.tourismniagara.com. All prices in this section are in U.S. dollars unless otherwise noted.

● Guinness World of Records

4943 Clifton Hill, (905) 356-2299. Hours: Dec.–Feb. Mon.–Fri. 11–5, weekends 11–7; Oct.–Nov. and Mar.–May daily 10–8; June–Sept. daily 9–midnight. Admission: Adults $6.50, children 6–12 $3.95, children 5 and under free. **All ages.**

If you want to know what is the biggest, loudest, tallest, or fastest, then pay a visit to this gallery with displays of world records in sports, science, and nature.

● Louis Tussaud's Waxworks

Clifton Hill and Falls Avenue, (905) 374-6601. Hours: May–Aug. daily 9 A.M.–1 A.M.; Sept.–Dec. daily 10 A.M.–11 P.M.; Jan.–Mar. daily 10 A.M.–8 P.M. Admission: Adults $6, children 6–12 $3, children 5 and under free. **All ages.**

This museum displays life-size reproductions of famous figures with historically accurate tableaux and costumes. My daughter is one of many kids who loves to see different costumes on people; this gallery gives children a chance to see figures in outfits from various time periods.

● Marineland

7657 Portage Road, (905) 356-9565. Hours: daily 9–6. Admission: Adults $21.95 plus tax (Canadian), children 5–9 $18.95 plus tax (Canadian). Free parking. **All ages.**

Marineland is probably the second most popular attraction in the Niagara Falls region. Here you can see killer whales, dolphins, and sea lions (there are shows every hour), visit the deer petting park, and ride the roller coaster.

● Minolta Tower Centre

6732 Oakes Drive, (905) 356-1501. Hours: Apr.–Oct. daily 8–midnight; Nov.–Mar. daily 9–8. Admission: Adults $5.95, children 11–18 $4.95, children under 11 free. **All ages.**

Get a great view of the falls from 335 feet high or rather, from 500 feet above the bottom of the falls. There are three tower levels including an indoor/outdoor observation deck.

● Niagara Butterfly Conservatory

Niagara Parkway, 5 miles north of the falls, (905) 356-8119. Hours: daily 9–6. Admission: Adults $6 Canadian ($4.50 U.S.), children 6–12 $3 Canadian ($2.25 U.S.), children under 6 free. **All ages.**

With over 120 species of butterflies (almost 2,000 butterflies), you and your child will have a magical time in North America's largest, man-made, glass-enclosed 11,000-square-foot butterfly sanctuary, which opened in December 1996. The building is kept at an even 85 degrees and has a 200-seat auditorium and a 250-seat cafeteria with both indoor and outdoor seating. (Wear brightly colored clothing and perfume if you want the butterflies to think you're a flower and land on you.)

● Niagara Falls IMAX Theatre and Daredevil Adventure

6170 Buchanan Avenue, (905) 374-4629. Hours: July–Labor Day daily 10–9, shows on the hour; rest of the year schedule varies, call for information. Admission: Adults $7.50 (plus tax), children 12–18 $6.75 (plus tax), children 6–11 $5.50 (plus tax). **Ages 5 and up.**

If you're one of those who love thrills and chills, watch one of these IMAX movies on the six-story screen (don't take small children—it's too scary for them), then head over to the Skylon Tower (see below) located next door, for great views of the falls.

● Niagara Falls Museum

5651 River Road, (905) 356-2151. Hours: Sun.–Fri. 9 A.M.–10 P.M., Sat. 9 A.M.–11 P.M. Admission: $6.75 Canadian, children 5–10 $3.95 Canadian. **All ages.**

With close to a million objects in the collection, there is something for the entire family here: Niagara Falls memorabilia, dinosaur fossils, and even Egyptian Mummies. The museum is located right near the Rainbow Bridge.

● Niagara Parks Botanical Gardens

Niagara Parkway North, (905) 356-8554. Hours: daily dawn–dusk. Admission: free. **All ages.**

Sixteen thousand plants and flowers make up the face of this garden clock. Other floral displays and gardens can be seen on this 80-acre site. This is the home of the Niagara Park School of Horticulture.

● Niagara Spanish Aero Car

Niagara Parkway at the whirlpool, (905) 356-2241. Hours: May 1–Oct. 9 daily dawn–dusk (weather permitting). Admission: Adults $5 Canadian, children 6–12 $2.50 Canadian, children 5 and under free. **All ages.**

Take a ride above the Niagara Whirlpool on this cable car that has been in operation since 1916. Take the 10-minute ride 250 feet high above the gorge on an 1,800-foot cableway for an incredible view.

● Queenston Heights Park

7 miles north of Horseshoe Falls. Hours: daily dawn–dusk. Admission: free. **All ages.**

This park commemorates the many battles of the War of 1812. It is also a great park for picnicking and hiking and for viewing the Niagara River.

● Skylon Tower

5200 Robinson Street, (905) 356-2651. Hours: daily 8 A.M.–11 P.M. Admission: Adults $6.95 Canadian, children 12 and under $3.95 Canadian. www.skylon.com. **All ages.**

View the Niagara Gorge from the tower's observation deck, which is 775 feet above the river. (The tower itself is 520 feet.) Built in 1965, the tower has seven levels, including a revolving restaurant (one revolution per hour) and an observation deck that will give you an 80-mile visibility range on a clear day. There are three exterior "yellow bug" elevators which reach the top in 52 seconds (and yes, they really do look like little yellow bugs from the American side).

NORTH TONAWANDA

● Herschell Carousel Factory Museum

180 Thompson Street, 693-1885. Hours: Mar.–June, Sept.–Dec. Wed.–Sun. 1–5; July and Aug. daily 11–5. Admission: Adults $3, children 2–12 $1.50. **All ages.**

Allen Herschell was one of the most famous carousel-makers in the late 19th century, and in 1883 he designed the first steam-driven carousel. Here you will see a hand-carved wooden carousel dating from 1916, and if you visit on the right day, you might even get a chance to see wood carving demonstrations. There is also a smaller carousel for younger children.

YOUNGSTOWN

● Fort Niagara State Park/Old Fort Niagara

SR 18F at the mouth of the Niagara River at Lake Ontario, 745-7273. Hours: Memorial Day–Labor Day daily dawn–dusk. Admission: free. Parking: $3 per car July 1–Labor Day. **All ages.**

Fort Niagara Park covers over 500 acres and has tennis and basketball courts as well as boating, fishing, and swimming facilities. Old Fort Niagara is on the state park grounds. This historical site was built in 1726 by the French. There are many interesting things at the fort to see; in particular kids love the drawbridge and cannons, and most of all, the fortified castle itself, restored to its 18th-century glory. Historical reenactments are held throughout the year, although special ceremonies and drills are conducted only from July through Labor Day.

Chautauqua-Allegheny Region

This region of New York state has much to offer families traveling through the area, with everything from Native American museums and Amish culture to scenic train rides. Visit a pioneer village or hike, bike, or canoe around the area. If you visit in the fall you can enjoy balloon festivals, apple festivals, and Octoberfests. This region is also known as the Grape Juice Capital of the World, because of the abundance of concord grapes grown here. Write or call the region's visitor bureaus for up-to-date information on current festivals and special events, or check the Web at www.C1web.com/.

The area code for the Chautauqua-Allegheny region is 716 unless otherwise noted.

CHAUTAUQUA

● Chautauqua Institution
On the lake, 357-6200 or 1-800-836-ARTS. Admission: Ticketing possibilities vary, buy tickets by the day or week, for evenings or Sundays. Call for a new schedule of activities each season (summer is June–Aug.). **All ages.**

The Chautauqua Institution is a special cultural learning destination which is a self-contained Victorian village where no cars are allowed. It was founded in 1874 as an educational center for Sunday-school teachers. Here at this lakeside summer community, families can stay overnight or a week, and can enjoy theater, art, dance, and music. Family members can participate in group classes or take individual classes. Grandparents, parents, and children can enroll in a chess class together, enjoy the 77-member symphony orchestra, walk along the lake, or just play a relaxing game of Scrabble on a front porch. There are storytellers, puppet shows, and musicians for children's entertainment. The institution is unique and offers families a chance to do things together that they might not normally get the chance to do. The site is on the National Register of Historic Places.

CUBA

● Cuba Cheese Shoppe
53 Genesee Street off Route 17, 968-3949. Hours: Mon.–Fri. 9–6, Sat. and Sun. 9–5. **All ages.**

I don't usually put cheese shops on my list of places to visit, but this one is an area institution. The Cuba Cheese Shoppe has 100 varieties of cheese as well as many other New York state products including maple syrup, honey, and crafts; the shop has been in existence since the late 1800s.

ELLICOTTVILLE

● Nannen Arboretum

Route 219, 945-5200. Hours: daily dawn–dusk. Admission: free. **All ages.**

Nannen is the only arboretum in western New York state, covering eight acres with 300 species of herbs and 250 other plants. Also on the site is a Ryoanji Japanese meditation area and Japanese gardens. Many paths are wheelchair-accessible.

JAMESTOWN

● Jamestown Audubon Nature Center—Burgeson Wildlife Sanctuary

1600 Riverside Road, 569-2345. Hours: Nature center, Tues.–Sat. 10–5, Sun. 1–5; Sancutary, daily dawn–dusk. Admission: free (separate fees for special events). **All ages.**

The Jamestown Nature Center is a 600-acre park on the grounds of the Burgeson Wildlife Sanctuary. Enjoy a hike on the five miles of trails. At the nature center there's a permanent exhibit of Roger Tory Peterson prints and a gift shop. Several special events take place each year, including a Snowflake Festival and an October Nature Art Festival.

● Roger Tory Peterson Institute of Natural History

311 Curtis Street, 665-2473. Hours: Tues.–Sat. 10–4, Sun. 1–5. Admission: varies per exhibit. **All ages.**

The institute puts on several wildlife photography and art exhibits each year. There are many outdoor trails for hiking, and a wonderful butterfly garden to view in the summer. For those interested in birds, bring your binoculars and field guide, as this is a great place for birding.

MAPLE SPRINGS

● Midway Park

Route 430 at Chautauqua Lake (off Route 17 exit 10), 386-3165. Hours: Memorial Day–Labor Day Tues.–Sun 1–sunset. Admission: purchase tickets per ride. Parking: free. **All ages.**

This theme park is celebrating its 100th anniversary in 1998. There are over a dozen rides, go-karts, mini-golf, bumper boats, an outdoor roller-skating rink, a swimming area, paddleboats, an arcade, a museum and gift shop, a food concession stand, and picnic grove. If all the above can't keep you and your group busy, I'm not sure what can.

OLEAN

● Rock City Park

Route 16, 5 miles south of Olean, 372-7790. Hours: May–Oct. daily 9–6. Admission: Adults $4, children 6–12 $2. **All ages.**

Located in the Allegheny Mountains, Rock City is the site of the world's largest deposit of quartz conglomerate, which happens to be over 300-million-years-old. Visitors can look at prehistoric ocean remains, see rock bridges, peek into crevices, and be amazed by huge towering boulders. There is a three-quarter-mile nature trail here, a rock shop, a picnic area, and a refreshment stand.

PANAMA

● Panama Rocks

Rock Hill Road off Route 474, 782-2845. Hours: May–Oct. daily 10–5. Admission: under $5 (prices vary and are subject to change). **Ages 4 and up.**

Panama Rocks is a privately owned scenic park and features some spectacular outcroppings—25 acres of primeval seashore rock formations, some as tall as 60 feet high. You'll see wildflowers in the spring, and mosses and ferns, as you navigate cliffs, caverns, and crevice passageways. You must sign a waiver of liability before you enter the site. There are many large roots to trip over and other hazards here and the crevices can be dangerous. Because of this I recommend this site for children who are over four and are fairly comfortable walking.

SALAMANCA

● Salamanca Rail Museum

170 Main Street, 945-3133. Hours: Apr.–Dec. Mon.–Sat. 10–5, Sun. 12–5. Admission: free (donations are appreciated). **Ages 3 and up.**

This museum is in a restored 1912 passenger railway depot with exhibits and video display on the history of western New York railroads. The main lobby and ticket office give a feeling of the past, when railroad travel was frequent. Also in Salamanca is the American Indian Crafts

(719 Broad Street), which features a wide assortment of Native American arts and crafts.

● Seneca-Iroquois National Museum

Route 17 (exit 20), 945-1738. Hours: Apr.–Sept. 9–5. Admission: Adults $4, children 7–13 $2, children under 7 free. **Ages 3 and up.**

This museum is on the Allegheny Indian Reservation. Exhibits cover the history and culture of the Iroquois Indians, with an emphasis on the Seneca Nation. My children especially liked the longhouse display, where you can really get a sense of a Native American dwelling. A small gift shop is also on-site.

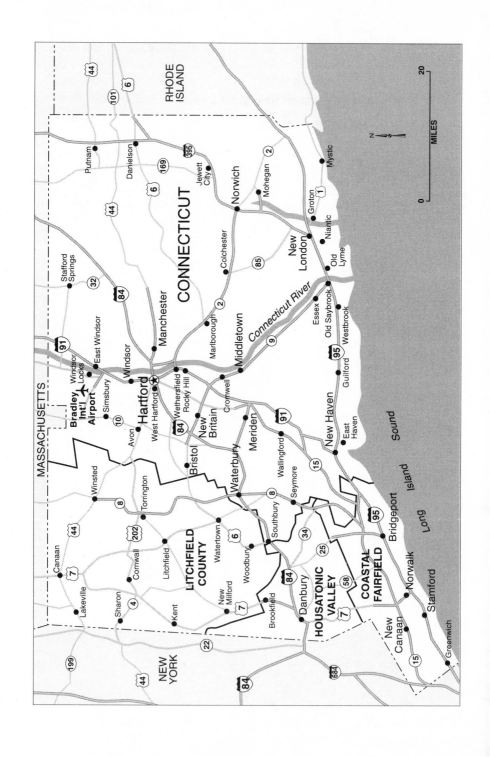

Western Connecticut

CONNECTICUT BORDERS SOUTHEASTERN New York state for approximately 100 miles and offers some great places to visit within easy access of New York. Connecticut is divided into 11 regions, three of which border New York state and have been researched for kid potential: Coastal Fairfield County, Housatonic Valley, and Litchfield Hills. To hook up to Connecticut on the Web, try these addresses: www.connecticut.com, www.state.ct.us/ and www.ctpassport.com/.

Coastal Fairfield County

This area of Connecticut, the closest to metropolitan New York, is the most heavily populated area of the state.

The area code for Coastal Fairfield County is 203 unless otherwise noted.

BRIDGEPORT

● The Barnum Museum
820 Main Street, 331-9881. Hours: Tues.–Sat. 10–4:30 and Sun. 12–4:30. Admission: Adults $5, children 4–18 $3.00, under 4 free. **All ages.**

One person I talked to while writing this book considers this "the best museum between New York and Boston." Established in 1893, this is a collection related to the career of P. T. Barnum, the circus giant, and includes circus material, videos, and memorabilia. There's a hand-carved miniature five-ring circus, clown costumes, and more. This museum is sure to please the many kids who love circuses.

● Beardsley Zoological Gardens
1875 Noble Avenue, 576-8082. Hours: Zoo, daily 9–4; Carousel, Apr.–Oct daily 10:30–3:30. Admission: Zoo, adults $4, children 3 and up $2, children under 3 free; Carousel, $1 per person. Parking Fee: $6 out-of-state vehicles, $3 CT vehicles. **All ages.**

Beardsley Zoo is located on 33 acres within the 130-acre Beardsley Park, and at the time of this writing, restorations were underway. This is a very nice zoo to visit, because kids can manage walking through the site easily. The zoo features over 120 species of animals. There is also a gift shop, snack bar, and picnic area. In addition, there's a carousel which is a wonderful treat for the kids after walking through the zoo (although the lines can sometimes be quite long). Call for information regarding the fun ZooFolk concert series that takes place each summer.

● Bridgeport–Port Jefferson Steamboat Company
For schedules and rates in Connecticut, call (203) 367-3043, and on Long Island call (516) 473-0286.

This ferry goes directly to and from Port Jefferson on Long Island. It operates year-round, and one can board it on foot, by car, or by bicycle. Sailing time is approximately one-and-one-half hours each way. We took the ferry from Long Island to Connecticut and then continued on to the zoo, which made a wonderful day-long adventure.

● The Discovery Museum

4550 Park Avenue, 372-3521. Hours: Sept.–June Tues.–Sat. 10–5, Sun. noon–5; July and Aug. Mon.–Sat. 10–5, Sun. noon–5. Admission: Adults $6, children ages 4–18 $4, children under 4 free. **All ages.**

This is an interactive art and science museum with 125 exhibits. The museum also features children's concerts, story hours, and family workshops. Children will have fun learning about electricity, energy, space, computers, light, color, and much more. The most popular exhibit is undoubtedly the *Challenger Learning Center,* where kids can experience computer-simulated space missions. They'll also enjoy looking in the gift shop which sells science kits, books, and toys.

● Polka Dot Playhouse

167 State Street, Pleasure Beach, 333-3666. Hours: Performances usually Fri. and Sat. evenings, Sun. matinees. Admission: Adults $15, children 12 and under $10. **All ages.**

Picnic on the beach overlooking Long Island Sound and enjoy some summer theater. The playhouse usually presents four productions between June and October; there is also a summer theater workshop for children. Call for a current schedule of performances.

FAIRFIELD

The town of Fairfield is one of Connecticut's oldest towns.

● Connecticut Audubon Birdcraft Museum

314 Unquowa Road, 259-0416. Hours: Tues., Sat., and Sun. 9–5. Admission: Adults $2, children 14 and under, $1. **All ages.**

The Birdcraft Museum highlights the surrounding area's natural history. The adjacent six-acre sanctuary includes trails and ponds and was the first privately owned bird sanctuary in the U.S. (it was founded in 1914). The museum is only a two-minute walk from the Fairfield Metro North train station.

● Connecticut Audubon Society Fairfield Nature Center

2325 Burr Street, 259-6305. Hours: Tues.–Sat. 9–4:30. Admission: Adults $2, children $1. **All ages.**

Enjoy a pleasant afternoon walking at this nature center, which has six miles of trails and a woodland habitat with marshes, ponds, streams, and meadows. There's also a facility for injured birds here, which is known as the Roy and Margot Larsen Bird Sanctuary.

● Ogden House and Gardens

1520 Bronson Road, 259-1598. Tours: mid-May–mid-Oct. Sat. and Sun. 1–4. Admission: Adults $2, children 12 and under $1. **All ages.**

The Ogden House is a restored 1750 farmhouse refurbished to portray the lives of its former owners, Jane and David Ogden. The wildflower and kitchen herb gardens are beautiful to look at in full bloom. In late September each year, harvest is celebrated with a fall festival. For $1 you can purchase an activity book from the museum shop that interprets the house for children.

GREENWICH

Greenwich, at the southwest corner of Fairfield County, is the Connecticut town closest to New York City.

● Audubon Center of Greenwich

613 Riversville Road at the corner of John Street, 869-5272. Hours: Tues.– Sun. 9–5. Admission: Adults $3, children $1.50. **All ages.**

At this center, you can explore 15 miles of trails set within 485 acres of woodland, meadows, and ponds. There is an interpretive center which contains an art gallery, a bird observation window, and a good book and gift shop. (At the same phone number, and located just half a mile away, is the Audubon Fairchild Wildflower Garden, listed below.)

● Audubon Fairchild Wildflower Garden

North Porchuck Road, 869-5272. Hours: daily dawn–dusk. Admission: free. **All ages.**

At this wildflower garden, you can enjoy eight miles of trails though native flowering plants and ferns. It is a very peaceful place to take children. Bring along a magnifying glass and take a closer look at the flowers.

● Bruce Museum

1 Museum Drive (exit 3 off I-95), 869-0376. Hours: Tues.–Sat. 10–5, Sun. 2–5. Admission: Adults $3.50, children 5–12 $2.50, children under 5 free, (all visitors free on Tues.). **All ages.**

This is a renovated natural history museum, which today has approximately 25,000 objects in three categories: fine and decorative arts, cultural history, and environmental sciences. A family favorite, the Bruce Museum offers many workshops, festivals, programs, and concerts. There is also a touch tank, a wigwam children can go into, and a minerals exhibit. (Also note that the Bruce Memorial Park and Playground is

adjacent to the museum and is a great place for picnics or for just letting
your kids get their ya-yas out.)

● Bush-Holley House

*39 Strickland Road, 869-6899. Tours: Feb.–Dec. Tues.–Fri. noon–4, Sun. 1–
4. Admission: Adults $4, students 12–18 $3, under 12 free.* **Ages 3 and up.**

This house is an example of a central-chimney saltbox (built around
1732) and it is also the site of one of the first (of only a few) American
Impressionist art colonies. American painters Childe Hassam and J. Alden
Weir painted here between 1890 and 1925. A collection of their works
and an artist's studio are on display. The museum offers several programs
for children including Summer History Week, in July, when children do
historic craft projects, and Art in the Yard, in which children paint for the
day with instructors. Call for a current schedule of hours and events.

NEW CANAAN

In addition to historic buildings and nature trails, the town of New
Canaan has charming boutiques, bakeries, bookstores, and other shops.

● New Canaan Historical Society

*13 Oenoke Ridge, 966-1776. Hours: Restored buildings, July and Aug.
Tues.–Fri. 2–4, Sun. 2–4; Drug Store, Costume, and Tool Museums, Sept.–
June Tues.–Sat. 9:30–12:30 and 2–4:30. Admission: free (donations
appreciated).* **Ages 3 and up.**

The historical society here operates five separate buildings with
seven museums and a library of local history. The Hanford-Silliman
House (1764) is furnished in the style of the day and includes a collection
of dolls, toys, and quilts. There is also a tool museum, schoolhouse, town
house, costume museum, and the Cody Drug Store.

● New Canaan Nature Center

*144 Oenoke Ridge Road, 966-9577. Hours: Tues.–Sat. 9–4, Sun. 12–4.
Admission: free (donations accepted).* **All ages.**

This extensive nature center has 40 acres of diverse habitats and two
miles of trails and boardwalks. The center also boasts a bird-watching
platform, a wildflower garden, a butterfly field, and an herb garden. The
discovery center has plenty of hands-on exhibits, such as a living bee
colony, a place to make animal tracks with rubber stamps, and a soil
exhibit. There are also fish tanks, snakes, turtles, newts, and, of course,
a gift shop. Call for a schedule of lectures, walking tours, live animal
demonstrations, and other programs.

NORWALK

Norwalk is only 40 miles northeast of New York City; the neighborhood around the Maritime Center has a variety of shops, boutiques, and restaurants.

● Maritime Center

In the SoNo neighborhood, South Norwalk. 10 N. Water Street near Washington Street, 852-0700. Hours: Memorial Day–Labor Day daily 10–6; Sept.–June daily 10–5. Admission: Adults $7.50, children 2–12 $6.50, under 2 free. Parking is available at the municipal lots for an additional cost.
All ages.

The maritime center is a large facility with an aquarium, a theater, and a museum located in a restored 19th-century foundry. At the aquarium there are 22 tanks with 125 species of marine life indigenous to Long Island Sound. Interactive and video displays throughout tell the story of life in the Sound. The highlight is the 110,000-gallon tank that contains sharks, stingrays, bluefish, and more. Children can handle crabs, starfish, and other sea creatures in the touch tank. There is also an IMAX theater appropriate for older children.

STAMFORD

For more information on Stamford, visit their Web site (www.futuris.net/city/).

● Bartlett Arboretum

151 Brookdale Road, 322-6971. Hours: daily 8:30–sunset. Admission: free.
All ages.

This arboretum is a 63-acre park with five miles of trails. The center has a wonderful program for children; it lends kids backpacks complete with crayons, sketch pads, a magnifying glass, card games, and activity suggestions. The visitors center has guidebooks, toys, and games. The arboretum also sponsors a summer concert series. Call for a current schedule of performances.

● Eco-Cruises aboard *SoundWaters*

4 Brewers Yacht Haven Marina, Washington Boulevard, 323-1978. Hours: June–Oct. sails approximately four times per month. Admission: Adults $25, children 12 and under $15. **Ages 5 and up.**

Aboard this 80-foot, three-masted sharpie schooner, take a two-hour eco-cruise led by trained naturalists and marine biologists. The company primarily has educational programs that focus on the coastal ecology of Long Island Sound. They offer floating classrooms for school groups and day camps, evening and weekend charters, and public sails. They also have Mother's Day, Father's Day, and Fourth of July special excursions. Call for seasonal sailing information and schedules.

● Stamford Museum and Nature Center

*30 Scofieldtown Road, 322-1646. Hours: Mon.–Sat. 9–5, Sun 1–5.
Admission: Adults $5, children ages 5–13 $4, children under 5 free.*
All ages.

This museum and nature center is set in a 118-acre park where there's also a working New England farm. On the farm there's a reconstructed barn that dates to 1750. The nature center was recently renovated and now has three miles of trails with a boardwalk. Near the parking area is the museum, which hosts a variety of art exhibits, natural history displays, and more. The center also has recently created an unusual playground, complete with a sandpit where kids can dig for bones and a replica of a beaver lodge which is actually a treehouse. There are also workshops, lectures, festivals, and summer camps for kids.

● United House Wrecking

535 Hope Street, 348-5371. Hours: Mon.–Sat. 9:30–5:30, Sun. 12–5.
Ages 3 and up.

Searching for treasures is probably one of the most fun things kids can think of to do. At this architectural salvage company, adults who are weekend or professional renovators will have a blast, but the kids might even have more fun. An old box, a picture frame, or a dresser with hidden drawers can become props for a kids' theater production or for a special restoration project. There is something for everyone here.

● The Varsity Club

74 Largo Drive in Riverbend Industrial Park, 359-2582. Hours: June–Aug. daily 10–6; Sept.–May weekends only 10–9. (Call to confirm hours; the club closes for private functions.) Admission: $1 per ticket, 12 for $10. Activities range in price from $2–$5. Unlimited activity bracelets are $14.95 (this does not include the new Skate Park). Children under 18 must place a waiver signed by one parent on file. **All ages.**

This facility is a 34,000-square-foot indoor recreational amusement center. Younger kids can try the softplay/exercise area, which includes tunnels, slides, and obstacles. Older kids can try the rock climbing wall called Mount Varsity, play miniature golf, or ride rides; or they might love the futuristic laser tag area and high-speed bumper cars. The Skate Park is their new facility for in-line skaters and skateboarders; it carries a separate fee.

● Whitney Museum of American Art

One Champion Plaza at Atlantic Street and Tresser Boulevard, 358-7630. Hours: Tues.–Sat. 11–5. Admission: free. Parking: free in the Champion Garage on Tresser Boulevard. **Ages 3 and up.**

The Connecticut branch of the Whitney Museum of New York City offers five changing exhibitions per year. It is small in size and ideal for introducing children to the arts.

WESTPORT

● Nature Center for Environmental Activities

10 Woodside Lane, 227-7253. Hours: Mon.–Sat. 9–5, Sun. 1–4. Admission (suggested donation): Adults $1, children $.50. **All ages.**

This nature center is a 62-acre wildlife sanctuary with three miles of trails and a trail for the blind. The 20,000-square-foot center has a live animal hall, a discovery room with natural science displays, a wildlife rehabilitation center, aquariums, and a marine touch tank. If that is not enough, there are also workshops, guided tours, and many special events. If you plan to visit the area, call ahead for current information.

● Sherwood Island State Park

Exit 18 off I-95, 226-6983. Hours: daily dawn–dusk. Admission: weekdays in summer $5 CT vehicles, $8 out-of-state vehicles; weekends and holidays in summer $7 CT and $12 out-of-state vehicles. **All ages.**

Who doesn't love to go to the beach? This is a one-and-one-half-mile beach with ball fields, a picnic area, and footpaths. Lifeguards are on duty from Memorial Day to Labor Day. You can swim, fly kites, play volleyball, play frisbee, or just get a suntan. There is also a nature trail, a small nature center, and a bird observation deck. Restrooms, changing rooms, and showers are available at no charge. In summer, a concession stand is open.

Housatonic Valley Region

The area code in the Housatonic Valley is 203 unless otherwise noted. For more information, visit acad.bryant.edu/~kbrook/housaval.html.

DANBURY

For more information on Danbury, visit their Web site (www.danbury.lib.ct.us/).

● Charles Ives Center for the Arts

Mill Plain Road, Westside Campus, Route 6, 837-9226. Hours: Performances June–Sept. Admission: tickets $10–$50. **All ages.**

This arts center has 30 acres of lawns and woods, with entertainment in the open-air gazebo in the summer months. Named for the Pulitzer prize–winning composer that many consider the father of American music, the center offers a wide range of musical performances, including Sunday in the Park (approximately four to five performances each season); this event is usually free and starts at 2 P.M. The music played in these free concerts ranges from classical and blues to pop and jazz. Call for a current seasonal schedule of performances (that have a fee). There are also children's programs, special events, and fireworks.

● Danbury Fair Mall

Exit 3 off I-84, 743-3247. Hours: Mon.–Sat. 10–9:30, Sun. 12–6. Carousel admission: $.50 per ride (money donated to children's charities). **All ages.**

I don't usually list malls as places to visit, but this one has a million-dollar double-decker carousel that was made in Italy. It is also Connecticut's largest mall with over 240 stores.

● Danbury Railway Museum

White Street and Patriot Drive at Union Station, 778-8337. Hours: Jan.– Mar. Thurs.–Sun. 10–4; Apr.–Nov. Tues.–Sun. 10–4; end of Nov.–Dec. call for schedule. Admission: Adults $2, children 5 and up $1, children under 5 free. www.danbury.org/org/drm/. **All ages.**

In 1995 Danby Union Station re-opened as a replica of how it appeared circa 1903. The goal of the museum is to educate the public about the role of the railroad in American history. You can take rides that last anywhere from one hour (in the rail yard), to all day (excursion to the Hudson River or a fall foliage tour). There is also a museum shop, as well as exhibit areas that display railroad artifacts. Please call ahead for current time schedule and rates.

● Stew Leonard's

Federal Road (exit 7 off I-84), 790-8030. Hours: daily 8 A.M.–10 P.M.

Believe it or not, I really have listed a dairy store here! Not only can you shop for milk and cheese here, but the children can visit the on-site miniature farm and petting zoo. A bit unusual perhaps, but certainly worth a visit.

RIDGEFIELD

For more information on Ridgefield, visit their Web site
(www.ridgefield.net).

● Aldrich Museum of Contemporary Art

*258 Main Street, Route 35, 438-4519. Hours: Tues.–Sun. 1–5. Admission:
Adults $3, students $2, children under 12 free.* **Ages 3 and up.**

The Aldrich Museum focuses on new artists and current events in
art and culture. Located in a historic building, the museum has works
by quite a few famous American artists in its collection, including Eva
Hesse, Jasper Johns, Roy Lichtenstein, and Andy Warhol, to name a few.
The outdoor sculpture garden is a real treat. The museum offers workshops for children; call ahead for a current schedule of events and tour
information.

● Weir Farm National Historic Site

*735 Nod Hill Road, 834-1896. Hours: Visitors center, Apr.–Nov. daily
8:30–5; Dec.–Mar. Wed.–Fri. 8:30–5; Grounds, daily dawn–dusk.
Admission: free.* **All ages.**

This site was the summer home of the American Impressionist
J. Alden Weir (1852–1919). The site comprises 57 acres and includes
his Greek Revival farmhouse, studio, and barns. If you have a child who
is artistically inclined, this might be just the place to visit and do some
sketching. Weir Farm was the first national park in Connecticut and is
the only park in the country dedicated to a painter.

Litchfield Hills Region

The northwestern county of Connecticut has the state's highest mountain,
17 state parks, and loads of antique shops. To find information about the
Litchfield Hills area on the Internet, go to www.litchfieldhills.org/.

The area code in Litchfield Hills is 860 unless otherwise noted.

BRISTOL

● American Clock and Watch Museum

*100 Maple Street (off Route 6), 583-6070. Hours: Apr.–Nov. daily 10–5.
Admission: Adults $3.50, children 8–15 $1.50, children under 8 free.*
All ages.

This museum boasts over 3,000 timepieces, from grandfather clocks
to watches, and many of them go off on the hour! The town of Bristol is

known for its watchmaking, and exhibits chronicle the history of the craft here. There is also a sundial garden and a museum shop.

● Lake Compounce Theme Park and Entertainment Complex

822 Lake Avenue (off Route 229), 583-3631. Hours: June–Aug. Wed.– Mon. 11–10. Admission: Adults $18.95 (unlimited rides), children under 48 inches tall $13.95, children under 3 free. **All ages.**

This park is America's oldest amusement park. It has over 25 wet and dry attractions, including roller coasters, rides, slides, and an antique carousel, and there will be even more after new construction is completed, which is taking place as of this writing. There are also special events and live entertainment, a lakeside train ride, and a lakeside pavilion for catered picnics. The park is also creating a new kiddie area with 11 rides for younger children.

● New England Carousel Museum

95 Riverside Avenue, 585-5411. Hours: Apr.–Oct. Mon.–Sat. 10–5, Sun. 12–5; Nov.–Mar. Tues.–Sat. 10–5, Sun. 12–5. Admission: Adults $4, children 4–14 $2.50, children under 4 free. **All ages.**

This museum features exquisite pieces of antique carousel art. There are displays of miniature carousels and an exhibit of an antique carving shop on the premises. This museum has a sister site in Mystic, Connecticut, which does have a carousel to ride (860-536-7862).

CANAAN

● Collins Diner

Route 44 at Railroad Plaza, 824-7040. Hours: Fri.–Sun. 5:30 A.M.– 7 P.M.; Mon., Tues., and Thurs. 5:30 A.M.–5:30 P.M.; Wed. 5:30 A.M.– 1:30 P.M. **All ages.**

The Collins Diner is one of only five diners on the National Register of Historic Places and that's why I've listed it here. Built in 1941 by the O. J. Mahoney Company it is blue and neon on the outside and gleaming stainless steel on the inside, with classic spinning counter stools and all the classic diner fare. Kids love it.

● Music Mountain

Falls Village off Route 7 (another entrance is off Route 6), 824-7126. Hours: June–Aug. performance times vary. Admission: Adults $18 ($15 in advance), students $10. **All ages.**

Music Mountain is the site of the nation's oldest chamber music festival, and now it also features jazz and folk music shows. Concerts are given on Saturday nights and Sunday afternoons from early June through August. Bring a picnic, stroll through the forest, and then take in a wonderful musical performance. Call for a current schedule.

KENT

● Kent Falls State Park
Route 7, 5 miles north of Kent, 927-3238. Hours: daily 8–sunset. Admission: $5 per car for CT vehicles, $8 per car for out-of-state vehicles. **All ages.**

This park is a perfect place for a picnic, with Kent Falls as the view. People are allowed to wade in the water with bathing suits. Toilets are available, as are grills and picnic tables.

● Sloane-Stanley Museum
Route 7 (just outside Kent), 927-3849. Hours: mid-May–Oct. Wed.–Sun. 10–4. Admission: Adults $3, children 6–17 $1.50, children under 6 free. **Ages 3 and up.**

This tool museum holds examples of many woodworking tools from the 1600s. Also on the grounds are the 19th-century ruins of the Kent Iron Furnace. Next door is the Connecticut Antique Machinery Association building, which has quite a few larger historic machines on view. At this writing, the machinery building is only open on weekends and is staffed by volunteers. Stop in to see if anyone is on hand when you visit the Sloane-Stanley Museum.

● Stosh's New England's Own Ice Cream
38 N. Main Street (located in the Old Railroad Station), 927-4495. Hours: Apr.–late May, early Sept.–Oct. daily 11–6; Memorial Day–Labor Day 11–10. **All ages.**

Stop in here for the best ice-cream in Litchfield County. The local train runs right behind the shop and the engineers usually toot the horn for the kids. There are also many other nice small shops in Kent.

LAKEVILLE

● Holley House Museum and Salisbury Cannon Museum
15 Millerton Road (Routes 41 and 44), 435-2878. Hours: mid-June–mid-Sept. weekends and holidays 12–5. Admission: free. **Ages 4 and up.**

The Holley House Museum is a 19th-century living history museum; the house itself incorporates both the Federal (1768) and Classical Revival (1808) styles of architecture. The Holley family lived in the house for over 150 years and during that time the household was run mainly by women. The museum's focus, therefore, is 19th-century history and the role of women. The collections include family furnishings, an ice house, an outdoor maze, a heritage garden, and, perhaps the most entertaining feature, the seven-holer (a seven-hole outhouse). Special children's programs such as a pre-Halloween storytelling program (with local ghost lore stories), are a regular feature. Call for further details.

The Salisbury Cannon Museum is a children's museum of revolutionary history featuring hands-on exhibits and activities for all ages. Many of the exhibits illustrate the activities of the local iron industry and the contributions of residents to the American Revolutionary War.

LITCHFIELD

● White Flower Farm
Route 63, 567-8789. Hours: Apr.–Oct. daily 9:30–5; Nov.–Dec. daily 10– 5. Admission: free. **All ages.**

This flower farm has 10 acres of display gardens and 30 acres of growing fields. Peak bloom times are June through September, and as you can imagine, the site is stunning. The garden store is open to the public. The White Flower Farm is nationally known for its English tuberous begonias.

● White Memorial Foundation and Conservation Center Museum
80 Whitehall Road (2 miles west of Litchfield Center) off Route 202, 567- 0857. Hours: Park, daily dawn–dusk; Museum, Mon.–Sat. 9–5, Sun. 12– 5, Admission: Park, free; Museum, Adults $2, children 6–12 $1, children under 6 free. **All ages.**

This is Connecticut's largest nature preserve, with over 4,000 acres and a total of 35 miles of trails. There are family campgrounds, boat launches on Bantam Lake, a bird observatory, and special observation stations for viewing birds and for photography. There is the Trail of the Senses and the Conservation Center Museum. An event in September called Family Nature Day is a really fun way to get the entire family involved. The Natural History Museum has several displays that feature the natural history and wildlife of the area, as well as some live animals and a small gift shop.

MIDDLEBURY

Middlebury is sometimes listed in the Waterbury Region of Connecticut, but I have listed it here because it is a popular attraction and is close to the southern area of Litchfield Hills.

● Quassy Amusement Park

Route 64, (203) 758-2913 or 1-800-FOR-PARK. Hours: mid-April–Memorial Day weekends only 11–6; Memorial Day–Labor Day daily 11–9. Admission: All-day ride ticket for children over 42 inches tall $11.50, for children under 42 inches tall $7.50. Beach passes only, adults $2.75, children 12 and under $1.75; Beach parking, $3. **All ages.**

This 20-acre park on Lake Quassapaug features over 30 rides and attractions, games, food, swimming, a petting zoo, and more! You can have a birthday party here, or just purchase a beach pass and enjoy yourselves at the freshwater lake. Call for more information on group and entertainment rates. This is true old-fashioned family entertainment.

SHARON

● Housatonic Meadows State Park

Route 7, 672-6772. Hours: daily 8–sunset. Admission: Park, free; camping, $10 per night. **All ages.**

Enjoy many outdoor activities here including hiking, fishing, canoeing, or just having a picnic. You can enjoy riverside camping here in the summer for a very reasonable price. Take a hike on part of the Appalachian Trail, which crosses the park.

● Sharon Audubon Center

Route 4, (203) 364-0520. Hours: Mon.–Sat. 9–5, Sun. 1–5. Admission: Adults $3, children $1.50. **All ages.**

The Sharon Audubon Center is a 684-acre park with 11 miles of self-guided trails through many kinds of habitat. The center has a nice bookshop and gift shop, natural science exhibits, and a children's discovery room. Outdoors there is a wildlife rehabilitation center, an herb garden, and a butterfly and hummingbird garden. On the last weekend in July, visit for the Annual Audubon Festival which features hands-on activities plus crafts, demonstrations, food, pony rides, and much more.

WASHINGTON

● Institute for American Indian Studies

38 Curtis Road (Route 99), 868-0518. Hours: Apr.–Dec. Mon.–Sat. 10–5, Sun. 12–6; Jan.–Mar. Wed.–Sat. 10–5, Sun. 12–6. Admission: Adults $4, children ages 6–16 $2, children under 6 free. **All ages.**

In a small building near the Steep Rock Nature Preserve, the Institute for American Indian Studies has exhibits of various subjects, including one on permanent display titled, *As We Tell Our Stories: Living Tradition and the Algonkian Peoples of New England.* The exhibit re-creates a 17th-century village and shows how people lived and interacted during that time. There is a furnished reproduction of a long house, a gift shop, and two art galleries. There are also craft workshops, films, and outdoor exhibits which include a simulated archaeological site.

WOODBURY

● Glebe House and Gertrude Jekyll Garden

Hollow Road off Route 6, 263-2855. Hours: Apr.–Nov. Wed.–Sun. 1–4; Dec.–Mar. by appointment. Admission (suggested donation): Adults $4, children $2. **All ages.**

This 1745 minister's farmhouse (also called a glebe) is the only garden in the U.S. designed by the English landscape designer Gertrude Jekyll. The house has its original paneling and period furnishings. Every August kids ages 8 to 12 can participate in a history camp that provides a glimpse into 18th-century life (this is an extremely popular event and three sessions are usually scheduled). In late September each year a colonial fair features all the entertainment that the original colonial fairs had, including a regiment, puppet shows, and more. The town of Woodbury is also known as a great place for antique collecting.

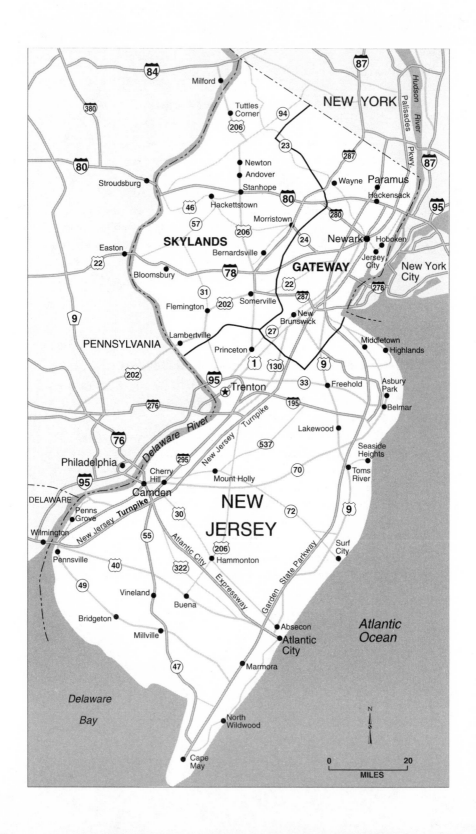

Northern New Jersey

NEW JERSEY, THE FOURTH smallest state, is only 32 miles wide in its midsection, but altogether it covers 7,468 square miles. Northern New Jersey shares a 50-mile land border with New York state, and is separated from the rest of New York by the Hudson River. (Pennsylvania and Delaware are separated from New Jersey by the Delaware River.) Of the six regions which constitute New Jersey, we will cover only the northern two, which border New York: the Skylands region of northwest New Jersey and the Gateway region, which makes up the northeast portion of the state. For more information on New Jersey, visit the Internet at www.nj.com or www.state.nj.us/travel.index.html.

Skylands Region

The area code in the Skylands Region is 201 unless otherwise noted.

For more information on the Skylands Region, visit their Web site (www.njskylands.com).

BASKING RIDGE

● Great Swamp National Wildlife Refuge

190 Lord Stirling Road, 635-6629 Morris County Education Center; (908) 766-2489 Somerset County Education Center; 435-1222 Wildlife Refuge. Hours: daily dawn–dusk. Admission: free. **All ages.**

The Great Swamp is actually 8,000 acres of the remains of Lake Passaic. This glacial lake never fully dried out, and therefore the wildlife refuge (some 400 acres) is made up of a freshwater marsh, a bog, a swamp, streams, fields, and woods. There are eight miles of boardwalks (yes, that's right), and for those of you who are avid birders, two observation blinds to get a better opportunity to glimpse the wildlife of the area. If this is too much for your kids to handle, an easy 3.9-mile (round trip) hike is also available. Don't forget those binoculars and insect repellent in the late spring and summer (we always seem to!).

BEEMERVILLE

● Space Farms Zoo and Museum

218 Route 519, 875-5800. Hours: mid-Apr.–Oct. daily 9–5. Admission: Adults $7.95 (plus tax), children $3.50 (plus tax). **All ages.**

Located right near the border of New York, this 100-acre zoo and museum awaits, with over 500 animals including lions, bears, tigers, monkeys, and more. This site has a very interesting history. The Space family began trapping wild animals that were threatening their livestock. When the caged animals were about to be disposed, the Space children pleaded for their lives. Consequently, their animal collection grew and grew. It is now the largest private collection of wildlife in the world. The museum also has old cars, carriages, wagons, sleighs, and other interesting antiques. They have a gift shop and snack shop on-site.

BERNARDSVILLE

● Scherman-Hoffman Wildlife Sanctuary

Hardscrabble Road (exit 26 off Route 287), (908) 766-5787. Hours: Tues.–Sat. 9–5, Sun. 12–5. Admission: free. **All ages.**

Formerly part of a private estate, this 265-acre site is now owned by the New Jersey Audubon Society. In the mansion itself, there are displays of birds native to New Jersey, and special programs just for children are offered, including summer day camps. After visiting the museum, take a hike on the 2.1-mile trail (especially in spring, to enjoy the wildflowers).

CLINTON

● Hunterdon Historical Museum
56 Main Street (off Route 78), (908) 735-4101. Hours: Apr.–Oct. Tues.– Sat. 10–4, Sun. 12–6. Admission: Adults $3, children 6 and up $1, children under 6 free. **Ages 2 and up.**

There are many historical villages listed in this book, and while they all have some things in common, each provides a different glimpse into life in the past. At this 10-acre park, there is a mill (with exhibits), a quarry, a blacksmith shop, a log cabin, and other buildings. One of the more famous pictures of New Jersey was taken here at the old mill with its waterwheel next to the 200-foot-wide waterfall. Call ahead for information regarding the annual craft fairs, harvest festival, and summer concert series.

FAR HILLS

● Golf House Museum
Liberty Corner Road, Route 512 (off Route 287), (908) 234-2300. Hours: Mon.–Fri. 9–5, Sat. and Sun. 10–4. Admission: free. **Ages 4 and up.**

If you and your kids happen to be a golf nuts, then you might be interested in this museum of golf and its artifacts. On the self-guided tour in the museum (housed in a Georgian mansion), you'll see golf balls and clubs from as far back as the 1600s. Also displayed are golf clubs that belonged to famous golfers and others figures (the most famous of these is probably President Kennedy).

FLEMINGTON

● Black River and Western Railroad
(908) 782-9600 or 782-6622. Hours: June–Aug. Thurs.–Fri. 11:30, 1, and 2:30 departures; Sat. and Sun. 11:30, 1, 2:30, and 4 departures; May–mid-Dec. Sat, Sun., and holidays 11:30, 1, 2:30, and 4 departures. Admission: Roundtrip, adults $7, children 3–12 $3.50, children under 3 free. **All ages.**

Take this one-hour, 11-mile train ride from Flemington to Ringoes either before or after your visit to the railroad museum listed below. The ride is one of those pleasurable things to do that most of us do not make time for. Plan one day to take this rail trip, and sit back and enjoy the scenery.

● Northlandz: Railway and Doll Museum

495 Highway 202, (908) 782-4022. Hours: daily 10–6. Admission: Adults $12.75, children 2–12 $8.75, children under 2 free. www.northlandz.com. **All ages.**

For those of you whose children love trains and model trains (and for those adults who do too), visit here to see one of the largest model railroad exhibits in the world (135 trains, 8 miles of track, and over 4,000 buildings!). The one mile self-guided tour takes approximately two hours. Not only are there model railroads, but also a doll museum, an art gallery, and a large pipe organ.

FRANKLIN

● Franklin Mineral Museum

Evans Street (off Route 23), 827-3481. Hours: Apr.–Nov. Mon.–Sat. 10– 4, Sun. 12:30–4:30; Mar. Sat. 10–4, Sun. 12:30–4:30. Admission: Adults $4, children $2; Combination museum and rock collecting, adults $7, children $3. **Ages 3 and up.**

Franklin used to be a major zinc mining town, but now, it is the home of a museum operated near the old zinc mine itself. Kids think it is so cool to see fluorescent minerals glow in ultraviolet light. You can even give them a chance to find some more rocks in the slag heap out back.

HOPE

● Land of Make Believe and Pirate's Cove

Route 80 (exit 12 off Country Road 11), (908) 459-5100. Hours: Memorial Day–June 23, weekends only 10–6; June 24–Labor Day daily 10–6; Sept. Sun. only 10–6. Admission: Adults $11, children 2–12 $14, children under 2 free. www.Lomb.com. **All ages.**

The Land of Make Believe is a water park designed primarily for preteens. Children do love this park, which comprises approximately 30 acres. Spend all day river tubing if you wish, or navigate a maze, take a hayride, or ride the carousel. There is a lot to do here and your kids will definitely be tired at the end of the day. Bring a picnic lunch and enjoy yourselves. The Land of Make Believe is the oldest and largest children's park in New Jersey (it opened in 1954).

MADISON

● Museum of Early Trades and Crafts

Main Street and Green Village Road (in the James Library Building), 377-2982. Hours: Tues.–Sat. 10–4, Sun. 12–5. Admission: Adults $3.50, children $2, children 5 and under free. **Ages 3 and up.**

Ever wonder what kind of job your grandfather or great-grandfather had? Ever think about the kinds of tools and instruments he had to work with? Well, at this interesting museum, visitors can see the tools used by old-time carpenters, bookmakers, cobblers, and more. For kids, there are several hands-on discovery areas. The museum completed a historic restoration in 1997.

MILLBROOK

● Millbrook Village

Old Mine Road, off Route 80 (last exit in western New Jersey), (908) 841-9531 or 1-800-543-4295. Hours: late June–Labor Day Wed.–Sun. 9–5. Admission: free. **All ages.**

Millbrook Village was a bustling town between 1870 and 1895 and was a ghost town by the 1950s. Located in the Kittatinny Mountains just north of the Kittatinny Point Visitors Center, the village has been restored, and now this farm community is open again for view. Take a leisurely walk around the village and visit the church and homes. Costumed guides lead visitors around the site and demonstrate various arts and crafts.

MORRISTOWN

● Morristown National Historical Park

Route 287 to exit 36 (3 miles south of Morristown), 543-4030 or 539-2085. Hours: Ford Mansion, Museum, and Visitors Center daily 9–5, Mansion tours hourly 10–4; off-season restricted hours, call for schedule. Admission: Adults $2, children under 16 free. **Ages 3 and up.**

During the winters of 1779 and 1780, George Washington made his winter camp at the Ford Mansion in Morristown; the mansion is now open to the public and furnished as it was during the late 18th century. At the visitors center, see the film that illustrates life in George Washington's era, and then examine a reconstruction of one of the soldier's huts, to get a very good sense of how the soldiers lived during that time.

● **Fosterfields Living Historical Farm**
Route 24 and Kahdena Road, 326-7645. Hours: Apr.–Oct. Wed.–Sat. 10–5, Sun. 1–5. Admission: Farm tours, adults $4, children 7 and older $2; Willows estate, $1 extra per person. **Ages 3 and up.**

If your kids (and you) have an interest in history, visit this 200-acre farm and experience life on a farm in the 19th century. On weekends, the farm has demonstrations of various farm activities. The Willows, a restored 1852 Gothic Revival estate on the property, is also open for tours.

NETCONG
See listing for Wild West City under Stanhope.

OGDENSBURG

● **Sterling Hill Mining Museum**
30 Plant Street, 209-7212. Hours: May–Oct. daily 10–5. Admission: Adults $8, children 17 and under $5. Tours begin at 1 and 3. **Ages 7 and up.**

The last operating zinc mine in the state has been transformed into a mining museum that older kids love. The site is located on over 30 acres, with outdoor (underground caves) and indoor (museum) exhibits. The museum provides an incredible lesson in geology and mineralogy; the cave with florescent minerals is a wonder to behold. I would not recommend this site for children under the ages of 6 or 7 because the tours last two hours and there is a lot of walking.

RINGOES
See Flemington, above, for information on the Black River and Western Railroad.

ROCKY HILL

● **Rockingham Historic Site**
108 County Road Route 518, (609) 921-8835. Hours: Wed.–Sat. 10–12, 1–4; Sun. 1–4. Admission: free. **Ages 5 and up.**

In addition to visiting the places where Martha and George Washington headquartered in 1778–79 (Somerville) and 1779–80 (Morristown), plan a visit here to see where the couple lived in 1783. George wrote his famous "Farewell Address to the Armies" here, and the table on which he wrote it is displayed with additional information. Each May the museum holds Children's Day with special events throughout the day.

This site is sometimes listed under Princeton but is actually located in the town of Rocky Hill.

SOMERSET

● New Jersey Renaissance Festival and Kingdom
Davidson Avenue (off exit 6 on I-287), (908) 271-1119. Hours: late May–late June weekends 11–6. Admission: Adults $10, children under 12 $6. www.NJKingdom.com. **All ages.**

The year is circa 1540, and you are in Renaissance England. Enjoy yourself as more than 150 costumed actors entertain you on seven stages. Watch music, magic, or dance performances. Let the kids take in a terrific puppet show or a comedy performance. Watch the actors play chess on the field-sized "living chess" board. The festival puts on 20 shows per day, so you have plenty of entertainment to choose from. There are two other such festivals: one is in Sterling Forest, in upstate New York (Finger Lakes region), and the other is in Tuxedo, New York (Catskills region). They're a wonderful way to spend a sunny summer day.

SOMERVILLE

● Duke Gardens
Route 206 (south of Somerville Circle), (908) 722-3700. Hours: May–Oct. daily. Admission: Adults $5, children $2.50, children under 6 free. Note: Visits are by reservation only; call at least one week in advance. **Ages 4 and up.**

Even though reservations are required here, this site has the distinction of being one of New Jersey's most popular attractions. Here at the Duke estate, you will tour several hothouses, each one representing a different culture: the Italian romantic garden, the English garden, the formal French garden, the Persian garden, and a Japanese meditation garden, among several others. This is a beautiful place and makes one want to immediately visit each of the countries represented (or at least take a load of books out of the library on garden design).

● Old Dutch Parsonage and Wallace House
38 and 65 Washington Place, across the street from the Duke Gardens (listed above), (908) 725-1015. Hours: Wed.–Sat. 10–12, 1–4; Sun. 1–4. Admission: free (donations appreciated). **Ages 5 and up.**

George Washington lived at the Wallace House between 1778 and 1779. The house is furnished with period furniture. While he was living there, he frequently visited the parsonage, which was owned by the founder of Queen's College (now Rutgers University). At the parsonage children can try on colonial clothing (most children, I think, love to try on any kind of clothing for dress-up, but to do so at a museum is a special treat). The parsonage is currently in the beginning stages of a restoration project. There are some original furnishings and artifacts. The parsonage and Wallace House are on the same schedule, and share tour guides.

● United States Bicycling Hall of Fame

166 West Main Street, (908) 722-3620. Hours: Mon.–Fri. 11–12, 1–3:30 (but the management suggests you call ahead just to make sure they are in). Admission: free. **All ages.**

Similar to the bicycle museum in East Aurora, New York (in the Western/Niagara-Frontier region), this bicycling hall of fame is located here because of the Tour of Somerville bike race. This museum, too has antique bicycles and memorabilia from our country's most famous cyclists.

STANHOPE

● Waterloo Village

Exit 25 off Route 80, 347-0900. Hours: mid-Apr.–mid-Nov. Wed.–Sun. 10–6. Admission: Adults $9, children 6–15 $7, children under 6 free. www.waterloovillage.org. **All ages.**

It will take your family an entire day's outing to see all there is to see in Waterloo Village. A restored colonial village with a general store, a church from 1859, and 23 other homes and buildings will keep all of you busy, as you explore and learn about our ancestors and how they lived. In the summer, call for a schedule of events—classical, jazz, and other musical concerts are often presented.

● Wild West City

50 Lackawanna Drive (Route 206), 347-8900. Hours: May and Sept.–Oct. weekends only 10:30–6; June–Aug. daily 10:30–6. Admission: Adults $6.75, children ages 2–12 $6.25. Special rides are $1.50 extra per ticket. These include the pony rides, the stagecoach ride, and the train ride. www.WildWestCity.com. **All ages.**

Gunfights, a hold-up at the local bank, rides on ponies, stagecoaches, and hay wagons: experience life in a reproduction 1880s Dodge City, and enjoy over 20 different live-action shows per day. Movies and TV shows have been filmed here; bring your jeans, boots, and cowboy hat and let yourself become a cowboy (or cowgirl) for a little while. In addition to all the Wild West happenings, the site also features a petting zoo. If you are feeling especially lucky try the Panning for Gold area, or just sit back and enjoy the shows or listen to live music.

VERNON

● Vernon Valley Action Park

Route 94, 827-2000. Hours: June 14–Sept. 1, daily 10 A.M.–11 P.M. Admission: Adults $27, children under 48 inches tall $15. **All ages.**

This park is one of the largest theme and water parks in the U.S. and with over 30 million gallons of water sloshing about the place, I think that is probably accurate. This amusement park has 75 rides, race cars, and even bungee-jumping—go ahead and try it if you dare (I decline, thank you very much).

Gateway Region

The area code for the Gateway region is 201 unless otherwise noted.

EAST RUTHERFORD

● Meadowlands Sports Complex

Giants Stadium, Byrne Arena, Racetrack, off the New Jersey Turnpike, exit 16W (northbound) or 18W (southbound), 935-8500 (Information) or 935-3900 (Box Office). Hours: vary per event. Admission: varies per game or concert. **Ages 3 and up.**

If you have football fans in your family or group and plan to be in the area during football season, then don't pass up a chance to visit Giants Stadium, possibly the most famous ballpark in the U.S. If your interests are more along the lines of basketball, ice shows, circus acts, and concerts, don't fear, the Byrne Arena provides those events.

EDISON

● Thomas A. Edison Tower and Museum

37 Christie Street and Route 27, (908) 549-3299. Hours: Memorial Day–Labor Day Tues.–Fri. 12:30–4, weekends 12:30–4:30; rest of the year Wed.–Fri. 12:30–4:00, weekends 12:30–4:30. Admission: free. **Ages 4 and up.**

Thomas Edison lived here between 1876 and 1886, until his laboratory became too small (he then moved to West Orange, New Jersey). Six years after Edison's death, a 131-foot tower and museum were erected in his memory on the site of his former laboratory. The contents of the original lab were acquired by Henry Ford and installed in a museum in Dearborn, Michigan, but visitors to the Edison Tower today can still see many of Edison's inventions on display.

JERSEY CITY

● Afro-American Historical Society Museum
1841 Kennedy Boulevard, 547-5262. Hours: Mon.–Sat. 10–4:30. Admission: free. **Ages 3 and up.**

Visit this small but interesting museum, located on the second floor of the Greenville Library to learn more about African-Americans and their culture and history. The museum has displays of dolls, civil rights movement information, and many other artifacts.

● Liberty Science Center
Liberty State Park, 251 Phillip Street (exit 14B off the NJ turnpike), 200-1000. Hours: March 31–Sept.1 Mon.–Sat. 9:30–5:30, Sunday and holidays 9:30–6:30; Sept. 2–Mar. 30 Tues.–Sun. 9:30–5:30. Admission: Science Center Exhibit Hall, adults $9.50, children 2–12 $6.50; Omni Theater, adults $7, children 2–12 $5; Combination tickets, adults $13.50, children 2–12 $9.50. www.lsc.org. **All ages.**

There is so much to do at this facility that you'd better be here at 9:30, when the center opens, or you can forget about doing anything else for the rest of the day—kids never want to leave (this is a good thing for the museum, right?). The Liberty Science Center is an interactive, hands-on, state-of-the-art science museum that has much to offer young visitors (and older visitors as well, if you like acting like a bug and crawling through a dark tunnel using only your sense of touch—yikes!). Let your young entomologists have fun in the Bug Zoo, and then move on to explore the fascinating Illusion Labyrinth, a 1,000-square-foot labyrinth with optical illusions to trick the most seasoned science center veteran. Or try the virtual reality basketball court, make mud pies, or have a theatrical thrill in the Omni Theater with the largest IMAX screen in the U.S. I think you'll agree there's plenty to do here for all ages. You also get a terrific view of Manhattan from the park. If you do have any time left over, board the Circle Line Ferry and take a leisurely visit to Ellis Island and the Statue of Liberty. Don't forget to bring your camera. (For more information on Ellis Island and the Statue of Liberty, see the chapter on New York City.)

LYNDHURST

● Hackensack Meadowlands Development Commission Environment Center (a.k.a. The Trash Museum)

2 Dekorte Park Plaza, 460-8300. Hours: Mon.–Fri. 9–5, Sat. 10–3. Admission: Adults $2, children 12 and under free. **Ages 3 and up.**

The museum's first name (the Hackensack Meadowlands Development Commission Environment Center) is its official name, but everyone knows it as the Trash Museum. And, believe it or not, kids really do find this museum fascinating (most adults do, too). Through photographs and other displays, visitors can see how the area looked in the 19th-century, and subsequently the importance of recycling. In the garbage sculpture room, you can see how much people throw away (and what some creative people have done with that waste). Outside, take a walk in the experimental park, where you also get a nice view of Manhattan.

MOUNTAINSIDE

● Trailside Nature and Science Center

452 New Providence Road, (908) 789-3670. Hours: daily 1–5. Admission: free. **All ages.**

My children absolutely love butterflies (doesn't everyone?), and here at Trailside a butterfly garden is one of the summertime features. There are also nicely groomed nature trails and an herb and wildflower garden, and a bird sanctuary. Peek in at the visitors center for the live reptile exhibit area.

NEWARK

● Cathedral of the Sacred Heart

89 Ridge Street, (973) 484-4600. Tours: 2nd Sun. of every month, after 12 noon mass. Admission: free. **Ages 5 and up.**

If you won't be visiting Europe in the near future, and you will be visiting this area, why not give your kids an architectural history lesson by taking them to a cathedral based on the finest examples of French and English Gothic architecture? The 200 stained glass windows are wonderful to view. In 1995, Pope John Paul II conducted services here while visiting the United States. If you need to brush up on your knowledge of gothic architecture, guided tours are available. Plan a visit while you are taking in the wonders of the Cherry Blossom Festival held in April each year. With over 2,500 cherry trees at nearby Branch Brook Park, the sight is spectacular (and certainly helps to alleviate those winter blahs).

● Newark Museum

49 Washington Street, 596-6550. Hours: Wed.–Sun. noon–5. Admission: free. **All ages.**

There is plenty to enjoy here for the entire family. Specifically geared to children are the Junior Gallery, the terrarium, and several aquariums. Children are also usually captivated by the Native American Gallery, and the costumes and textiles in particular. This museum has a good collection of American painting and decorative arts, and in addition to all the above, they also operate the Fire Museum and Ballantine House (next door), an opulent late-Victorian (1885) home that once belonged to the wealthy Ballantine brewing family.

● New Jersey Historical Society

52 Park Place, 483-3939. Hours: Tues.–Sat. 10–5. Admission: free. **All ages.**

Sometimes small history museums are the best ones for kids. At the new Kids Center in this museum, children can try on period costumes or visit an interactive exhibit called Histories Mysteries. There is also a new area called Teenage New Jersey 1941–1975, with real letters from teenagers, music to listen to, videos, and more. It's a terrific way to spend a rainy afternoon. The society has family workshops that relate to the exhibits (usually from 1–2 on Saturdays). The society moved to this new location in June 1997.

PARAMUS

● Bergen Museum of Art and Science

320 East Ridgewood, 265-1248. Hours: Tues.–Sat. 10–5, Sun. 1–5. Admission (suggested donation): Adults $2.50, children $1. **All ages.**

Most kids are fascinated by dinosaurs and here they can see the famous Hackensack mastodon skeleton. They can also enjoy themselves in the children's discovery room where they can play with frogs and snakes. Kids will be intrigued by the Lenape Indian display and will want to spend a lot of time with all the hands-on science exhibits. This museum offers a lot to visitors and you can easily spend several hours here enjoying the various exhibits.

● The New Jersey Children's Museum

599 Industrial Avenue, 262-5151. Hours: daily weekdays 9–5, weekends 10–6. Admission: Adults and children $7, children under 1 free. **Ages 1–8.**

Visiting the area and not quite sure what to do? Feel stuck in the hotel? How about a trip to this interesting children's museum, where your children can climb into a real fire engine, explore a castle, dig for fossils, shop in the grocery store, play with puppets, pretend to fly a real helicopter, play office, or work on real computers. The list goes on and on. The museum itself is located in a renovated industrial building.

SCOTCH PLAINS

● Bowcraft Amusement Park

Route 22, (908) 233-0675. Hours: daily 11–7. Admission: price is per ride ($.50–$2) (no admission or parking fees). Miniature golf is $3 per person. **All ages.**

Who needs the latest fancy turbo-blaster ride when you can have old-fashioned train rides, bumper cars, and paddleboats? This small park is your ticket to nostalgia—if you are under 50, you probably visited a park like this when you were a kid. There is also an 18-hole miniature golf course, and the standard amusement park arcade.

● Scotch Plains Zoo

1451 Raritan Road, (908) 322-7180. Hours: weekdays 10–5, weekends 10–6. Admission: Adults $6, children 1–12 $3. **All ages.**

Sometimes the Bronx Zoo is just too big and takes too much energy, but you'd really like to go see some animals. Try this small zoo, where you can see hippos, lions, giraffes, tropical birds, and more. You can even let the kids have a pony ride (usually available only on the weekends).

TETERBORO

● Aviation Hall of Fame and Museum of New Jersey

Teterboro Airport, Route 46, 288-6345. Hours: Tues.–Sun. 10–4. Admission: Adults $5, children 12 and under $3. **Ages 3 and up.**

This is really a neat place for kids, and usually it's not too crowded. The museum illustrates the history of aviation in the state of New Jersey. It has displays of rocket engines, helicopters, propellers, and other fun plane-related stuff. Several famous pilots have trained here, including Amelia Earhart and Charles A. Lindbergh.

WEST ORANGE

● Edison National Historic Site

Main Street and Lakeside Avenue (Edison's Laboratory), 736-5050. Hours: daily 9–5; hour-long tours begin at 10:30 and leave every hour on the half-hour. Admission: Adults $2, children 16 and under free. The $2 fee includes both the laboratory and Edison's home, Glenmont (see below). Edison's Papers Web site: www.edison.rutgers.edu. **Ages 4 and up.**

The town of West Orange has the distinction of being the home of Thomas Edison from 1887 until his death in 1931. He developed over 500 patents at his laboratory here, including ones for motion pictures and the phonograph. (Before moving to West Orange, he lived in the town of Edison, see listing above.) Not only can you view the first movie ever filmed *(The Great Train Robbery)*, watch an informative film about Edison, and see his chemistry labs, you will also visit his extensive library as part of the tour, which still contains his desk and over 10,000 books. Then you can walk over and visit his home, which is equally wonderful (see below).

● Llewellyn Park West/Glenmont (Edison's House)

Main Street and Lakeside Avenue, 736-0550. Hours: Wed–Sun., 11–4; hour-long tours begin at 11 and leave every hour. Admission: Adults $2, children 16 and under free. The $2 fee includes both the laboratory and Glenmont. **Ages 4 and up.**

Edison lived here with his wife, Minna, for most of his life. Their grand piano and pipe organ, which they often played while entertaining, are still here to see. It is nice for visitors to see a house with original furnishings. It gives children (and their parents) a sense of time to see how others lived in another era. Llewellyn Park is actually the first closed community in the United States. Glenmont is one of 125 private residences in the park. Access is provided to Edison's home only after purchasing a pass at the visitor center at the laboratory listed above.

Annual Events

■ New York City

■ MANHATTAN

January
Chinese New Year and Parade (January or February)
Winter Festival in Central Park

February
Chinese Lantern Day
Chinese New Year and Parade (January or February)

March
Easter Parade (depends on year)
Greek Independence Day Parade
Radio City Music Hall Spring Spectacular
Ringling Brothers and Barnum and Bailey Circus, Madison Square
    Garden
St. Patrick's Day Parade (March 17)

April
The Greek Day Parade

May
Annual Asian Pacific American Heritage Festival
Brooklyn Bridge Day Parade
Cinco De Mayo Festival
Martin Luther King, Jr., Memorial Day Parade
Ninth Avenue International Food Festival
Ye Old Village Fair, Greenwich Village

June
Buskers Fare Festival (end of June–early July)
International Cultures Festival
Puerto Rican Day Parade
St. Anthony Festival
Salute to Israel Parade

July
American Crafts Festival
Buskers Fare Festival (end of June–early July)
Celebration of Nations Festival
The Great July 4th Festival (4th of July from Fulton–Battery Park, in
    Lower Manhattan)
Lincoln Center Out-of-Doors Festival (July–August)

August
Battery Park Festival of Families
Festival of the Americas
Greenwich Village Jazz Festival
Harlem Festival
Lincoln Center Out-of-Doors Festival (July–August)
Summer Seaport Festival (early August)
Tap-O-Mania (Macy's Parade of Tap Dancers—at 34th Street and 7th
    Avenue, near Broadway)

September
Feast of San Gennaro
Labor Day Weekend Big Apple Balloon Festival (end Aug.–beg. Sept.)
Medieval Festival at Fort Tryon Park

October
Annual Greenwich Village Halloween Parade
Columbus Day Parade
National Horse Show
Oyster Festival at the Merchant's House Museum

November
Macy's Thanksgiving Day Parade
New York City Marathon
Veteran's Day Parade

December
Christmas Tree Lighting at Rockefeller Center
Lincoln Center Holiday Tree Lighting
New Year's Eve Celebration, Times Square

■ BROOKLYN

May
International Children's Festival of Theater and Music (at the Brooklyn Academy of Music (mid-May)
Norwegian Independence Day Parade (May 17)

June
Brooklyn Pride Parade

July
Celebrate Brooklyn (free concerts at Prospect Park)
Nathan's Famous Hot Dog Eating Contest (on Coney Island)

August
Brooklyn's County Fair (at Floyd Bennett Field)

September
Atlantic Antic—Street Fair
Harvest Fair
West Indian–American Day Carnival

■ QUEENS

April
Arbor Day Fair (Queen's Botanical Garden)

July
Thunderbird American Indian Mid-Summer Pow-Wow

September
Queens County Fair

October
Apple Festival

■ BRONX

April
Bronx Zoo–Spring Break Out

May
Folk Parks (Annual Outdoor Festival of Traditional Music and Dance) at the New York Botanical Garden

June
Bronx Day at the New York Botanical Garden

October
Columbus Day Parade
Mardi Gras Festival at Pelham Bay Park

■ STATEN ISLAND

March
Staten Island Children's Museum Annual Fashion Show

August
Richmond County Fair

October
Pumpkin Festival at Victory Plant Center

Long Island

■ NASSAU COUNTY

May
Long Island Mozart Festival, Oyster Bay
Old Bethpage Village Restoration–Spring Festival, Old Bethpage

June
African American Street Fair, Hempstead
Annual Summer Festival, Freeport
Maritime Folklife Festival, Freeport

July
Independence Day Celebration (4th of July), Old Bethpage
Star-Spangled Banner Blast (Grucci Family fireworks), Wantaugh–Jones
  Beach State Park (4th of July)

August
Scottish Games, Old Westbury Gardens, Old Westbury

October
Long Island Fair, Old Bethpage
Oyster Festival, Oyster Bay

■ **SUFFOLK COUNTY**

March
St. Patrick's Day Parade, Montauk

April
Spring Festival, Cold Spring Harbor

May
Arts and Crafts Festival, Southampton

June
Harvest of the Bays, Hampton Bays
Strawberry Festival, Mattituck

July
Greek Hellenic Festival, Mattituck
Hallockville Summer Festival, Riverhead
Lobster Fest, Orient
Sand Castle Contests, Amagansett
Sand Castle Contests at Hither Hills State Park, Montauk

August
Annual Polishtown USA Street Fair and Polka Festival, Riverhead
Sand Castle Contests, Amagansett
Sand Castle Contests at Hither Hills State Park, Montauk
Summer Fair, Amagansett

September
Historic Seaport Regatta, Greenport to Sag Harbor
Historicfest, Sag Harbor
Long Island Fall Harvest Festival, Riverhead
Shinnecock Pow-Wow on the Shinnecock Reservation, Southampton
   (August/September–Labor Day weekend)

October
Apple Festival, Cutchogue
Fall Festival, Montauk
Fall Festival and Craft Show, Riverhead

Eastern New York

■ HUDSON VALLEY REGION

January
Annual Horse Drawn Sleigh Rally (depending on snow conditions),
   Wappingers Falls

March
Annual Ice Sculpting Contest, Poughkeepsie

April
Nyack Street Fair, Nyack

May
Great Hudson Valley Balloon Race, Wappingers Falls
May Merriement (Shakespearean Renaissance Faire), Annandale-on-Hudson

July
An Old Fashioned Family Fourth of July, Cleremont
July 4th Parade, Hyde Park
New York Renaissance Festival (end of July–mid-September), Tuxedo
New York State Firefighters Competition and Field Day, Hudson

August
Dutchess County Fair, Rhinebeck
Kites Over the Hudson, Newburgh
New York Renaissance Festival (end of July–mid-September), Tuxedo

September
A Celtic Day in the Park, Staatsburg
Civil War Weekend, Monroe
Fall Harvest Festival, Wappingers Falls
New York Renaissance Festival (end of July–mid-September), Tuxedo
Oktoberfest (late September–October), Bear Mountain

October
Annual Fall Foliage Festival, Port Jervis
Oktoberfest (late September–October), Bear Mountain

December
Historic Hyde Park Christmas, Hyde Park

■ CATSKILLS REGION

January
Winter Ice Carnival, Livingston Manor

May
Annual Civil War Reenactment, Bethel
Annual Kite Festival, Loch Sheldrake
Kite Festival, East Durham

June
It Takes a Village—Catskills Celebration, Monticello
Summer Festivals (Summer-long ethnic/cultural festivals), Hunter

July
Annual Medieval Festival, Monticello
Annual Strawberry Festival (4th of July weekend), Livingston Manor
Annual Ukrainian Festival, Glen Spey
Children's Day Parade, Kingston
Hang Gliding Fun Fly-In, Ellenville
Independence Day Celebration at Hanford Mills Museum (4th of July),
    East Meredith
Irish Traditional Music Festival, East Durham
Lumberjack Festival, Deposit
Peaceful Valley Bluegrass Festival, Downsville
St. Joseph's Italian Festa, New Paltz

August
Annual Little World's Fair, Grahamsville
Ulster County Fair, New Paltz

September
Hudson Valley Food Festival, Kingston
Hudson Valley Garlic Festival, Saugerties

October
Delhi Harvest Festival, Delhi
Giant Pumpkin Party and Children's Parade, Grahamsville
Maple Leaf Festival, Downsville
Octoberfest, Deposit

November
Holiday Arts and Crafts Fair, Loch Sheldrake

Central New York

■ CAPITAL-SARATOGA REGION

March
Annual New York State Chocolate Festival, Albany

April
Capital Springfest, Albany
St. Clement's Saratoga Horse Show, Saratoga Springs

May
Annual Riverpark Canalfest, Waterford
Annual Tulip Festival, Albany
Dressage at Saratoga, Saratoga Springs

June
Market Fair (18th-century market fair), Johnstown
Newport Jazz Festival–Saratoga, Saratoga Springs
Riverfront Arts Festival, Troy

July
Independence Day Celebration (4th of July), Albany

August
Altamont Fair, Altamont Fairgrounds
Capital District Scottish Games (August or September), Altamont
   Fairgrounds

September
Capital District Scottish Games (August or September), Altamont
   Fairgrounds
Larkfest (third Saturday in September), Albany

November
Festival of Trees at Albany Institute of History and Art (end November–
   beginning December), Albany

December
Altamont Fair Festival of Lights, Altamont Fairgrounds
Festival of Trees at Albany Institute of History and Art (end. November–
   beginning December), Albany
Victorian Street Walk, Saratoga Springs

■ CENTRAL LEATHERSTOCKING REGION

May
Art in the Sky Kite Festival, Cazenovia
Iroquois Arts Celebration, Howes Cave
Two Rivers Ethnic Festival, Binghamton
Whitney Point Regatta and Craft Fair, Whitney Point

July
Country Festival, Cooperstown
Family Fun Day and Bullthistle Balloon Fest, Norwich
Genesee Street Festival, Utica
Honor America Days Celebration (end July–mid-August), Rome
Independence Day at the Farmer's Museum (4th of July), Cooperstown
JulyFest, Binghamton
Spiedie Fest and Balloon Rally, Endicott

August
Honor America Days Celebration (end of July–mid-August), Rome
Iroquois Indian Festival, Howes Cave

September
A Taste of the Arts Festival, Rome
Harvest Festival, Cooperstown

October
Apple Fest, Endicott

December
Christmas at Lorenzo, Cazenovia
Joy to the World Festival, Cazenovia

■ FINGER LAKES REGION

January
Lights on the Lake, Syracuse

April
Central New York Maple Festival, Marathon

May
Dogwood Festival, Dansville
Finger Lakes Balloon Festival, Canandaigua
Ithaca Festival (last weekend of May), Ithaca

Lilac Festival, Rochester
Marquette International, Corning

June
Annual Otsiningo Pow-Wow and Indian Craft Fair, Apalachin
Fireman's Field Days, Apalachin
Living History Weekend (Confederate Encampment), Geneseo
Maplewood Rose Festival, Rochester
Monroe County Fair, Rochester
Rochester Harborfest, Rochester
Sterling Renaissance Festival (end of June–mid-August), Sterling
Strawberry Festival, Owego
Wolcott Strawberry Festival, Sodus Point

July
A Festival of Arts, Corning
Arts and Crafts Festival, Watkins Glen
Carnival on the Bay, Sodus Point
Convention Days (Celebration of First Women's Rights Convention),
    Seneca Falls
Downtown Arts and Crafts Festival, Canandaigua
Fireman's Carnival, Hammondsport
Fireman's Fair, Hector
Yates County Fair, Penn Yan
4th of July Extravaganza, Watkins Glen
4th of July Gala, Sodus Point
Grass Roots Festival of Music and Dance, Trumansburg
Schuyler County Youth Fair, Watkins Glen
Sterling Renaissance Festival (end of June–mid-August), Sterling
Summer Festival, Geneseo
Symphony Concert and Fireworks (4th of July), Syracuse

August
Central New York Scottish Games, Syracuse
Empire Farm Days, Seneca Falls
En Plein Air—Open Art Festival, Owego
Fingerlakes Dixieland Jazz Festival, Hector
Genundowa Native American Festival of Lights, Hammondsport
Grand Prix Festival and U.S. Vintage Grand Prix, Watkins Glen
Great New York State Fair, Syracuse
Italian Festival at Lakeside Park, Watkins Glen
Oktoberfest, Syracuse
Park Avenue Summer Artfest, Rochester
Sterling Renaissance Festival (end June–mid-August), Sterling
Tioga County Fair, Owego

Trumansburg Fair, Trumansburg
Waterfront Arts Festival, Canandaigua
Women's Equality Day, Seneca Falls

October
Apple Festival, Ithaca
Oktoberfest, Dansville
Rockwell Museum Chili and Chocolate Cookoff, Corning
Zoo Boo (Halloween festivities), Burnet Park Zoo, Syracuse

December
Annual Holiday Open House, Auburn
Festival of Lights at Sonnenberg Gardens and Mansion, Canandaigua

Northern New York

■ ADIRONDACKS REGION

February
Lake George Winter Festival, Lake George
Saranac Lake Winter Carnival, Saranac Lake

May
Annual Whitewater Derby, North River
Memorial Day Parade, Lake George

June
Annual Blues Festival, Glens Falls
Fort Ticonderoga Great Encampment of the French and Indian War,
    Ticonderoga
Summerfest at Shepard Park, Lake George

July
Annual Scottish Military Tatoo at Fort Ticonderoga (first weekend July),
    Ticonderoga
4th of July Celebration (4th of July), Ticonderoga
Free Concerts at Shepard Park (July and August, Wednesday nights), Lake
    George
Independence Day Celebration (4th of July), Saranac Lake
Willard Hanmer Guideboat and Canoe Race, Saranac Lake

August
Annual Lake George Family Festival, Lake George
Free Concerts at Shepard Park (July and August, Wednesday nights), Lake
    George

Music Festival in the Adirondacks, Paul Smiths
Warren County Country Fair, Warrensburg

September
Adirondack Hot Air Balloon Festival, Glens Falls and Queensbury
Apple Festival, Lake George
Lake George Jazz Festival, Lake George
Lakeside Festival, Lake George
Taste of the North Country, Glens Falls

October
Farm Fun Day, Lake George
Oktoberfest, Wilmington

■ THOUSAND ISLANDS–SEAWAY REGION

April
Arbor Day Festival and Craft Fair, Adams
1000 Islands Spring Boat Show, Clayton

June
Kidrific Weekend (end of June), Alexandria Bay

July
Buskers Rendezvous (street performer's festival), Alexandria Bay
1812 Can-Am Pageant, Sackets Harbor
Fireworks over Boldt Castle (4th of July), Alexandria Bay
French Festival, Cape Vincent
Grindstone Creek Pow-Wow, Pulaski
Harborfest, Oswego
Roaring Twenties Weekend, Alexandria Bay

August
Antique Boat Show, Clayton
Antique Raceboat Regatta, Clayton
Festival of North County Folklife, Massena

September
Bravo Italiano Festival, Watertown
1000 Islands International Balloon Festival, Alexandria Bay

October
Autumn Festival, Alexandria Bay

Western New York

■ NIAGARA FRONTIER REGION

January
Annual Festival of Lights (mid-November–January), Niagara Falls

May
Buffalo Heritage Day, Buffalo
Greek Hellenic Festival, Buffalo
International Kite Festival, Niagara Falls
Niagara Falls Community Faire (end May–June), Niagara Falls
Old Fashioned Farm Festival, Somerset
Tulip Festival, Batavia

June
Allentown Outdoor Art Festival, Buffalo
Annual Strawberry Festival, Lockport
Family Fun Weekend at Old Fort Niagara, Youngstown
Juneteenth Festival, Buffalo
Kidfest! at Hyde Park, Niagara Falls
Niagara Falls Community Faire (end May–June), Niagara Falls
Shakespeare in Delaware Park (end of June–mid-August), Buffalo
Strawberry Fest, Youngstown
Taste of the Tonawandas (end of June or early July), Tonawanda
Thunder Over Niagara—Military Airshow, Niagara Falls

July
Canalfest (mid-July), Tonawanda
Independence Day at Herschell Carousel Factory Museum (4th of July),
    N. Tonawanda
Italian Heritage and Food Festival, Buffalo
Niagara County Fair (end July–beg. August), Lockport
Picnic in the Park (4th of July), Batavia
Shakespeare in Delaware Park (end of June–mid-August), Buffalo
Taste of Buffalo, Buffalo
Taste of the Tonawandas (end of June or early July), Tonawanda
Waterfront Festival-Summer Concert Series at LaSalle Park (Tuesday and
    Saturday evenings in July and August), Buffalo

August
Annual Toyfest, East Aurora
ArtFest, Lewiston

Caribbean Festival, Buffalo
Erie County Fair and Expo, Hamburg Fairgrounds, Hamburg
Irish Festival, Lancaster
Niagara County Fair (end July–beg. August), Lockport
Polish American Arts Festival, Buffalo
Scottish Festival at the Amherst Museum, Buffalo
Shakespeare in Delaware Park (end of June–mid-August), Buffalo
Waterfront Festival-Summer Concert Series at LaSalle Park (Tuesday and
    Saturday evenings in July and August), Buffalo
Youngstown Volunteer Fire Company Annual Labor Day Field Day,
    Youngstown

September
Harvest Festival and Craft Show, Lewiston
Jazz Festival, Lewiston
Niagara County Peach Festival, Lewiston

October
Arts and Crafts Show, Castile
Heritage Days, Tonawanda
Niagara's Apple Country Festival, Lockport

November
Annual Festival of Lights (mid-November–January), Niagara Falls

■ CHAUTAUQUA-ALLEGHENY REGION

February
Winterfest at Island Park, Wellsville

March
Winter Carnival, Ellicottville

April
Annual Hot Dog Day and Family Weekend, Alfred

May
Lucyfest (Lucille Ball Festival of New Comedy) (end of May), Jamestown

July
Allegheny County Fair, Angelica
Annual Great Wellsville Balloon Rally, Wellsville
Folk Fair, Panama

August
Sky Jam (balloons, music, fireworks), Jamestown

September
Renaissance Fair, Alfred

October
Foliagefest, Panama

December
Angelica Christmas Walk, Angelica
Annual Victorian Christmas Festival, Alfred

Western Connecticut

March
Maple Sugaring Festival, Norfolk

May
Civil War Battles and Reenactment, Madison
Dogwood Festival, Fairfield
Garlicfest, Fairfield

August
SoNo Arts Celebration, South Norwalk

September
Durham Fair, Durham
Kids' Day, Stamford
Mum Festival, Bristol
Norwalk Oyster Festival, East Norwalk

Northern New Jersey

February
New Jersey Flower and Garden Show, Somerset

April
Cherry Blossom Festival, Newark

May
Spring Somerset Craft Festival, Somerset
Tour of Somerville (national cycling race), Somerville

June
New Jersey Renaissance Festival (Memorial Day weekend), Somerset

July
New Jersey Festival of Ballooning, Readington
St. Ann's Italian Festival, Hoboken

August
Magic of Alexandria Balloon Festival, Pittstown

September
Fall Somerset Craft Festival, Somerset
Jewish Renaissance Fair, Morristown

October
Bell Atlantic Hudson County American Heritage Festival, Jersey City
Millbrook Days, Millbrook Village

November
18th Century Encampment, Fort Lee

Resources

Internet—World Wide Web Information

With the explosion of information available on the World Wide Web or Internet, I thought it would be an added bonus for readers to have the addresses (URLs) of as many of the places I describe as possible. For the ease of the reader, I have added the URLs to the information at the head of the individual listings; included below is a list of some of the more general Web sites that might also be of interest. Please note that Web site addresses, admission fees, and hours of operation change regularly, so calling ahead to verify is advised. These are just jumping off points—visiting one site will lead to a zillion more! Have a blast searching for information!

TRAVEL (GENERAL)

Travelocity: http://www.travelocity.com
Pathfinder Travel: http://pathfinder.com/travel
World Travel Guide: http://www.wtgonline.com
Lonely Planet: http://www.lonelyplanet.com
Vacations: http://www.vacations.com
Fodor's: http://www.fodors.com
Your Personal Network: http://www.ypn.com/living/travel
Travelers Saving Site: http://home.sprynet.com/sprynet/inetmktg
Great Outdoors Recreation Group: http://www.gorp.com
Citylink: http://www.neosoft.com:80/citylink
Travel Web: http://www.travelweb.com/thisco/global/travel.html
The Travel Connection: http://travelxn.com

PARENTING

Parents Place: http://parentsplace.com
Parents Forum for Parenting Publications of America: http://
family.com
Family Planet: http://www.familyplanet.com
Kids Source Online: http://www.kidsource.com
Sesame Street **Magazine:** http://www.ctw.org

NEW YORK STATE

New York State: http://iloveny.state.ny.us
New York Museums: http://cityinsights.com/nymuseums.htm
Gannett Suburban Newspapers: http://nynews.com

Local Parenting Publications

All of the following can be picked up for free at local libraries and
children's stores, or ordered by calling or writing the publisher. If you
visit the Web site www.family.com you can find some of the following
publications on-line.

NEW YORK CITY

Big Apple Parents Paper
Family Communications, Inc.
36 E. 12th Street
New York, N.Y. 10003
(212) 533-2277

New York Family
141 Halstead Avenue, Suite 3D
Mamaroneck, NY 14534
(914) 381-7474

LONG ISLAND

Long Island Parenting
P.O. Box 214
Island Park, NY 11558
(516) 889-5510

HUDSON VALLEY

Westchester Family
141 Halstead Avenue, Suite 3D
Mamaroneck, NY 14534
(914) 381-7474

Hudson Valley Parent
174 South Street
Newburgh, NY 12550
(914) 562-3606

FINGER LAKES

Rochester Area
   Genesee Valley Parents
   1 Grove Street, Suite 105-B
   Pittsford, NY 14534
   (716) 264-9955

Ithaca Area
   Ithaca Child
   P.O. Box 6404
   Ithaca, NY 14851
   (607) 273-2005

Syracuse Parent
   Syracuse Parent
   P.O. Box 6818
   Syracuse, NY 13217
   (315) 471-7610

WESTERN

Buffalo Area
   Western New York Family
   287 Parkside Avenue
   P.O. Box 265
   Buffalo, NY 14215-0265
   (716) 836-3486

CONNECTICUT

Connecticut Family
141 Halstead Avenue Suite 3D
Mamaroneck, NY 10543
(914) 381-7474

Connecticut Parent
315 Peck Street
New Haven, CT 06513-0580
(203) 782-1420

NEW JERSEY

The Parent Paper
105 Main Street
Hackensack, NJ 07601
(201) 342-4613

Index by Age Group

Alphabetical Index